Baby Father 2

Patrick AUGUSTUS

Published in United Kingdom by:
The X Press,
6 Hoxton Square, London N1 6NU
Tel: 0171 729 1199
Fax: 0171 729 1771

This edition published in 1998

Printed by Caledonian Book Manufacturing, Glasgow, Scotland.

Distributed in UK by Turnaround Distribution, Unit 3, Olympia Trading Estate,
Coburg Road, London N22 6TZ
Tel: 0181 829 3000
Fax: 0181 881 5088

ISBN 1-874509-15-8

ABOUT THE AUTHOR

Born in south London of Jamaican parents, Patrick Augustus has worked for many years as a musician and record producer. As well as being the author of four novels, he has written and directed several plays, is a regular radio contributor, and is a founder member of *The Baby Fathers Alliance*, a pressure group for separated fathers. Aged 33, Augustus is currently living in Spain where he is writing his next novel.

OTHER BOOKS BY THE AUTHOR

Baby Father
Baby Father 3
When a Man Loves a Woman

THE MEN

Gussie Pottinger

Beres Dunkley

Johnny 'Dollar' Lindo

Linvall Henry

AIN'T TOO PROUD TO BEG

Men have been unfaithful to women since the beginning of time, so what's the big deal? Like his male predecessors throughout history, Johnny 'Dollar' Lindo couldn't understand what all the fuss was about. It was, after all, a minor misdemeanour rather than the end of the world. Yes, he had got off with another woman, but that hot night of illicit love had more to do with confidence boosting than satisfying his lust. It was proof that he still had it in him to pull a criss-looking woman. Typical mid-life crisis stuff men go through when they, like Johnny, hit their thirtysomethings.

Understandably Lesley was none too happy when she found out about her man's infidelity and there was 'nuff cuss and quarrel. "Bastard" was only one of the names she called him, the others were even worse! Then she threw him out. Suddenly Johnny was free and single and able to check as many women as he wanted. Life couldn't have been more straightforward. But where kids are involved nothing is quite so simple. He soon began to miss his children bad. His daughter Winnie and his baby son Jacob needed a father as much as a mother. Every child has their image of what a family should be and it invariably follows the nuclear model. Without him, they weren't a family and somehow Johnny couldn't see his children growing up to thank him for not being there for them when most of their friends were enjoying the full benefits of a two-parent home. His best bet, he decided, was to try everything in his power to get back with their mother and to make a new go of it.

Easier said than done. Lesley had refused to answer his letters and wouldn't take his phone calls. She even restricted

1

his access to the children. "That's the price you've got to pay, Johnny," she reasoned. "Nothing in life is free. You should have considered that when you were making love to your outside woman. But instead you let your dick do your thinking for you." She warned him not to even think of coming round to their home, on pain of an injunction. Out of shame he stayed away. And when they met up in that moment after Beres, Gussie and Linvall's triple wedding, Johnny had already given up hope. Yet, though he had braced himself to say: "Look, we've got to deal with this and get it settled through lawyers," when he opened his mouth, what actually came out was, "Can I come back...?" Just like that. He didn't know where it came from. Maybe it was the atmosphere of perfect love and harmony at his best friends' joint wedding. Maybe it was the look of love in their eyes as they each said those magic words 'I do' at the altar. Whatever it was, Johnny wasn't too proud to beg.

The triple wedding must have softened Lesley's heart too. Johnny's happiness had vaulted like the temperature in a heatwave when she agreed to allow him to accompany her to Carnival where, he was confident, he could eventually smooth over much of Lesley's rough memories of his 'transgression'.

Carnival at the end of August, was strictly level vibes. It was the second day, the Monday, 'standing room only' day when breathing space is at a premium. Most people agreed it was better than the Sunday. Though it wasn't the warmest summer day, the occasional showers couldn't dampen the spirits of the one million revellers jammed into the square mile of Notting Hill enjoying themselves. 'Leave Your Troubles At Home' was the motto for this year's two days of unrivalled free entertainment, Caribbean style. It seemed like the whole world had come to Carnival and certainly most of the tourists in town were present. Those who could get a squeeze from an acquaintance who lived in the area, were able to watch the proceedings from the balcony of one of the many elegant Victorian houses on the route of the procession. Everybody else moved with the flow in the drizzle; they had no choice.

No amount of downpour was going to trouble Johnny Dollar. With his darkers on despite the grey clouds, he cut a tall and elegant figure in the light-grey collarless suit, and a gleaming white shirt which seemed to bring out the colour in his ebony hue. Cocked back on his head, was a new Trilby. With his woman by his side and his daughter bringing up the rear a few paces behind them, Johnny was walking tall. With baby Jacob safe at home with his grandmother, Johnny didn't have a worry in the world. Even a hurricane couldn't trouble him today. Despite the crowds and the hustle and bustle of Carnival, this was the best chance he had had to woo his woman back in six months and he didn't intend to waste it. 'Not even an earthquake could stop me,' he assured himself. After all, Carnival was their spot. At Carnival, they could be like they used to be; like they were when they first met as teenagers, all those years ago when they only had eyes for each other; when the most important thing in their lives was to make each other smile. Their shared memories of Carnival went back fifteen years and more, and as they eased their way through the All Saint's roadblock, he took every opportunity to recall the good times. Up ahead, the music was loud, the crowd even more dense and the energy at fever pitch, but as long as they stayed out of the thick of things, he could make himself heard-and if he could make himself heard, Lesley would surely see reason and take him back.

However old you are, you aren't at Carnival if you don't pass through All Saint's Road to check 'what ah gwan' and to scan the gallery of happy faces for anyone you know. On All Saint's Road, long lost friends are united and new friendships and romances are forged. All Saints Road is the place to be!

"Bwoy, didn't that used to be old Free-I's shop!" Johnny pointed to a store across the road which had been temporarily boarded up for the duration of the two-day festivities.

Lesley followed the direction of Johnny's finger. The newly painted sign in fancy type above the store read: *'A.J. Cartland, Cabinet Makers of Distinction'*.

"You mean Free-I, the rastaman? No that can't be it," Lesley said after focusing for a moment. "That can't be the run-down store Free-I used to own."

She had dressed sensibly for Carnival in a figure-hugging pair of white jeans and a thick woolly sweater. Around her neck she had a silk scarf to keep out the wind and she had even brought an umbrella, "just in case."

"Nah I'm telling you, that's it. That's definitely Free-I's store."

"Well if that's the place, the building's been done up nice."

"You remember old Free-I, don't you?" Johnny turned his head to his daughter behind him.

Winnie, sipping the juice out of a coconut through a straw, looked at her father with a quizzical expression. She hadn't heard a word he'd said. Though only eleven years old, she looked and behaved like a girl of fifteen or sixteen. She had that 'air' about her which suggested that she was streetwise. This was partly due to artificial considerations such as the plaited sculpture on her head which had taken her mother twelve hours to create and made her look very grown up. Lesley had given her daughter permission to use make-up and wear jewellery to Carnival. But this was a special dispensation. Tomorrow, she would have to hang up her glad rags and start looking her age again, but today she was going to make the most of it.

"I just wish this crowd would hurry up and get a move on," a frustrated Winnie told her father. "By the time we get to where I want to go I will have missed everything."

Her attention was on the huge street party further up, where the legendary Goldfinger ragga sound with its huge loudspeakers set up on the pavement were duelling with the up-and-coming Fever Inc., currently London's top jungle sound, set up on the opposite side of the road with speakers to match. It was a 'clash of the titans', jungle versus ragga. By nine o'clock that evening, a champion would be declared when the police eventually managed to shut down one of the combatants. For now, there was no way the ravers were going to allow 'babylon' to distress the two 'boom' sounds for another half hour at least.

Like most girls her age, Winnie would normally have been there to blow her whistle for the junglist crew. But today, she was more interested in checking out Goldfinger, where, her best friend Aisha had reliably informed her, the young D.J. Pickney would be chatting on the mike. Not only was D.J. Pickney "safe" and "criss" her girlfriend had enthused, he was also their age.

"You probably don't remember Free-I," Johnny said. "You were probably too young at the time. Yeah, I remember now, you couldn't have been more than five or six when we used to live up this side of things..."

Johnny reached back to his daughter and pulled her tenderly up alongside of him, a straw still clenched between her teeth even though the coconut water was now right down to the jelly.

"Let me tell you about the rastaman," Johnny said, chuckling to himself.

"Oh you're not going to tell her about Free-I are you?" Lesley said.

"Yeah, why not?" Johnny was still chuckling. Just the thought of Free-I was enough to set him off in a fit of mirth. "Winnie's old enough to hear about Free-I... He was one of the most upful black men in the community at that time and that's something we should pass on to the youts. Jah know. Because you see, all man like Free-I, that's our history and your history's supposed to help you understand the world, seen? You remember how back in the day everybody around this area knew Free-I? Everybody knew that however bad things got, there was one black man out there who wouldn't let the shitstem beat him down. Free-I was synonymous with hope for all those who knew him. You imagine how many people there are who heard about Free-I and when they were in a certain desperate situation they were reminded of him and suddenly everything looked, you know, copasetic."

Lesley agreed with a smile and a nod of her head. She had to admit that thinking of Free-I never failed to cheer her up. It was just that she didn't want her daughter thinking that the way to make a living was the way Free-I did.

"But you gotta do what you gotta do and that's what he had to do to feed his wife and pickney. And you know he had 'nuff ah those. Remember the sign on his shop? 'Rasta don't work for CIA'. Remember that?" Johnny asked, tickling Lesley cautiously. From the smile on her face she remembered vividly. "In big huge letters right across the front of his shop window, 'Rasta don't work for CIA'." Johnny laughed some more. "He was asking for it with that sign. It was an open invitation to the police to step right in and distress him... He bought a brand new Mercedes once, which everybody said was a 'wicked' car. He went up to this breddah who was an artist, and told him to paint the Lion of Judah on the bonnet in red gold and green. And he got him to paint quotes from Marcus Garvey's teachings around the rest of the car.

"That's why he didn't send his children to school, none ah dem, because like the sign said, 'Rasta don't work for CIA'! Speaking to his rasta bredrin he would say, "Yuh see me is not like unuh fally dread, because me don't send my pickney to the mad house dat unuh call school. It's a madhouse!"

If Johnny had looked down, he would have seen his daughter sigh impatiently. She was hardly listening to him. The voice of D.J. Pickney was calling, echoing through the mega-speakers further down the road, shouting out requests to anyone who knew him. For the moment though, Winnie couldn't answer the pint-size MC's call. She was trapped in a six o'clock roadblock and unless the crowds shifted soon, she wouldn't be getting a close-up look at D.J. Pickney. There was virtually no forward movement in the crowd, everybody was jammed too tight. And there was nothing Winnie could do but wait, unless she had wings. She was close to the reputedly 'criss' D.J. Pickney and yet so far away.

Johnny didn't mind the fact that the crowd wasn't moving. In fact, he preferred it. It was intimate. He hadn't been this close to his woman since she had found out about him cheating on her. Now, with her body squeezed up close to his, he was happier than he had been in a long time. What's more, he was on a roll and he had the captive attendance of several ears, not just those of his woman and his daughter, but even of those trapped in the jam around him.

"You see," Johnny continued, addressing his daughter more loudly than was necessary to be heard above the din, "Free-I, was the local ganja man. A skinny, short man, but with massive dreadlocks. He used to own that shop across the road. It was a little record store back then, but more time people knew him as 'the ganja man', because he always had the best weed in the area. Trust me. It was like a legal ganja shop where you could buy your herbs over the counter. Most people went to the shop to buy a five pound draw and maybe a record. But in dem times, slackness was the only kind of reggae really selling. Everybody seemed to want slack records so a lot of artists were making them. Free-I refused to sell anything but the most conscious and upful music. And when I say conscious, I mean the most hardcore, no retreat no surrender, super duper consciousness. Seen? He would tell anyone that listened that slackness was a sickness and he was going to lick it in the head with some 'blouse an' skirt' cultural cure. So he sold strictly rasta music to the small clientele who had heard of Count Ossie & the Mystic Revelations, Ras Michael & The Sons Of Negus and artists like that. Rasta reggae, y'know. And apart from the occasional lost Scandinavian tourist passing by, it was strictly a ganja shop. He sold it openly and didn't business with no hide and seek. Whenever he got stopped by the police anywhere in London, he would tell them, 'Phone

Patrick Augustus

Portobello Road Police Station, tell dem you have Free-I, the herbsman who sells ganja 'pon the corner. Because I sell dem their draw more time. When dem nuh have no black youts to come an' frisk up an' tek their ganja, they come to me, seen!' Even when the police came to raid him, he'd ask them if they wanted to buy a draw or an ounce. I remember one time when he went to court. They asked him to swear on the Bible and he said 'No.' Then they brought some other thing to swear on and Free-I still said no. So the judge said stiffly to Free-I's solicitor, "would you tell your client to do one or the other," but Free-I told them he wasn't going to swear at all. The judge was getting angry and was about to send Free-I down for contempt when the jury sent a note to the judge to ask why the Dread wouldn't swear on the Bible. He told them to read James 3 or 6 in the Bible to find out. "It says do not swear on anything on heaven or earth, because only evil and wicked people do such things." The judge interrupted him with a voice of disdain, "Oh, it's biblical reasons!" And this is Free-I to the judge: "Your honour, you is a dog an' Selassie I is God... You send your lickle Robbing Hood an' dem merry lickle men fe come rob me t'ings... How long unuh gwine teef black people t'ings...? It's over four hundred years now, bwoy, an' you still ah teef me t'ings. Gimme back me herb! I WAAN BACK ME HERB!! The whole ah unuh TEEF...!" No judge liked to preside over any case involving Free-I, because they knew what was coming – total disrespect. And when it came to sentencing, Free-I would address the judge, saying: 'Now yuh see Mr. Grudge, when you sentence me, yuh know, you just lighten my burdens, because when I go to jail, I don't have to work. I jus' cock up my foot all day an' don't do nut'n. When I'm in jail, you gotta feed me and you've got to clothe me. And unuh had bettah keep me cell warm! So you see, it just eases my burden. You can only sentence me to what God 'llow you, so just do whatever Jah tell yuh fe do..." And it didn't stop there. When they sent him to jail, he would make as much of a nuisance of himself as he could. He would insist on white inmates cleaning out his cell because, "I don't work for Esau, he is here to work for me and serve me." The warders would soon tire of hearing Free-I bawling at dinner time, "Me waan some ackee an' saltfish inna this blouse an' skirt place yah! Unuh hear me?! ...'Bout yuh cyaan come bring me no ackee an' salt fish... Unuh is James Bond, unuh send rocket to the moon an' you cyaan bring me no ackee and saltfish on yah?!" The warders would all be relieved when Free-I's sentence was over. They were only too happy to go up to him and say, "Free-I, we're going to give you parole now." But hear Free-I now, "Yuh gwine gimme what?! You don't give my people nut'n. Your name is Caesar – you *seize* people t'ings!'" And he'd say, "Listen man, jus' tek me back to my cell... You cyan keep me here one day longer than Jah 'llow you to'."

By now, tears of laughter were streaming down Johnny's eyes. The people jammed tightly in the crowd around him were also in stitches. Lesley couldn't help laughing aloud, even though she had heard the Free-I stories several times before. Even Winnie seemed to have forgotten about D.J. Pickney and was giggling. Nobody seemed to mind that the police had begun to shut down the sound systems and that the crowds were now dispersing. The Carnival was almost over for another year.

"I see Free-I as John the Baptist living in the wrong dispensation," Johnny continued as they made their way home on the tube. "That same way is how John the Baptist flexed back in dem times."

Patrick Augustus

THE SEVEN WEEK ITCH

So here I am, walking home to Brixton wondering if I rushed into things and whether I made a mistake by getting married. I mean one moment I was free and single, and yes, happy, and now I'm not. I'm not free, I'm not single and I can't say I'm as happy as I used to be. I still can't believe how it all happened and how quickly I turned my back on bachelor life and went marching to the sound of wedding bells. It was like I lowered my guard for a minute and the vows were signed, sealed and delivered.

Oh Marcia was cool the first few weeks of our marriage. That's what they call the 'honeymoon period'. Neither of us could do enough for each other and we both made sure that the new arrangement didn't mean too much compromise. Lacquan was happy with the situation as well and I began to believe that my worst fears about married life were unfounded.

It didn't take long for Marcia to start behaving like a wife and making me feel like a husband however. It started with little things, like letting everybody she came across know that we were now officially married. I couldn't even leave my filofax lying around without her calling every woman listed and informing them that she, Marcia Henry, was my lawfully wedded wife. She claimed she only made those calls to let everybody know my new home address now that we have moved in together, that she was actually doing me a favour! And I couldn't say nothin', because she's like: "What's the big deal? You shouldn't mind my calling up your women friends now that we're married. Because we're one, your friends are mine too. Unless of course there's something you're not telling me."

That wasn't the end of it. Next she suggested that I cut my funki dreds and go close-cropped. Okay, I thought, I can deal with that, it's not the end of the world. I love my funki dreds and everything, because it's part of my style, but I love Marcia more and I figured it was a small price to pay for her happiness. But that didn't satisfy her. She would come home after shopping at Marks & Spencer and pull out a woolly jumper or a pair of grey slacks she felt I ought to wear. She's touched my style so many times in the last month, it's getting outta order.

"You're thirty years old, you know Linvall, you're too old to be wearing those ragamuffin clothes," she'd say, forcing the jumper over my head. After a few shopping trips, even she could see she wasn't going to win that one, so she started criticising my eating habits instead. "And another thing," she said recently, "it would be nice to spend Sunday together as a family..."

"No," I sighed, "football is not more important than my family." With the next breath I was agreeing to take a sabbatical from my Sunday League commitments with Brixton Massive FC, "but do we really have to go to church?"

She insisted. It wasn't up for discussion. "The family which prays together stays together," she said, with a new-found religious fervour.

At this point, I thought married life couldn't get any worse, but I had another thing coming. Marcia's got this 'wife' thing so sussed that my life ain't mine no more. How can I tell my spars that I can't step with them because my woman's got every minute of my day accounted for? I ain't kidding. It's like now, I've got to dip into the grocery store on my way home, because just as I was leaving the studio, Marcia calls up from work and says, "Can you pick up some food on your way home?"

"Sure I can." What choice did I have? 'Pick up some food on your way', sounds innocent enough, but it's not. It's like that all the time; always checking up on me and it's driving me crazy. I don't like the idea of being under manners. 'Cause I left home a long time ago. Who is it that's always saying that I'm a big man now and then treats me like I'm the same age as Lacquan?

It's damn outta order! Especially when she calls me up at Gussie's place. Where am I every Friday evening if not out with my spars like every other Friday? But no, she has to check to see if I'm actually there, just in case. Damn! Can you imagine how embarrassing it is when you're with your boys having a laugh and your missus calls you up to ask what time you're coming home? *I'll be home when I get home!* Believe. *And you don't need to wait up either.* I mean what is it, man? I got married for better or worse, but I don't remember nothing about no curfew! And imagine how I feel when I get home five minutes late and she starts asking, "Where've you been?" "Who've you been with...?" And when the inquisition starts, there ain't no 'ifs' or 'buts'; the excuses had better be good because Marcia's got a bullshit detector permanently trained on me.

I don't doubt that she loves me, but she's too conscious of the fact that I'm a successful fashion photographer and therefore bait for many women. If we're out driving and someone calls out to me from a car or a bus stop, she's always got to ask, "Who's that?" or, "Was she an ex-girlfriend?" It's like Marcia's squeezing me too tight, man. I mean, what's the problem? I said that I was going to be faithful and I have been. No way is just any and any woman going to turn my head as easily as they used to, I'm a married man now. Marcia's gotta give me the benefit of the doubt. But no, just because she's never known one man who was faithful to his woman, she's got to distress me.

Maybe Gussie had the right idea by chucking his wife on his wedding night. I don't know how he did it or why, but the point is that when you realise your marriage isn't working, you get out and suffer the consequences. I don't know how he got a judge to believe that his marriage to Chantelle had never been consummated. If there's one thing I know about my spar Gussie, it's that he could never have had a sweet-looking honey like Chantelle in his bed without giving her the agony. But the judge took his word for it and annulled the marriage.

What's really bugging Marcia is that I spend my days working with some criss babes in shorts, bikinis and less. It was never a problem when I was on my own, but taking pictures of glamorous women when you're married can seriously distress your domestic affairs. No joke. And I've had my chances too. Last night for example, when I went out for a drink with one of the models after a shoot. She was all inviting and everything, but I wasn't flirting with her, I was just being friendly. Though it crossed my mind to join her in the back of the cab to her place, it was already past my curfew time. So it takes me another hour to get home and when I eventually arrive, Marcia's like, "Where are you coming from?"

"I'm coming from talking to a magazine editor about a new photo spread."

"Do you want to try again?" she asked, daring me to continue lying.

"What do you mean by that?" Up to now my head was still fuzzy from the alcohol earlier, but I began to sober up. She said she was giving me another chance to tell the truth. Even as I felt myself steaming I knew the best thing was to stay cool. I felt a rush of alcohol in my head and knew I was beyond good advice.

"Get off my case, Marce! Damn! Can't a man come home from work without his wife calling him a liar? I'm home, that's all there is to it. Take it or leave it. I don't care if you don't believe me."

"You mean to tell me that you've been in a meeting and you come in smelling of booze? Then you ask me what's wrong! Don't do this to me, Linvall, don't try to make me think I'm crazy."

"Nobody's saying that you're crazy."

"Because here I am struggling to get the house together and working like a dog while you're spending all our money going out for drinks with friends – male or otherwise! You don't seem to care about the needs of everybody else around you, Linvall. You don't even know if your son needs a new pair of trousers or not and if we can afford it."

I couldn't believe what I was hearing. But I simply stood

there with my mouth half-open. For a small woman, Marcia had a mouthful of distress at her disposal. She was right though, I didn't know if Lacquan needed new clothes or not.

"If you could only see what I'm going through for a change," she continued mournfully. "I don't want to be like this. I've got better things to do with my time than to keep trying to track you down. But I didn't get married to be made a fool of, Linvall. You're behaving like nothing's changed, like the wedding was all about signing a piece of paper. Wake up. Get real. You're a married man with a grown up son, your duty's here at home, not out on the street."

Then she noticed the expensive silk shirt I was wearing. "Where did you get that from? Why are you wearing it?"

"It was a present from Gussie," I said. No way was she buying that, but it was the truth and I challenged her to call him to verify it.

"Alright then," she conceded, "but wasn't there something in your diary about doing a bikini shoot with some models today? That's why you're wearing this 'pass-the-riddim' shirt, isn't it? You sure you're not using this work thing to cheat on me?"

I sighed. "Look, I'm a photographer. Taking pics of beautiful women is my job. The only way I'm not going to notice the attractive model on the other side of the camera lens is if I'm blindfolded. But I need to look to take the shot, right?"

Marcia wasn't convinced, so now she's on a new tip about me looking for a 'better' job.

Crissakes! If she had her way, she'd force me out of my career. The other day for example, I had to get up at dawn for an early shoot. I knew she'd be up by then so I asked her to wake me. When I woke up, it was after nine. "Why didn't you wake me?" I asked her and without batting an eyelid she answers, "You needed the rest so I didn't think it necessary..."

Basically, I'm under heavy manners and I don't

appreciate it. I need my space, 'cause I'm a creative kinda guy. I mean, photography isn't just about clicking a button. I need time on my own to be able to sit down and focus, because I'm a man of ideas and sometimes you need a rest from people. When it comes to the evening, I like to switch off without becoming stressed out. And to be honest, being a newly-wed and a father all at the same time, is stressing me out. Perhaps I shouldn't have rushed to get married.

I'm not saying that marriage hasn't got its good sides. The time since the wedding have given me the stability I needed in my life. Sometimes there's nothing better than just kicking back with your wife and kid in a family kinda vibe. After years on the singles scene, I'm hitched to one woman and I can't deny it's been a positive change in many respects. I'm looking better, feeling better and eating better. I even put on some weight, nothing serious, just a coupla pounds, but everybody seems to notice. And that's cool too, but I don't want it getting out of hand. So it's down to the gym in the morning for a session on the step machine.

And that's another thing about this marriage lark. Bustin' sweat never used to be a problem. When you're single and regularly checking different women you have to keep in trim. With me, it was up early every day for a jog, football training one evening a week and then a game on Sunday in season. That's all I needed to keep my muscles toned. But married life puts a different perspective on your priorities and Marcia makes a wicked cheesecake which my stomach is weak for.

We decided to get married before thinking about where we were all going to live. Marcia's old place was only big enough for herself and Lacquan, so we postponed the honeymoon until next summer and went house-hunting instead. In no time at all, through Marcia's contacts, the housing association got us a moderate three bedroomed, newly-built house behind the Police station in Brixton. A little too close to comfort for me, but Marcia reasoned that at least we wouldn't get broken into. So we moved in and for the first few days it was chaotic. There were no carpets and other bits and pieces of DIY needed to be sorted out. Marcia took time off work and really got into the 'togetherness' of making a home and playing house.

When it was all finished it looked beautiful. The pastel coloured walls seemed to go with all Marcia's African figurines and my little art deco touches. We spent a small fortune in getting a new leather three-piece suite to fit into the compact living room. When it was all done, our new home looked so beautiful that Marcia cried, "because I don't want any of this to ever end. At last we can get on with our life together. I've been waiting twelve years for this day. Twelve years for you to finally say, 'Let's get married'..."

However good she felt about everything, she had no intention of easing up on me one bit. It seemed like the better she felt, the more suspicious she acted towards me.

"I want to trust you, but I know you too well. I know you find it hard to resist women. Your flesh is weak, Linvall. Your flesh is too damn weak!"

"So that's what it's all about, eh? Jealousy?"

"No, not at all. Let me remind you that my son, not my husband, is the most important person in my life. My concern is for Lacquan. I don't want to have to put him through all the trauma of a break-up just when we are together as a family for the first time. Maybe I'm a fool, but the romantic side of me so much wants our marriage to work that I'm not going to give you an opportunity to disrespect it... Do you remember back in the old days when we first met, how you used to tell me I was an Egyptian goddess and whisper in my ear, 'a goddess like you shouldn't be sleeping alone tonight. If you'd only allow this good knight to give you a good night...' Do you remember Linvall? You always had such sweet words, the sweetest. But when I look back, they were just words. I didn't feel like Isis, because you never treated me like Isis."

When I reflected back, I didn't see it like that at all.

"I recall treating you like a goddess on more than one

occasion," I protested. "The way I remember it, it was you who didn't want anything to do with me when you realised during your pregnancy, that I didn't intend to settle down and get married to you at once. Wasn't it you who forced me to pretend to Lacquan for more than ten years that I was his uncle and not his father? Wasn't it you who told him that his father was in America all those years? So don't blame me if our son's getting into trouble at school now that he knows the full truth. Look, I love Lacquan as much as you, he's my son after all. I had hoped that he wouldn't have any more disciplinary problems at school now that we are official, but it hasn't happened. But don't I try and help him with his studies and reason with him? Didn't I encourage him to go to the Book Shack's Saturday School with Johnny Dollar? At least I'm trying."

There was no two ways about it, Lacquan was doing very badly in school. He was doing everything he wasn't supposed to do, like talking with an attitude and using words he knew he wasn't supposed to use. Only in his first term in his new secondary school, the headmistress had already asked to see Marcia and myself. For some reason, Lacquan was just not interested in his studies. He once came top in his junior school class, but was lagging behind everybody else now.

In Marcia's view, she and I shared the responsibility of spending time with our son. From where I stood, it wasn't an equal split. After all, I was spending most evenings with him. She felt that was only natural after all the years she had spent being both a mother and father to him and besides he was a boy child and needed his father more. If he had been a girl, Marcia volunteered, she'd be at home most evenings instead. Her father had always been there for his son and she didn't see any reason why I shouldn't be there for Lacquan twenty-four seven. In her view, that had to be my number one priority.

"You learn what's important in life when you come from a close-knit family like I do," she said. "As far as I'm concerned my family is my rock. When my sisters are happy, then I'm happy too."

"I couldn't agree more. But what I'm saying is: is it necessary for me to spend most of my evenings with Lacquan? After all he's eleven years old, he's a big boy now. When I was a kid my father was too busy trying to provide for us to spend much time with me. That doesn't mean I wasn't getting all the love that I needed, because I was. It's just that an eleven year old boy doesn't need to hold his father's hand to cross the road."

"Yeah, but the difference is," Marcia said, "in those days the parents' job was done if their kids were wholesome and had three meals a day and clothes on their backs and a roof over their heads and didn't bring shame on the family. It's harder for kids out there today. Your job as a father is not done unless you prepare your son for what's waiting for him when he leaves home every morning. You've got to make sure he's independent and can take care of himself when the time comes. You've got to make sure that he's happy. All those things."

I couldn't argue with that either. Marcia was right. When she is being reasonable like that it makes me feel good that we are a family. I love her and probably always will. Because no matter how I feel on a day-to-day basis, she's part of me. But I just can't help worrying that things are going to get painful between us. Because at the end of the day, I'm a man and no matter how much good sex Marcia can give me, she can't give me any new sex. What's going to happen when I get tired of being tied to one woman? 'Cause if these three months of marriage feel like thirty years, what's it going to feels like in six months time?

WHY DO FOOLS FALL IN LOVE?

Gussie's mind was playing tricks on him. The more he tried to forget the horrifying memory of his wedding night, the more it appeared written large before him. He and Chantelle had been locked in a steamy embrace in the hotel's honeymoon suite, promising each other the sweetness. In breathless tones she said he would get nothing less than the 'slam' and he replied that he would give her the full 'agony'. That was as far as they got to consummating their marriage. A moment later, his new bride whispered nervously, "There's just one thing... I used to be a man."

Gussie clenched his jaw and twisted the throttle of the Harley as far as it would go, to overtake the cars up ahead on the dual carriageway, with nature's rolling hills flashing past on either side of him. Thinking about Chantelle raised his blood pressure and he didn't care that the speedometer needle was on 80, nor if he got pulled over by the police. He had intentionally avoided the motorway, for despite the cold he wanted to see something of the countryside.

He had bought the motorbike from Linvall more for fun and kudos than anything else. Even though the Harley Davidson engine was notoriously sluggish and its road handling left a lot to be desired, it was every schoolboy's dream to one day own one and, for Gussie, that dream had become a reality at the age of thirty-five. Moreover, it had turned out to be a good purchase. With all his domestic distress of recent weeks, the bike was a way of ridding himself of a lot of angst and anger. After walking out from Chantelle in their honeymoon suite at the Park Lane Hotel, he took a taxi home, climbed on the Harley and just drove into the night with no particular place to go, and when he got there three days later, he turned the bike around and rode back again. He had even managed to pull a couple of women on the bike, so now he always carried an extra helmet, just in case!

Today, he had somewhere to go. He had decided to spend

the week alone in a little cottage in a secluded Welsh valley.

Gussie glanced at his watch. It was a quarter to one. He was tired and hungry. He swung off the road at the next turning and rode through a quiet village before pulling up in front of a pub. A couple of youths standing beside a moped nearby turned to admire the black man climbing off the big motorcycle.

"Hey mista!" one called. "Let's have a go on your bike!"

"Let me have a shag with your sister first!" Gussie called back.

"I haven't got a sister!" the boy called back.

"Pity," Gussie replied, "you would have enjoyed riding the bike an' all." Then as he locked the back wheel and set the alarm, he added, "Beautiful machine the Harley Davidson, innit?"

Gussie had changed and he knew it, but there was nothing he could do about it. He had become coarse and arrogant and disinterested in things he had previously felt passionate about. The shock of his wife's true identity had turned his world upside down. Too ashamed and disgusted to share the truth of his dilemma with anyone, he had bottled things up to the point of bursting. That buppie veneer of the successful young black bachelor that he had so carefully nurtured had disappeared. And where once he was driven to making his business secure, his Mighty Diamond shop in Hatton Garden had more or less run itself while he 'recovered' from his 'stress'. .

His friends quickly saw the deterioration of their spar. Beres, Johnny and Linvall who knew him better than most, were as surprised as everyone else that Gussie's marriage had ended after the first night. But he had refused to talk about it, explaining only that he didn't need more than one night to discover how "nasty" Chantelle was. All he would say was, "I'm getting divorced in the morning, most definitely. 'Cause I can't take it no longer."

Gussie had heard many rumours about his marriage break-up, none of which were on the money. His friends joked that Chantelle had walked out on him, when she discovered that Gussie wasn't going to buy her the crown jewels. Others suggested that Gussie had a dark side, which Chantelle only discovered on their wedding night.

And even though Gussie reassured them continually that he had gotten over the whole thing and put it all down to a "mistake", his friends could see that what went down was still gnawing at his heart. They were thankful that Gussie had decided to get back in control of the Mighty Diamond shop; that at least was a sign that he was getting back to normal. But then he came up with this "lost in the wilderness" business and they realised Gussie still had a lot of things to get out of his system. October was the wrong time to be lost in the wilderness trying to find some peace and rest.

With his open-faced helmet on the table beside him, Gussie tucked into the hearty meal of roast beef and Yorkshire pudding. The few locals in the bar having their midday pints raised an eyebrow when the black man stepped in through the saloon doors. But that didn't bother Gussie. He had seen it all before. Word had probably spread through the town by now that a 'sambo' had blown in, he thought, grinning to himself. He glanced out of the window at his bike and for a moment thought he was Marlon Brando in *The Wild One*. His fantasy was cut short, however, as the memory of his wedding night flashed before him again... He was back in the honeymoon suite, paralysed, unable to believe what he had heard or utter a single sound. Refusing to make sense out of nonsense, it was like he was on another planet. How could it be? He hoped he was wrong. He had to be wrong. Chantelle had to be a woman. Seeing her on the bed naked, he couldn't tell the difference. It had to be a joke. But from the look in Chantelle's eyes, he realised that this was anything but a joke. This was serious and calculated to blow his mind. He tried to get up and leave, but his body wouldn't allow him to move a muscle, as the full horror of what his new 'bride' had told him sank in. His heart began to pound. His senses were numbed. His reality became a psychedelic nightmare from which he couldn't escape.

He kept on seeing her at the church, in her wedding dress, making promises in front of everybody. And he was thinking of his promises too, "Love and honour for better or worse..." This was probably the 'worse' they were talking about, and he didn't want it. He wanted better. He wanted to stop seeing Chantelle's face and he wanted the sound of her saying, "I used to be a man... I used to be a man... I used to be a man," to stop ringing in his ears.

It was driving him nuts, bolts and screws. How could she have duped him so easily? Now that her honey-coated lies came echoing back to him it seemed so obvious that she was a devil in disguise, however smooth and slick. And more importantly, how could he have fallen for her?! And why the hell was he talking of Chantelle as 'her' or 'she' when in truth he married an 'it'? Just thinking about it made him ill, and though he tried hard to erase the memory, the loudspeakers of his mind kept blasting in his ears: "YOUR WOMAN WAS A MAN! YOU MARRIED A MAN, YOU KISSED A MAN AND YOU ALMOST..." *Stop there, stop there!* Gussie's soul cried out in loud, unspoken words. It was more than he cared to contemplate. What actually happened was bad enough without him having to consider what could have been if Chantelle had waited another moment to reveal her secret. His sexuality was not up for discussion. If he hadn't discovered that 'she' was a 'he' before the relationship was consummated, he would have done the honourable thing and committed suicide. He didn't have the slightest hesitation. He would have ended his life immediately. No question about it.

Gussie was brought back to the here and now by the silky sounds of Nat King Cole oozing out of the pub's jukebox:

When I fall in love, it will be forever...

Over by the bar, one of the customers, now a little worse for drink, was serenading his woman.

When I fall in love, it will be forever...

Gussie listened dispassionately. As good as they were, old King Cole's songs of love were not for him. Since the wedding, not even the great Marvin Gaye had been able to soothe him. Gussie had become cynical about love and romance and for the first time since he could remember, his collection of Al Green records had no effect on him. The question was, would he ever love again? Would he ever *really* love again, or would he simply wade in his own despair until he was old and grey? Who was it that said that the end would come in a fiery holocaust when the sun would rise in the West and set in the East and that the men would look like the women and the women like the men?

He looked up. The clock above the pub fireplace said 3 o'clock. Gussie sighed, picked up his helmet and made his way over to the bar to pay for his meal. He hadn't meant to spend this much time in the pub, but he had a lot on his mind. Despite the terrible blow he had received, he was far from finished. Only he was hip to the secret of his marriage and it had to stay that way. As importantly, he had to get back on the fast track. Back to life, back to reality.

Outside, it had started to get dark and there was a cold bite in the air. The chrome on the Harley glistened, though the bike looked a lot more crooked on its sidestand than Gussie had remembered. On closer examination, he discovered to his dismay that the rear tyre was flat. But how? The three inch nail sticking out of the tyre just below the rear mudguards was the answer. Gussie cussed out loud, the alarm hadn't even sounded. He remembered the two kids on the moped and how he had teased them. He glanced around the pub car park, but they were long gone. There wasn't a soul in sight.

The AA man wasn't overjoyed about having to drive Gussie

and his motorbike all the way to mid-Wales, but he had no choice. Gussie had wisely invested in the five-star recovery service which guaranteed that the breakdown vehicle would take you to the destination of your choice. Although he hadn't been to the cottage before, Beres had assured him that it would be easy to find.

He had first told his friends of his plans two weeks previously. At first, they all laughed. Why did Gussie think that if he got away from it all, he would be able to better judge what he wanted from a woman? But Gussie didn't see the funny side of it. He wasn't prepared to keep making mistakes about women. He had to get things right, and if he was to find the woman he was looking for he would have to be adventurous and industrious. His current way of assessing women wasn't working. He needed to start afresh without all the prejudices of his earlier relationship to distort his views and most importantly he didn't want his relationship with Chantelle hanging over him clouding his judgement. So he was going to spend forty days and forty nights alone in the wilderness (or rather seven) and when he was ready to come back to London, he would be a stronger person and more confident about the kind of woman he was looking for.

On hearing Gussie's plan of action, Johnny couldn't stop laughing, he said that it sounded like the act of a desperate man. And he chastised Beres for offering Gussie his parents' summer cottage in Wales to indulge his fancy. Johnny had a better idea to solve Gussie's problems. He passed his friend a leaflet which he had been handed earlier that morning outside Brixton tube station. It was an invite to a symposium entitled, *How To Love A Black Woman*. Gussie read the leaflet quickly. He already knew the plot of this one. Such symposiums were now standard in black London life. He wasn't impressed. He needed something much more personal than that. He envied his friends who had their women and who, despite all the problems of their relationships, seemed to have an understanding with their partners which kept them together through thick and thin.

"I'm not trying to save the black race," he told Johnny. "I just want to find the right woman."

Johnny teased him, refusing to allow his spar to start moping about his miserable self again. They had already done the best for him that they could. When Johnny met a single woman he always made sure that he informed them of his good friend Gussie who he was sure they would like. What more could Gussie ask for?

Maybe it was a stupid idea, Gussie considered, now that he had arrived at the little cottage. It was a secluded, two-bedroomed cottage at the outer fringes of a sheep farm and was at least a kilometre away from the nearest neighbours. At one time, it had been used by the farmhands, but for the last five years, Beres' school teacher parents had rented it from the farmer at a very reasonable rate as a weekend home. It looked beautiful and serene, but would he really be able to take being so far from civilisation? Anyway, it was too late to be considering that now. He gave the AA man a large tip. Unimpressed, the man mumbled something about his wife reporting him missing to the police, before driving off.

The key to the front door was where Beres had explained that it would be: underneath a loose brick, under a step at the back of the house. Gussie let himself in. The cottage was dark and cold. There was no electricity. But it was clean and tidy even though Beres' parents, Mr and Mrs Dunkley, hadn't been there for a month.

It took nearly an hour before Gussie managed, with great effort, to get a log fire blazing in the open fireplace downstairs. By then, he was so exhausted that he fell asleep in the armchair even though it was only nine o'clock.

He awoke the next morning to the unfamiliar sound of sheep bleating outside. He peered out of the window to see his motorbike being examined warily by a vicious-looking black ram with curled horns. Gussie decided against stepping outside the cottage for the moment. Besides, it was only seven in the morning. Instead, he decided to explore the cottage in the crisp daylight. The downstairs consisted of one large room. The end at the front of the house was used as a sitting room, with a couple of armchairs in front of the small fireplace, where the embers from the fire he had lit the night before were now dead. Towards the back of the house, the room became a kitchen, with a little dining table. It was all very basic, but homely. Upstairs, were two tiny bedrooms, one overlooking the front of the house and the other the back. From the bedroom windows, Gussie could see right across the valley. He could see the large farmhouse in the distance and the fields that separated them, dotted with sheep that looked like white specs in the distance. Beyond the farmhouse was a cluster of houses which he assumed was the nearest village that Beres had told him about. The nearest town was Aberystwyth, but that was some way beyond the hills, and Gussie didn't intend to go that far. He was here to get away from towns and people.

Yes, maybe it was a stupid idea, but he couldn't come up with anything better. The Chantelle episode had really shaken his belief in women and in himself. There was no guarantee that this period of meditation would work but he couldn't carry on playing the game as he had been and failing so dismally. He had to do something different. And this was as 'different' as he could imagine.

There was no TV in the cottage. That suited Gussie fine. Beres had explained that when his parents were there, they kept in contact with the outside only through a battery-operated wireless. They didn't even have a phone there. You had to go down to the pay phone in the village to call out. What was more, the cottage had only the most basic of comforts. There was an outside toilet, but no bathroom.

Gussie soon figured out the best way to have a bath. With all the pots and pans boiling with water on the wood stove in the kitchen, he filled the small tin bath with care. It was going to be a tight squeeze, but he had seen it done in cowboy films. When there was enough water in it, he squeezed his six foot two frame into the bath and relaxed as best he could, feeling like Clint Eastwood. He sat in deep thought for several hours, climbing out of the bath only to add more boiling water from the stove and to light a stick of incense which he had earlier found in the kitchen.

At the age of thirty-five, Gussie Pottinger conceded that he didn't want to become a prisoner of loneliness. He didn't know exactly what he wanted out of life, but he knew it included a loving wife and a family. He wanted to get married, to have that security and support behind him, but that it wasn't easy finding the right woman. Despite everything that had happened, he still had hopes that he would one day meet, the woman he would want to spend the rest of his life with. Someone to build a home and start a family with. Family was a thing that he personally took very seriously and he was determined not to become a baby father. He wanted to be a father to his children on a permanent basis and not just by appointment.

As he sat in the tin bath, he considered everything that had happened to him since he met Chantelle. If she hadn't come into the Mighty Diamond to look at some jewellry, his life would still be the way it was before. He would never have discovered that his father had had a child out of wedlock. And his mother would never have had to admit that he was not his father's son, but that his father didn't know it. Ultimately, if Chantelle had never crossed his path, he wouldn't have made the greatest mistake any man could make in marriage.

So where did he go wrong? Was it simply that Chantelle was a 'woman' who brought evil with her? He thought back to the women he had dated in the past. He had to admit that he suspected several of them of one form of madness or another. Like Barbara, who he had dated for a while in his teens. He could never understand why she took such pleasure in digging her fingernails into the skin on his back and dragging until it bled. She seemed to get a kick out of that for some reason. And then there was Arlene. She was a personnel manager at one of the large Oxford Street department stores. Her kick was making love at a different location each time. It was easy at first because there was his place, then there was her place, then there was his car, and a few of his friend's places and then there were hotels. But after a few months of hunting around for a new venue for their daily sessions, things started becoming tiresome, but still Arlene insisted. No new venue, no sex. There had to be some madness in that. 'Normal' people just aren't like that. When he thought about it, it was not unreasonable for Gussie to conclude, that the problem was perhaps in his choice of women.

Where was that 'significant other' that people talked of? When he checked the real deal, Gussie couldn't help but feel that his mistake was in always going after the prettiest woman he set his eyes on. He always liked to be seen with a woman who other men regarded as 'criss', pure and simple. And when he was bewitched with physical attraction, his normally probing mind would slip into neutral while he got off on vanities, unable to see if a woman was dressed up in disguises of various forms. And each time he believed that he had found Miss Right she turned into Miss Wrong. He had thought that he could buy a woman's happiness. With a successful diamond business to his name, he had the money to buy a woman whatever she wanted and he had once believed that that was sufficient. He couldn't have been more wrong. No matter how much you sat down and thought about it, nothing could prepare you for waking up to discover that your wife is a man. It had distorted his sense of himself, but he needed now to rise up above it and become that man who truly understands, and be one with the real world, not the world of micro miniskirts. He was looking for a love queen not a sex queen. He vowed to never again allow infatuation to cloud his judgment.

He was no longer interested in hearing advice from his friends like 'seek and you will find'. All that was foolishness. It was advice like that which had got him into his marriage predicament in the first place. He was seeking and he found Chantelle. He didn't intend to allow a mistake like that to happen again. This time, he was going to leave it all up to statistics.

His meditation found him searching for an objective way of determining his 'ideal' woman. Was there such a thing as an objective evaluation? Didn't everything need a subject to evaluate it. For example, could he really talk of an objective evaluation of his Harley? To him, it was worth a few grand, but to someone with no interest in riding motorbikes it might be worth nothing. And could you talk of a 'value' for the bike if there was no one around to consider it? When he thought about it deeply, Gussie couldn't come up with any examples of truly objective evaluations of anything outside mathematics and science, which dealt with certainty, necessity and precision. Was it possible to evaluate women with the same certainty as mathematics?

Then in a blinding flash, it came to him. What he had to do was find a new way of looking at women. He had to discard his previous notions of what a woman, the woman he wanted, would be like. The opinions he had held about women since his youth had proved false and he had to look doubtfully at everything else he had built on those opinions. He had to do this if he was to make a choice that would establish a lasting relationship. The task seemed enormous, but it was nothing more than he had expected. That's why it was so important that he was alone, in the wilderness, far from everybody else he knew and all other distractions, the matter would get his full attention over the next few days. He would raze his previous opinions to the ground and start again with a totally new premise. What he would do in future, he decided, was to avoid the pretty women. If anything, if he was to consider a wife again, he would go for the conventional wife-mother, however frumpy or dumpy she may be. Right now, he wasn't interested in anything else. At the end of the day he simply wanted what everyone wants, the right partner. Most definitely. In future, he resolved, he would use his intelligence more when it came to choosing a partner. He would take more than five minutes in evaluating whether or not a particular woman was the future wife he was looking for.

But what exactly did he require from the kind of woman he was looking for? Oblivious to the fact that he had become wrinkly from sitting too long in the tin bath, he wrote down a list of his desires in a notebook. At the top he wrote 'HONESTY' in big bold letters and underlined it. After the shock revelations on his wedding night, honesty was the number one priority in choosing a woman. 'Independence', 'decent looks', 'down-to-earth' and, of course, 'family oriented'. At first he felt that age didn't matter, but it did. If women his own age made him feel immature and insecure, he needed a woman between the ages of 22 and 30 years old. Even a woman with a child from a previous relationship was worth considering. As long as she still had a whole lot of love to give him. Dating a woman with kids was not a problem, in fact, he expected it at his age and his large, hazel eyes lit up briefly with the thought of having a child of his own one day.

That was it; his fundamental requirements. Then he wrote down a list of the type of women he wanted to avoid including: 'Women with no ambition'. Most definitely.

He read over his list of requirements for the fifth time. What it boiled down to was that he was looking for a soul mate, somebody to share his life dreams and encourage his ambitions. There were still some good women out there who weren't already taken, he was sure of it. There had to be. Women who were looking for a man like him, with a good sense of humour; a man who was sensitive, caring and adventurous. He was more than ready to offer the right woman a future with fun, stability and a lot of love and potential.

Submerged in lukewarm water, he dozed off and dreamt of the 'perfect wife'.

RUDE BOY BUSINESS

Only a crazy man allows someone else to be a father to his child. I should know, because I've become something of an expert on the matter since having to maintain two families. My daughter, Lara, I can't do much about. The law says that she is to live with her mother. That is the price I have to pay for divorcing Sonia after she walked out on me. Vernon was a different matter, he came free of charge. "Love me, love my son," Caroline said when we started dating. But I couldn't imagine how complicated that was going to be once we were man and wife.

Becoming a househusband wasn't something I had reckoned on when we got married. But I can't deny that I knew what I was doing. I had my eyes open and there was no sign of any shotgun at the wedding. If I had wanted a housewife, I wouldn't have married a rising star of the legal profession. But it's one thing to marry a woman who's never going to cook or clean for you, and another thing entirely to take on those chores yourself. But that's the way it is, we're a partnership and as such, whoever's not working wears the apron. Anyway, Caroline's earning potential is likely to be greater than mine for some time to come so it makes better financial sense for me to wash the dishes.

I didn't exactly leave my job at Dan Oliver's car showroom, I was eased out. Quite simply, they didn't like the fact that their top salesman was a black man. And when, after an exceptionally good month during which I sold a dozen new Jaguars to one Arab client and my commission surpassed the managing director's salary, it all became too much for them.

"It has nothing to do with your being black," they said, and just in case I thought otherwise, they paid me off with six months basic salary. Caroline was adamant that I should take them to the industrial tribunal, that the Commission for Racial Equality would support me and that I had a prima facae case of racial discrimination, but conceded that these things were hard to prove. Faced with the prospect of a drawn out legal case, I opted to take the money and run. It was a cop-out, I know, but I wouldn't have been able to handle it. I'm using my anger in a positive way. The whole thing has made me determined to work for myself again. There's no sense in being an employee. With the money I've got in the bank, I'll be setting up a little something of my own. I've got ideas, I just haven't settled on one yet.

Househusbandry held no terror for me. After all, I had to be both father and mother to Lara after Sonia left me. I knew how to clean and I've learned how to cook. The one thing I don't like, is having to babysit for that brat Vernon, Caroline's seven-year-old son, while she's away in Brussels.

It wouldn't have bothered me if Caroline had told me from the beginning that she had a kid, after all I had a kid from a previous relationship also. But she sort of dropped it on me when I was already besotted with her and when it was really a case of: *when a man loves a woman, she can do no wrong...* It wouldn't have bothered me, after all I expected nothing less from Caroline with regards to my own daughter; if it wasn't for the fact that Vernon is 'the devil's child'. I'm not kidding. Of course Caroline can't see it, she's got a rosy picture of her son. She can't see how unruly he is, but believe me, the boy needs some serious discipline!

How bad can a seven-year-old boy be? Forget about mischief, because Vernon's beyond that. At his tender age, he's declared total war on his stepfather and has learned to use the tactic of disobedience in disrespecting me.

Vernon doesn't miss an opportunity to remind me of how much he dislikes me. He doesn't need to, but he feels he ought to anyway. When his mother told him that she was thinking of getting married to me, he told her not to. He didn't want her to tie the knot, because he considered me "so ugly". No other reason apparently. At first Caroline, with all her modern ideas about upbringing, was reluctant to force him to get used to the idea and refused to allow me to do it for her. "Spare the rod and spoil the child," my old headmaster at Millfield public school used to say, almost regrettably, just before he beat you. Until I met Vernon, I disagreed with that statement most vehemently. Anyway, we eventually got married, with Caroline promising that she wouldn't expect me to kiss and cuddle my stepson.

So here I am, a surrogate father to Vernon and feeling uncomfortable about it. Not just because he needs a good slap in his neck-back, but also because I couldn't imagine that his real father would approve. I know I wouldn't want any other man bringing up my kid. It's bad enough only being able to see Lara at weekends, but if Sonia brought some man in to replace me as her father, I wouldn't be too happy. So I tread carefully where Vernon's concerned and let him get away with a great deal. I just don't want him going to his father at the weekend and starting static.

How bad can a seven-year-old be? Gussie couldn't believe it when I told him. He suggested twisting Vernon's ear until it tears. Fortunately for the brat, I didn't take Gussie up on it. The problem is that Vernon is vindictive and spiteful, if you let him disrespect you and get away with it, he lives to disrespect you another day.

Caroline's only been gone a few days, but with Vernon in the same house, it feels like a lifetime. When she told me she was going to Belgium to fight a landmark case in the European Courts, I knew straight away that she expected me to do the honours and take care of Vernon while she was gone. I felt like telling her there and then: "I can't take your rude pickney in any way shape or form!" But she already suspected me of being jealous of all the attention she was paying to Vernon and her career, so I ended up saying nothing and got lumbered with him. Once his mother was gone, Vernon refused to acknowledge me or obey me. Even when I drive him to school in the mornings after serving him breakfast and getting him ready, he says nothing. No "see you", no "thank you", nothing. And when he comes home from school he flops down on the carpet in front of the television, looking up only to eat the dinner I place in front of him.

Though he refuses to communicate directly, Vernon makes his views known one way or another. He's stopped doing his chores like emptying the dustbin every evening, and instead he's started treating me as his personal maid. If he eats a banana, the skin is left lying on the carpet for 'Miss Beres' to pick up or slip and slide on. Despite his young age, Vernon knows how to leave a subtle but devastating hint lying around. This is why I say he's 'the devil's child'. The banana skin is his way of telling me, that for all he cared, I could break my neck. It's not paranoia either, I know what I'm talking about. I've had to live with the boy and quite frankly, he's evil. Like, for example in the mornings when he wakes up, he goes in the bathroom to brush his teeth and always makes sure that he removes my toothbrush from the mug containing the family toothbrushes, and places it on the side of the sink. That's how we first got into the argument. After all this had been going on for four days in a row, I finally had enough of his misbehaving. He was outside playing rudie with a few of his local friends. When I told him to get in, he ignored me. Finally, I dragged him, despite his yelling and screaming and kicking. He spat in my face. He actually spat in my face! He just didn't know when to stop. I wiped the spittle off with a handkerchief and confronted him straight, telling him in no uncertain terms the way things were and how he was going to behave from now on.

"All the fun and games are over young man. Welcome to the real world. In the real world, you're just a little boy, and little boys have to learn how to be responsible men. You're going to learn that whether you like it or not."

Vernon said nothing, but simply shrugged me off. I had to grab him again and with his feet flying at me from all directions, I picked him up to take him in. I hadn't got very far however, before his friends started calling the neighbours for help, and yelling that I was beating up the kid!

"You know what, this two masters business can't work. Two masters can't run this house. From now on we do things my way," I said dragging him in and slamming the door closed behind us.

He still didn't get the message. He cussed and shouted that he needed to be outside with his friends.

"I can't breath inside the house because your stinking breath is killing me. I need fresh air!"

"So you want fresh air?" I asked. "If you want fresh air, you can go in the garden until it gets cold. But I'll tell you now, you're not going out to play with all those out of order friends of yours. They should be in their beds by now anyway."

When Vernon realised that he wasn't going to get his way, his main object was to release himself from my grip.

"Alright, ease off!" he screamed. "I'll tell mum when she comes that you hurt me! You're not my dad, you know. Just because you're sleeping with my mum, you think you own the place!"

"What the f...!"

I couldn't believe what I had just heard. Where did he learn stuff like that? I let him go, wondering who had won the moral victory, him or me. Then the brat pulled out his next stroke which was to cry as loudly as possible, until the neighbours were coming around wondering if everything was alright.

The tears didn't draw my sympathy. I can't stand to see a boy-child bawl his eyes out for no reason. My dad always used to say to me, "Son, you are the man of the house while I'm gone." Even as a child I realised what that meant; I had to behave in that certain way which I had often seen my father doing. My father never cried and I was left with the belief that boys don't cry. Vernon's tears then, had the wrong effect on me and I had to resist the urge of really giving him something to cry about.

Though Vernon had calmed down, I began to feel uneasy. Had I gone too far? Stepfather or not, did I really have the right to physically restrain another man's child? I became so nervous, I spent the rest of the evening trying to reason with this seven-year-old terror. I felt I had to explain my actions and why I was insisting that he had to behave himself. As usual, Vernon ignored me and I soon realised I was wasting my breath. He clammed up with his arms folded and never said a word. In the vacant stare in his eyes I saw that he was planning something and it bothered me. Why was I letting this seven-year-old get to me like this?

That night I went to bed with a troubled mind. I had lost my cool. I had let a child distress me. I was more than a little worried, not knowing what Vernon's next move would be, but he was definitely planning something. I really shouldn't have got heavy with him. More than anything I wished that he would accept my apology and understand how out of order he was being. What was that he said about me sleeping with his mother?

That I had replaced his father in his mother's bed was a vexed issue with Vernon. Caroline said he was just being protective of her, that little boys were often that way about their mothers. So I agreed for the first month of our marriage to slip out into the spare room early in the mornings before Vernon woke up, so that he wouldn't find us in bed together. It was crazy, but Caroline thought it was best, just until he got used to the idea. Thinking about it now, it would have been better to get him used to it from the start. Now that he knew what the real deal was, he wasn't taking it any better than if he had known from the beginning.

I tossed and turned all night long, wondering why I was bringing up another man's child. Why wasn't Vernon somewhere else with his father? The further the better. Why wasn't my daughter with me instead of with her mother? All I got that night was a couple of hours sleep, or maybe three.

Vernon was still silent in the morning. At least it was Friday and in the evening I was able to pack him off in a taxi to his father's for the weekend. I needed the break. Caroline would be back the next day, if only for a day. I was determined to make her stay sweet. Until then, I was going to give more consideration to the business ideas I had been toying around with.

However, I wasn't to get much peace that evening. Vernon had only been gone to his father's an hour, when the phone rang. It was Colin Simmons, Vernon's dad and he was irate as hell.

"You pussyhole! Me hear seh you've been brutalising my yout. Threatening to put him out in the cold all night. You're sick! They should lock people like you up. Come and pick on somebody your own size. Come on, come on... Come on, you bumbaclaat!"

"Now steady on..."

"Kiss me raas! Me personally ah go deal wid you, you bully! You haffe learn dat Vernon is not no fatherless pickney you can distress anytime. Hol' tight there, you raas, me comin' fe you!"

With that there was a click of the phone as the line went dead.

Patrick Augustus

HOW ABOUT A LITTLE SLAP AND TICKLE?

With the skill of a man who knew all the cooking short cuts, Johnny added a splash of olive oil and tilted the frying pan at all angles for the oil to cover the base. He tossed in the fish and threw his head back as it sizzled with an upward rush of steam, then he fried it gently on a low heat. Next, it was the turn of the herbs and seasoning, and that was just about it. Perhaps a dash of lime or lemon later would add the finishing touch, but there wasn't much more to it than that. It was natural enough to cook for himself. He always had. He had been independent from an early age and didn't need a woman to feed him. Besides, he had spent an evening watching *A Taste of Africa*, a television programme showing the varied cooking from every part of the African continent; exotic delicacies cooked on open fireplaces.

He looked at his watch. The fish was done, the rice was steamed to perfection in an old dutch pot and there was still a few minutes before Lesley would reach back home.

When he got up that morning, the washing of several days was still piled up high in the kitchen sink and it didn't look like it was going to wash itself. He went through things quickly in his mind. He had to get everything looking spick and span. With what seemed to him like a mighty effort, he had pulled on a string vest and set about not only washing the dishes, but vacuum cleaning and window cleaning, not to mention scouring the bath to a shine. He had opened the windows for most of the day and even scented each room with a different fragrance. Anything to make an impression on Lesley when she returned from her holiday.

With a little determination, dreams can come true. Johnny Dollar had his dreams and they were beautiful ones, but if he figured that everything between Lesley and himself was going to be nothing but sweetness and niceness since she took him back, he had another thing coming. He was always quick to remind her of how sorry he was for the pain he had caused her and he hoped and prayed that they could make it work this second time around. After all, it was she who had said she couldn't go through life without him. He knew that despite everything, she still loved and cared for him. There had to be reasons for their love, reasons far greater than he could immediately perceive. Sure, she was still angry, but at least he was home now, where he belonged with his woman and his children. Even though she hadn't completely got her feelings of resentment out of her system.

Johnny had moved back home the day after Carnival. Back to the secure and stable family situation which he had enjoyed before Lesley's discovery of his infidelity. It was just like the old days, well almost.

Lesley had offered so little resistance to his return, that Johnny got swell-headed. Of course she wanted him back. Why shouldn't she? When you've been together fifteen years, you can always work things out. It was going to take more than the fact that he now had a child by another woman to distress all the good times they had had together. "Without unuh support, where would I be today?" Johnny asked Lesley earnestly.

Okay, she was upset and angry when she found out and all of that, fair enough. All that was understandable. He appreciated being given a second chance to prove himself. He was already halfway back in her heart, but this time he would make sure that he didn't mess things up. He had to at all costs, to avoid hurting her a second time.

"This time I'm going to think positive and try not to live negative," he told Lesley. "This time I won't make promises I can't keep. But here's one promise engraved in stone: My intentions are never to be unfaithful to you again."

Within himself he knew that anything could happen, after all, he was a man and with men it only takes one hot moment with an attractive woman for their resistance to crumble; yet he was so convinced that he would never be unfaithful to Lesley again if she took him back that he was willing to lay odds on it.

"That's as close to a guarantee as any man can give," he

told the sceptical Lesley.

And he really had meant it when he proposed to her at Carnival, but now when he thought about it, there was no need to hurry things. *Fools rush in where angels fear to tread!* a voice echoed in his ears. *Fools rush in where angels fear to tread!* It was one of those proverbs that Johnny had never quite understood the meaning of, but it didn't take a genius to realise that it was a call to maintain the status quo. They had got on fine the last fifteen years, living ostensibly as man and wife without getting married, why change a winning formula? But once you've already proposed, it's hard to take it back before the woman's given you an answer.

If Johnny had paused to read the irony in his woman's eyes when he asked her to marry him, he would have realised that there was no need to trouble himself too much with excuses. Marriage was the last thing on Lesley's mind. It was going to take more than "sorry" for her to forgive and forget Johnny's "indiscretion" as he put it. She called it adultery, plain and simple. And nothing, nothing in this world could make her want to marry him. Having him around in the house didn't help either and she had only allowed him back for Winnie's sake. How could she forget, when everytime she looked at Johnny, she was reminded that he was another woman's baby father.

Once, not all that long ago, Lesley had worshiped her man. She had put him on a pedestal where he could do no wrong. Now, nothing he could say would make her trust him again. 'A leopard can't change its spots' was one of her mother's favourite sayings. "Yuh evah see a leopard with stripes?" she would regularly ask her daughter rhetorically. "Impossible!". There was even a time when Lesley would have walked to the end of the earth for her man, but he had succeeded in burning all her illusions. How could he now talk of romance between them? She could see clearly now, and saw Johnny for exactly what he was. Romance would only confuse the issue.

Yet, as crazy as it sounded, she still loved him. So many

friends had reasoned with her and advised her to forget about Johnny Dollar and build a new life for herself and her children. "You're better off without him," they said. And they were right, she knew it. And if he was any other man, Johnny Dollar would have been history long time. But this wasn't just any man. This was her childhood sweetheart and the father of her two children. As Johnny had discovered on their first date at the Chrysler Ballroom in Norwood all those years ago, it only took a tiny bit of magic to turn Lesley's love on, but nobody had ever taught her how to turn it off.

When she checked it though, Lesley found that she wasn't doing all that badly at all. She seemed to have the best of everything for the moment. She hadn't fully embraced Johnny's return to the family home, because she discovered that she could love him without being in love with him or, indeed, without *making* love to him.

"No matter how much you claim you love me," she told him. "I'm not going to fall for that old fairy tale again. I only allowed you to come back home for Winnie and Jacob's sake – bless their hearts. I didn't want them to suffer just because their father can't control his willy. Why did I put all my trust in you in the first place? For what? You've lied and cheated and lied and cheated... And it never stops. So from now on, I couldn't care less what you do and who you do it with. You can come and go as you please, like you've always wanted. But please, no more tears and no more promises. It's too late for that and I've got my own life to live."

She was in no doubt that she could manage well without him as she had done when she kicked him out in the first place. She didn't need him for anything, not for health, strength or wealth and, for the moment, the jury was still out on whether the kids would fare better with their father or without him. That depended entirely on the defendant. If Johnny played his part as a role model, then, maybe it couldn't do any harm. Otherwise his role as a father was completely redundant.

Still, having Johnny around meant that somebody else

could do the babysitting while Lesley took the opportunity to go out with her own friends for a change. Sometimes she would be in the house with all her girlfriends, preparing to go to a particular party. They'd all gather downstairs in the living room, discussing outfits and putting the finishing touches to each other's hair and talking loudly and excitedly about all the 'good catches' that were likely to be at the party, and Johnny would just have to kick back and take it all. And even though he would huff and puff disgruntled when he overheard them as he did the ironing or while he was changing baby Jacob's nappies, Lesley seemed not to care. Then she informed him that her mother had agreed to look after Jacob and Winnie for two weeks, while she took a deserved holiday to Gambia in December with her friend Alison. Johnny was incensed.

"Isn't Alison the one who's man crazy? Isn't she the one you're always saying can't control herself in the presence of anybody who hasn't got breasts? Isn't Alison the one who can't talk to a man for more than a couple of minutes without wanting to get into their pants?"

"Yes that's right," Lesley confirmed with an ironic smile. "It's the same Alison. It's going to be fun going on holiday with her."

Johnny muttered and spluttered and protested, but what could he do? As he had done for the past three months since Lesley had allowed him to return, Johnny had to bite his tongue to keep from exploding in an outburst.

It was wishful thinking on Johnny's part that once he moved back home, he and Lesley would be able to put all the hurt and heartache of the past behind them. He was naive enough to think that everything would be like it had been before, that he would be back in her bed and they would be making beautiful love together as they used to. It wasn't to be. Johnny's bed was the sofa in the living room, and three months later he was still there! To Johnny, a grown man having to sleep on a sofa in his own home was shameful, but at least he was with his family. It would have been even more shameful if word got out that he was the lodger in his own home and that he wasn't sharing his woman's bed. He didn't even want Winnie to find out, so he would wait until she had gone to bed, before pulling out the duvet and a pillow from the airing cupboard, and he would get up early, before his daughter did. He didn't want her to see him asleep on the sofa.

Poor Johnny, he couldn't understand why Lesley was treating him like a complete stranger. Wasn't he trying? Hadn't he been completely faithful since Carnival? At first he thought she just wanted to have a little time by herself. So he decided to leave it a night. One night became two, which quickly became a week, then a month. By now he was tired of sleeping on the sofa, but Lesley had insisted that he had to get used to it. More than once, Johnny considered staying out all night and crashing at somebody's house with the hope that he could come home the next day with everything sorted. And more than once he decided against it. Lesley was suspicious of him as it was. The last thing he needed to do now was to stay out all night and get Lesley thinking that he had been with another woman. If that happened, he feared, it would almost certainly prolong his exile from her heart.

Poor Johnny, he couldn't bring himself to believe that Lesley really didn't care who he slept with. Despite everything, he accepted Lesley's unreasonable conditions to his return. Such was the burden of a man who couldn't afford to upset the delicate balance of his relationship with the mother of his children.

Perhaps if he had considered the cost of his one particular night of passion with Pauline before it happened, he would have thought it a price too high to pay. It wasn't the first time he had been unfaithful to Lesley and because he had managed to sweet her up all the previous times, he didn't think it was any big deal. But who can say when that time comes when a woman decides enough is enough? Johnny was convinced that what tipped the scales this time was the fact that his infidelity had resulted in a child. That if Pauline hadn't gone and got herself pregnant, Lesley wouldn't still be holding a grudge.

It wasn't the first time that Johnny had failed to understand where his woman was coming from and it wouldn't be the last. Again, Lesley couldn't care less about the kid, that was Johnny's problem and he could play 'worl'-a-gal' to his heart's content now. As far as she was concerned, the alms house business was a thing of the past. Johnny had scarred her beyond repair. Ever heard the saying "Once bitten, twice shy"? she asked him.

"Look I know how you feel." he said sympathetically.

"You'll never know how I feel... How could you?"

"Well alright... But just to let you know, you can have me whenever you want," he assured her undaunted.

"Just to let me know?" Lesley couldn't believe his offer.

"Yes. All I know is that I love you and want to be with you. I'm ready and waiting, anytime you are. All you have to do is show me how to get you to love me."

What pissed Lesley off the most was when Johnny talked so much foolishness. He kept saying that he never expected things to come to this. But how couldn't he have known? How did he expect her to feel when she discovered that he was the father of another woman's child. Johnny wasn't that naive, he couldn't be. How could he not see that she was still angry. Very angry.

The view of his family and friends was that Johnny had made his bed, so he had to lie in it. They had little sympathy for him. It wasn't their fault that he had two pickneys of exactly the same age, by two different women. Why hadn't he listened when they'd predicted how he was going to get burned? It was no use showing up at all hours of the night and day looking for a shoulder to cry on either. It wasn't that people didn't understand, it was just that everybody had their own problems to deal with. To everybody that knew him, the continuing saga of Johnny's comedy of romantic errors, rated on a level with the omnibus edition of *Eastenders* in their lives; it always provided them with a few good laughs, but they wouldn't go out of their way to get involved in it.

The last thing Johnny expected from those he turned to in his hour of need was stress. As if things weren't bad enough in his domestic life, his friends handled him like he was the living duppie. It was easy enough for them to say that his problems were all his own making. Linvall, Beres and Gussie wouldn't be taking it so lightly if they were in his position. Getting two women pregnant at the same time was a situation any man could find himself in, after all he wasn't the only man with a wandering 'lunchbox'. Look at all those big-name black celebrities, Johnny had challenged his spars. He reminded them of how many baby mother's 100 metre champ Greg Owen had and how nobody distressed him about it. Linvall seemed to understand that point and meditated on the matter for a while over a cold beer. Beres on the other hand was unimpressed and reminded Johnny that he wasn't Greg Owen and even if he was, he'd still be out of order.

"You can't just go around having kids all over the place. You're not a stud you know."

Johnny huffed and puffed. "Alright, guilty as charged. Bwoy, you don't half go on about it, Beres. Give it a res', man. Anyway, the way I see it, what's done is done and my real problem right now isn't that I've got two baby mothers, it's that those two women are Lesley and Pauline. That's like fire and brimstone – either way, you're bound to get burned... Funny how dem seh, 'Jah nevah give a man more than him can bear'!"

Johnny heard the taxi when it pulled up outside. He heard Lesley's voice as she climbed out. And he heard Alison's voice call out, "See you tomorrow!"

He added the finishing touches to the table. He lit the candles and made his way quickly to the front door. He opened it wide just as Lesley was about to insert her key in the lock.

"Surprise!" he cried out, beaming all over his face and

showing her in with a wave of his hand.

Lesley looked uncertain, an eyebrow raised. She stood on the doorstep, unsure of what was going on.

"Let me take your suitcase," Johnny offered, relieving her of her luggage. "Did you have a nice flight and holiday?"

Lesley took her sunglasses off and stepped in, still cautious. She looked around in the living room. She hadn't expected it to be this tidy. Her nose was hit with the aroma of herbs and spices. Then she glanced over at the dining table, set for two and candles burning with their subtle flames.

"Yes I did have a nice time, thanks. It looks like you're expecting someone?"

Johnny smiled with pride in his eyes.

"I was expecting you of course, all this is for you."

Removing her wide straw hat and jacket, Lesley sat down on an armchair exhausted.

"I've already eaten," she said. "They served lunch on the plane. It was really good for a change. I couldn't eat anymore."

Johnny looked deflated. All his preparation was to nought. Lesley didn't even make the effort to show she was pleased. He sat down on the sofa opposite her.

"So, did you have a good holiday in Gambia or what?"

"Yeah... we did, we had a really great time. You know how Alison is, she's a party girl. So we ended up having a lot of fun."

Johnny was trying to read between the lines.

"And you didn't miss me at all?"

"No, funnily enough I didn't even think about you the whole two weeks. I forgot about you completely. I thought of Winnie and Jacob a lot though. Where are they anyway? Don't tell me you've sold the kids while I've been gone."

"Don't be silly," Johnny replied. "Winnie's staying over by Aisha's house tonight. And your mum's still looking after Jacob. I know they were supposed to come back home today, but I arranged it specially, so that we could spend the night together."

"Oh there was no need for that, really there wasn't."

Lesley closed her eyes briefly, she was exhausted. What she hated most about package holidays, was the mad rush on the last day to get everything done in time for departure and then the waiting around at airports for hours.

Johnny didn't know whether to speak or to allow her to rest for a moment. He could understand that she was tired, but he yearned for some tender loving care and he wasn't getting it.

"So..." he asked cautiously, "did Alison get off with anyone?"

"What was that?" Lesley asked, opening one eye slowly.

"Did Alison get off with anyone? That's the only reason she's always going off on holidays, isn't it, she's looking for a man."

"Yes she did meet someone actually, a really handsome guy called Musa. Those African guys are so charming... But then, you know all about that, don't you Johnny?"

Johnny bit his lip nervously. He knew exactly what Lesley was getting at and from his wide-eyed look, she knew he got the message. It was a low punch. Lesley didn't have to remind him that his other child was being brought up by the African guy his baby mother Pauline was living with.

"And what were you doing when Alison was getting off with this African guy?" Johnny continued.

"I was barefoot on a deserted beach," Lesley recalled vividly, "the waves lapping at my toes and a cool breeze blowing through my hair, under the full moon up in the velvet, midnight sky."

"Are you crazy?!" Johnny jumped up anxiously. "I thought we discussed safety and all that and you promised you wouldn't go off walking at night by yourself."

"Oh but I wasn't by myself, I was with Issa..."

Johnny froze in his tracks. He looked across at Lesley, fear registered in his eyes, his worst fear. Lesley averted his gaze and picked up a newspaper from the bookcase beside her.

"So what's been happening over here in the last two weeks? Anybody famous die?"

Johnny was deaf to her question. "Issa? Who's Issa?" he asked.

Lesley sighed. She didn't want to talk about it, but if Johnny insisted on hearing more he was going to get burned.

"He's a fisherman out there. A really cool guy and handsome and charming as well. He's a friend of Musa's. We met them both on the beach, so we had to invite Issa to dinner. We went out as a foursome. And then when Alison went off with Musa it became a twosome. You know Johnny, meeting him was the best thing that happened to me on the holiday. He had so many funny stories to tell, because his family have been fishermen in that village for hundreds of years." She laughed. "You know, the fishermen out there remind me of the fishermen in Jamaica— none of them can swim!" She laughed again. "And if you saw the state of the boats they go out in... No thank you!"

Johnny was still motionless, staring at her, hearing nothing.

"So... did you sleep with him?" he asked slowly.

"Johnny!" Lesley exclaimed in mock horror. "That's none of your business. You've got no right to ask that kind of thing."

"What do you mean? I've got no right to ask my woman if she slept with another man?"

"Your woman? Let's get one thing straight Johnny, I'm not 'your woman'. You gave up that privilege, remember?"

Johnny threw his hands up in frustration.

"Awww come on Les, I thought we were past that. I thought all that was over with?"

"How can it be over? You made another woman pregnant, didn't you? How can that ever be over? Do you think your other child is going to thank you for not being around? Do you think Winnie and Jacob will call you 'Dad' when your mind is on the other side of town with the other pickney? You must be joking!"

Johnny held his head in his hands. He felt like he was drowning in a turbulent sea. Why was she giving him all this stress? He also knew what it was like to love and lose. He had lost her and he had paid for it, but Lesley had to stop living in the past and holding it against him.

"Awww come on. This isn't how it was supposed to be, Les. You've got a right to be angry and I understand, but you've just come back from holiday and I've tried to set everything up nice, so that we could spend a quiet evening in together. I mean, it's been months, Lesley. Trust me."

It had been almost a year since they made love. The very thought of it brought water to Johnny's eyes.

"Give me one reason to trust you?" Lesley challenged.

"Because I've changed. I've been home every evening and I haven't even gone out to play football, let alone check woman. How much more proof do you need that there's nothing for me out 'pon street? My life is here, with you and the kids. Take me back Lesley, believe me, everything's going to be beautiful"

"Well, I won't hold my breath," Lesley said, determined not to compromise. "One thing I realised in Gambia was that all these years with you, all I've been doing is waiting in vain to exhale. Face it Johnny, you threw away the good thing you had."

Johnny put his arm around her. "Look, I've got an idea..."

"Beginner's luck."

Undaunted, he said: "Forget about the dinner, let's go to bed."

"Well pull out the sofa then. Don't let me stop you. I'm tired too, so I'm going up to bed."

Lesley got up to go. Johnny caught her by the arm and pulled her close towards him.

"I said I want to go to bed – your bed."

Patrick Augustus

UNFINISHED BUSINESS

I can take care of myself when I have to, physically or otherwise. I don't go down to the gym five times a week for nothing. It keeps my muscles toned and my mind alert. But I've always found the idea of two grown men fighting rather distasteful. I've been to enough dances with Johnny where men were throwing blows and bottles at one another, generally over a woman, and to be honest, it looks ridiculous. Not just childish, but ridiculous. It's embarrassing representing the same species as them let alone the same race!

The prospect of Vernon's father showing up with violence in his eyes, or worse, a machete in his hand, filled me with dread. I had met Colin Simmons on only one occasion when he came by to drop off a birthday present for his son. He wasn't the most impressive guy I've met and I found it difficult to understand what could have possessed Caroline to marry him, or conversely how she could be attracted to me after living with him. For one thing, he's short where as I'm tall and although I wouldn't deny that he has a modicum of intelligence, he's foul-mouthed and bad mannered enough to make me think otherwise. In short, he's on the coarse side of smooth.

We didn't exchange more than a nod with each other, there seemed little else to say. He was the 'ex' and I was the man who had moved in to give Caroline some proper loving. That put him in a more difficult position than me. I sensed that he felt uncomfortable about being a guest at the house which he had always treated as his own, even after he and Caroline separated. I don't know if she noticed it or not but when he came by with the present, I felt that Colin had an air of humility about him. Anyway, while I stretched comfortably on the living room sofa listening to the radio, he was reluctant to leave before throwing a little weight around, just to make his presence felt.

"So you've moved your man in," he said with a sarcastic

Caroline info...
mind, we would like to con...
some more. Either the message didn't g...
immediately or he chose to ignore it. Either ...
continued in the same manner: "Yeah I bet you're such a
great couple together, like Romeo and Juliet, eh...? Is that it
Caroline? Or is it like Antony and Cleopatra, like Napoleon
and Josephine, Bonnie and Clyde...?!"

Caroline didn't need to hear any more and she gently
shoved her ex-husband out of the door.

I had to ask her afterwards what had possessed her to
marry him. She said she really couldn't remember. She was
young at the time and fresh out of college. But it didn't take
her long to realise how selfish and childish he was.
Unfortunately, she was pregnant with Vernon at the time
and decided to give Colin more rope. It was a waste of time
of course and for the first few years of Vernon's life she
ended up looking after two kids – Vernon and his father.

Fortunately, Colin didn't show up after his threats on the
telephone. Hopefully it meant that he'd thought the wiser of
it. That was fine by me. I hoped the matter would end there
or that I would at least get an opportunity to explain my
position, but somehow I knew in the back of my mind that
it was far from over.

Saturday morning, I got up early. Caroline would be back
from Brussels for the weekend in a few hours and I wanted
to get all the shopping in quickly so that we could have the
rest of the day to ourselves. She had been gone less than a
week, but already I was yearning for her. Life had seemed
quiet and empty without her and, yes, I was in need of some
tender loving care.

Sainsbury's was packed with shoppers by the time I got
there. It was the usual thing for a Saturday, but I was
nevertheless overwhelmed by the swell of people. I

51

way through with great difficulty and grabbing a basket, manoeuvred my way through the obstacle course to the necessary shelves. I was in and out in an hour, which wasn't bad for the time of day.

The shopping was all done by midday and when I got home, I quickly got everything tidy and hoovered around the house, cleaned the bathroom, made sure the bath had a gleam on it. With an hour to go before she arrived, I thought everything was done. It was a good job I cast a quick glance around the house, for under the sink the washing basket beckoned filled with dirty laundry. I threw as many clothes into the washing machine as I could, but soon realised I was going to have to go for a second load. Oh well, the 'magic' doesn't always work. Caroline would return home to find half as many dirty clothes in the basket as there would have been and that had to be worth something.

I suddenly remembered that I hadn't showered yet. I wanted to smell fresh when Caroline arrived, so without hesitation, I made my way to the bathroom, pulling my sweater over my head as I went. I stepped into the shower and turned the tap to full on and let out a holler as a jet of cold water hit me in the face. The water quickly warmed up and I soaped myself thoroughly, then I let the water gently massage every part of my body, relaxing me. For a moment, my thoughts drifted through the events of the last four months.

After marrying Caroline at the end of August, I moved in with her and her son in their terraced house in Tooting. It was only supposed to be a temporary thing, while we got ourselves sorted out. But I didn't reckon on Sonia, my ex-wife getting the Child Support Agency on my case with such speed. Before I knew it, she was claiming for the house which, true, we owned jointly, but for which I was still paying the mortgage. Minor details such as who was paying the mortgage didn't trouble Sonia, as long as she wasn't paying it. She wanted the house. Before long she was squeezing me from one side with the CSA and from the other, with her lawyers Messrs Bailey, Hobbs and Lincoln Solicitors. I finally conceded and handed over the keys to my home and signed everything over in her name. That still leaves me paying the mortgage, but it was better to reach that settlement than to wait for the CSA to skin me alive. So now my daughter's living with her mother and her mother's girlfriend in my big house overlooking Streatham Common. I don't need to say how painful all of this is to me. To be frank, it's a subject I avoid at the best of times. The only way I can avoid thinking about it is to immerse myself in work. I've been doing some market research and coming up with figures for a little business project. With the money that I was paid from Dan Oliver's, I should be able to set up a nice little business and hopefully be able to build back up a portion of the capital I had before I had to sign it away in child support.

I stepped out of the shower and dried myself with a towel which I wrapped around me before stepping out. I figured that I had maybe another ten or fifteen minutes before Caroline was due to arrive. I was making my way across the top landing to our bedroom to pull out a clean shirt from the wardrobe, when I was startled by a cry from downstairs.

"Yaow, yah bloodclaat!"

Horrified, I looked down the stairs. It was the diminutive figure of Colin Simmons, with fire in his eyes and pointing a threatening finger up at me. Next to him was Vernon, with a big smile on his face, enjoying every bit of it.

"You is the bumbaclaat me ah look for! Come down, nuh raas!"

"Look, I think you better..."

"Don't tell me I better nut'n, y'hear?! 'Cause yuh is a pussyclaat! You think you're big when you're beating up a seven-year-old, don't you? Well come nuh, let's see how you stand up to someone your own size."

"What the f...!"

"COME DUNG NOW!!!" Colin screamed at the top of his voice, his brow sweating and his eyes glazed. He wasn't pointing his fingers any longer either, but holding his fists up in a boxing stance.

"Alright, I'll come down... All I need is a moment to put some clothes on. I can see you're not going to heed reason, so if you want war, I'm ready."

I never got a chance to change my clothes however, before the sound of the key turning in the front door lock cut through the tension in the air. In the next moment, Caroline stepped in laden with duty free bags from her journey, looking surprised to see her ex-husband standing there. As soon as he saw her, Colin moderated his tone, dropping his phoney patois. I walked over to my wife, took her bags from her and placing them aside, I hugged her briefly. If Colin wasn't present, it would have been tenderly.

"Caroline, I've got to protest at the way this man," pointing to me, "has been treating our son while you've been away." Colin said.

Caroline had hardly had time to step in the door and from the expression on her face, it was clear that she wasn't happy about walking into her house in the middle of an argument.

"Do you know what he threatened to do to Vernon while you were away? He threatened to lock Vernon in the garden all night long if he didn't behave. For goodness sake, the boy is seven-years-old and he threatens to lock him outside!"

Caroline looked across to me. I just shook my head.

"Before you make those kind of accusations you wanna check the facts," I said.

"Liar!" Vernon hissed.

I could have slapped him, but this wasn't the right occasion.

"You see what I mean?" Colin said to Caroline. "How could you leave our son in the care of this man? He's unfit to be anywhere near small pickney."

"Vernon," said Caroline with a severe tone, "you had better stop lying. You'll be in a lot of trouble young man, if I find out that all of this is because you're not telling the truth."

"I am telling the truth!" Vernon cried out, his mother's accusations bringing water to his eyes. "Why is it that you're always picking on me? He started it. He said he would lock me in the garden until it was cold."

Caroline was unsure what to do, but eventually decided that it would be better to not have Vernon present. She sent him up to his room to go and read a book until it was time for him to leave with his father. Vernon did so reluctantly realising that he was going to miss out on the real action.

"All I'm saying," Colin resumed, when we had removed ourselves to the living room, "is that he's using psychological whatdyamacallit to disturb my son. And I don't like it."

"Oh don't exaggerate," said Caroline flopping down on an armchair. "The trouble with you, Colin, is that you have no sense of humour..."

He thought about it for a second then replied, "Well, I don't think that's very funny."

"You see what I mean? Come on now, you know what Vernon's like, he does have a tendency to misbehave. That's probably what this is all about, isn't it darling?" Caroline turned to me standing beside her and caressed my arm playfully.

I smiled at her and nodded. Yes that's exactly what it was about. "I was trying to get him to..."

But Colin didn't want to listen to me. He interrupted and continued his appeal to his ex-wife.

"Well Vernon doesn't misbehave when he's with me. He's always really well-behaved and we have a great time when we're together. That's because I'm a great father and I'm patient with him and I understand what he needs in his life and give I him that support."

"Good for you," said Caroline sighing. She had heard it all before. I thought it was a pretty pathetic appeal. And I didn't believe it for one second. If he was such a great father, he would be at home bringing up his kid full-time instead of just at weekends. Being a good father means being a good husband too and by all accounts Colin had been deficient in that category as well. You can't have the former without the latter. What's the use of being such a good father if you're such a crummy husband that your wife flings you out?

I could have said all these things, but I didn't. I wasn't going to get involved in what Caroline had to sort out between her ex, herself and her son. In this more than anything I really wasn't part of their family. So I simply stood back and watched Colin make his play. It wasn't long in coming.

"As a matter of fact, I don't care how much my son misbehaves, there is no way I want this man or any other man laying a finger on him. Why should Vernon obey him anyway, he's not the boy's father... You know what the real problem is?" he said very deliberately, looking only at Caroline. "The boy's upset because you have a man sleeping in your bed every night who is not his father. He's confused and upset."

"Beres happens to be my husband actually," Caroline reminded him.

"Husband or loverman, what does it matter. The point is that the boy is confused. That's why I don't have girlfriends staying overnight when he's with me at weekends, because he's only ever been used to seeing me in bed with Mummy. I don't want to confuse him any more."

Right now, I didn't much care what Colin Simmons' beef was. I wanted him out of the house. "You're talking a load of rubbish," I told him, "and besides I want to be alone with my wife if you don't mind."

"As a matter of fact, I do mind," he said, looking at me disdainfully.

"Caroline, ask this man to leave before I do something I'll regret." I said.

I knew it was an uncomfortable situation for her to walk into. After working hard in Belgium all week, the last thing she wanted to come home to was an argument between her sweetheart and her ex, but this domestic problem needed to be sorted out now.

Before she could ask Colin to leave, he pompously reminded her of the fact that legally, the house was still his. He was still in his own home and if anybody was to leave, it should be me.

"You ever hear the saying every man's home is his castle?" he sneered at me. "Well this is my castle and there's no room in here for more than one king."

"What?!" I couldn't believe what I was hearing. I turned to Caroline for a denial.

"Yes, it's true. I meant to explain all that to you," she said, confirming Colin's revelation with a nod of her head. "But with all this work I've had, I totally forgot. Technically, the house is still his."

She went on to explain that although they had reached a divorce settlement whereby Colin was signing over the house to her, the legal details hadn't quite gone through yet.

Colin glared at me with a triumphant look. I could have punched him in the mouth. My mind was confused. I was wondering how I had got myself into this position in the first place. How could I be living in another man's house? It was bad enough having to bring up another man's child, but to now discover that on top of that I was living in the other man's house, made me feel uncomfortable about sleeping with Caroline, even if she was only his ex. A feeling of distaste soured my thoughts. I wanted to leave, right there and then. But where would I go? I didn't have my own house anymore either. And why should I go anyway? I married Caroline for better or worse and my place was right beside her in that house.

My deliberations were brought to an end by Caroline, who asked whether I would mind running over to the chemist for her and picking up some things. I could see from the look in her eye that it was a ploy to get me out of the way for a while in order to ease the tension.

"Look, I'm really sorry about this, Beres," she said. She

hugged me briefly. "I'll make it up to you," she whispered in my ear. "I'll get rid of Colin and we'll get together for something sweet and sexy. Oh, how I've missed my baby."

Then she kissed me on the cheek. I was weak for her and was already imagining how sweet and sexy the rest of our weekend would be. I agreed to to her request. Caroline followed me to the door.

"It'll give me some time to talk to him," she explained, "I'll calm him down and get rid of him before you get back."

I took my leave and decided to return after fifteen minutes. It wouldn't take me longer than that.

So many things were going through my head as I made my way down to the chemists on the High Street and I could see Vernon's smiling face through all of it. The boy was evil pure and simple. I wouldn't be surprised if he had orchestrated the whole thing. Maybe Colin and his son had worked as a team, so that Vernon would rile me up to the point where I would lose my cool and then he would go and get his father who then turns on me for disciplining his son. I was sure I was being set up to look stupid and to turn Caroline against me.

Now I really was being paranoid. The conspiracy theory was too far-fetched. I had better things to do with my time than fight some phoney imaginary battle with Colin Simmons and I supposed that he had a life to be getting on with too.

I suspected that things hadn't been resolved, as I returned to the house. Vernon was outside with the same baby gangsters that I had previously stopped him from playing with. When they saw me approaching, Vernon whispered to them and they all started laughing at me. I glared at Vernon and he simply glared back.

As I figured, Colin was still in the house. He wasn't just in it, but was making himself very comfortable, lying down on the sofa with his feet up on the coffee table. He grunted as I walked in and continued reading the magazine in his hand. I turned to Caroline with a quizzical look. She shrugged her shoulders. "I tried, but he's refusing to leave, not before he gets to see for himself how you're treating Vernon. He's just being childish, I know, but there isn't much I can do about it before everything's settled legally. I know he's just using it as an excuse, but he's insisting that he doesn't want to get in our way and that he just wants to spend one night here to satisfy himself that Vernon is happy at home with his step-father. I suppose that's fair enough, isn't it?"

I couldn't believe what I was hearing. What the hell was 'fair enough'? She had just come all the way from the European Parliament where she was representing a group of black pensioners who had been treated unfairly by the customs people when they went over to France on a day trip. If that was unfair, how could it be fair to have someone invade your home and refuse to leave? But Caroline insisted, we really didn't have a leg to stand on. Legally, we couldn't remove Colin from his own home. And as long as he wasn't causing a disturbance, she couldn't really call the police to have him taken away. She added that she could see his point and if I thought about it, I could too, because if I thought that my daughter was being mistreated by her step-father I would want to investigate, wouldn't I? "At the end of the day," she concluded, "it's best to humour him for one night than to let him ruin the whole of our weekend together."

This was just some bee in Colin's bonnet and she knew him well enough to know that he would eventually get tired of being a full-time father.

I wasn't so sure it would be only a temporary thing. But Caroline was the lawyer, she knew best. I resolved to hold my peace for the moment. All I wanted to do was spend some hours alone with my wife, before she flew back to Belgium the next day.

Patrick Augustus

SWING YOUR OWN THING

"...You want to sleep in my bed?" Lesley repeated impatiently. She really didn't need any of this when she was this tired on her return from holiday. "Please Johnny, you know the rules," she said, pushing him aside forcefully. "Don't make me have to ask you to leave."

Johnny looked stunned. How could Lesley continue treating him in this way? *Because you're a sap!* Living in a loveless relationship was bad enough for him, without having to listen to the back-chatting echo of his inner voice. All he wanted was one little ride.

"That's all you've ever done, take me for a ride," Lesley added, reading his thoughts. "Maybe I'm sick and tired of it."

The determined look on her face spoke a thousand words.

"How long is it going to take you to understand that you can't do anything for me. I don't want your money, nor your loving. And because I don't need sex like you do, I can survive without you. And if I can't, there are more handsome bastards out there than you."

She didn't say another word, but simply made her way upstairs to her bedroom.

Johnny watched her ascend the stairs silently, before he went back into the living room. He flopped himself down on the sofa and lay there for a long while, staring up at the ceiling without batting an eyelid. He didn't want to sleep. He was too hyped up. He flicked on the TV set and stared at the screen blankly. He still believed in miracles, but Lesley's pain had obviously not disappeared as he had hoped. He was getting desperate and didn't know what to do. Several months without sex had made him feel this way.

Involuntary celibacy does funny things to a man's head. In his mind Johnny pictured Lesley's familiar breasts and her round bottom and was reminded of how much he missed caressing them both. To hell with her, he thought proudly, then decided in the next moment that he didn't mean that at all. The montage in his head continued. How could he possibly forget that first time with her, at her father's house all those years ago? He remembered vividly how excited he had been by her nakedness and how it had been difficult to contain himself. And how, despite being older and more experienced than her, it was Lesley who had been in control and had been patient with him. He remembered also how she quickly learned the art of fondling him intimately where it mattered. No, he hadn't forgotten that first time. He thought of Lesley again and how beautiful her skin must feel after two weeks in the African sunshine. If only he could...

And yet, she didn't come home hungry for it like he was. Why was that? Had she slept with someone while she was out there? This 'Issa' guy she mentioned, most likely. Jealousy was eating away at his heart and he could barely control himself. His heartbeat quickened and he started breathing heavily, like he was hyper-ventilating. Without pausing for thought, he lifted himself off the sofa and jumped out of the living room, and climbed the stairs two at a time. He walked into Lesley's bedroom without knocking.

Lesley stood semi-naked in front of the closet, frowning. She cocked her head towards him, deliberating.

"What do you want?" she said.

Johnny admired her in all her splendour. He glanced at the large double bed in the centre of the room, which he had tidied immaculately earlier in the morning after ironing the sheets. He turned his gaze back to Lesley. Even though it was the wrong move, Johnny couldn't stop himself grinning as he admired her. Dressed in only a thin bra and black silk panties, the softness of her full-body and those comfortable hips, neither too wide nor too narrow had weakened his resolve. His lust for those curves stiffened his reserves to attention.

"You don't know?" he asked. His mouth was dry. Licking his lips he walked over and slipped a warm hand around her waist. She peered up at him, lips tight.

"Whatever you're looking for, you won't find it down there," she said, moving his hand away. "Please keep your business, away from me," she added, pointing to his crutch

The rebuff was frustrating. *Here we go again*, Johnny thought, as he flopped himself down on the bed. He lay silently on his back, flesh quivering. Moonlight cast a soft glow through the sash windows. Massaging his temple with his fingers, he stared up at the ceiling light, deep in thought. His efforts had got him nowhere slowly.

"It's driving me crazy!" he cried out. "How's a man supposed to live in the same house as his woman without having sex? I can't take it anymore!"

"Good," Lesley answered coldly. "Now you can relate to what I was feeling when I learned that you had a child by another woman."

Why was Lesley so casual about the whole thing?

"You must be getting it some place!" Johnny blurted out finally.

By now Lesley had slipped on a set of metallic-grey satin pyjamas and was standing, arms folded, with her back to the dressing table, an impatient look on her face.

"...And if you're not getting it," Johnny continued, "let's get it on."

"Oh Johnny, you really are Mr Pitiful. So you want it that bad, eh?" Lesley laughed.

For a moment, Johnny's hopes were raised. It sounded like an offer. Maybe he was at last making an impression. Yes, he really did want it that bad, and the sooner the better. He lifted himself off the bed and for the second time went over and pulled her close to him until his lips touched hers.

Lesley pushed him back forcefully.

"I'm on my period," she said, staring deep into his eyes. If there was one thing that could cool Johnny down, it was that.

"Oh, well I'll see you in five days," he replied.

On the Monday, Johnny got up early like he usually did on

weekdays, awaked from his slumber by the incessant buzz of the alarm clock in the middle of the sweetest dream which had him all curled up on the sofa. It felt like getting out of bed on the wrong side. He had barely moved a muscle and already the day had started off bad for him. He was neither suffering from a hangover nor was anything distressing him, yet he felt miserable.

It was another one of those 'clean up the mess before you go to work' mornings. He rolled up his duvet and tucked it behind the sofa as he had been doing for the past three months. It was getting to be a drag. Living like this was doing him no good. He had stayed awake most of the night as he usually did, in the vain hope that Lesley might feel some sexual urge for which he could be ready and waiting in an instant. There had to be a way he could get back into his woman's heart and into her bed. What good was a relationship if it didn't have sex? Why was Lesley still holding out?

He sat down on the living room floor in his shorts and went through his normal routine. First, there was the stretching. He eased his legs into the splits and felt the bite of the muscles at the back of his thigh. Then he turned himself over onto his stomach and began to push himself up and down, using his fists for support. He counted a hundred pushes before flipping himself onto his rear and counting a hundred sit-ups. Then he flicked on the TV breakfast news. After a few minutes of yesterday's news, he went to wake Winnie so she could get ready for school. Feeling the muscles in his lower abdomen tighten, the irony struck him that he was as fit as he ever was, his battery fully charged, and yet all his excess stamina was going to waste, because Lesley still felt a way about something he had done months before. There just had to be something else eating her. Why was she acting up? That was the kind of thing that was bound to drive him back to his old ways, looking for women outside his domestic situation. He had been in the wrong to start off with and he had paid for that wrongdoing many times over.

She had caught him in a lie, but he had promised that it wouldn't happen again. Now he needed some co-operation from her.

He had tried reasoning with her right through the night. Okay, she had a dose of PMT or PMS or whatever, but in a few days, when it was all over, he wanted things to be back to normal between them.

"Maybe we should start all over again," he had suggested, "start from scratch. Let's forget all that has been, or could have been and just start afresh as lovers, like we did when we first met. I understand, baby, believe me, I understand... But we both need to have a little more give and take in this relationship. That's the formula for a successful family life. Once that's worked out, everything will be alright." At least, that was what Johnny thought. And if after that Lesley still felt she wasn't getting the things she wanted out of the relationship, he would understand.

That was just it, Lesley had replied. He didn't understand, couldn't. What did he know about the thoughts that were running around in her head? Things were different now and they could never be like they once were. Playing away from home was one thing, but kids were a serious matter and Johnny now had a life outside of their relationship to deal with.

"Where there's a kid involved, it's already too late for learning give and take, sharing and understanding one another and friendship... I still can't believe how you dissed me. It was like a nightmare. I always thought that kind of thing happened to other people. I just wasn't prepared for it. I've tried so many times to forget the fact that you've got another child out there, but it's impossible. Besides, my mother warned me that if I allowed you back in my bed after what you've done, I may as well call myself a 'whore'."

Johnny slapped his forehead. Of course, her mother had to be behind all this. Since his infidelity was found out, Lesley's mother had cursed him with unremitting venom and kissed her teeth every time he opened his mouth in her presence. She held a grudge against him and wouldn't rest until she saw to it that Johnny was out of her daughter's life completely. Johnny had tried to ease things off, but it was no good. When Lesley's mother had demanded that he leave the house – "And when I say leave, I mean *leave!*" – he had packed his bags and left without fuss or quarrel. But now he was back, the woman was getting dyam outta order! She even had the nerve to come chat some nonsense about: "Johnny, I don't want you having any more kids with Lesley..." Dyam outta order! He had only bargained to have a relationship with the daughter, but now the mother-in-law was thrown in for free!!

Lesley on the other hand had always felt that Johnny wasn't only having a relationship with her, but also with her family, and if he didn't get on with her family, he didn't get on with her. Johnny didn't really check it out until things started going wrong between them, but he got to realise now that what Lesley had always said was true. Ever since the discovery of his infidelity, he had got involved with her mother verbally and he now felt like he really was having a relationship with her too. The funny thing about it was that Lesley's mother had stood by her husband all these years despite having had a rough time in her marriage, yet she'd encouraged Lesley at the drop of a hat to leave Johnny. Every time the mother heard Johnny's name she would dig wounds and open up new sores. And the worst thing was that Lesley listened to her!

So no, he got "*no* sex" last night, and was going to get "*none* tonight *either*." He was frankly fed up with the involuntary celibacy business. He wasn't a blasted monk, after all!

Johnny was a man, living with a woman who felt vulnerable and he was feeling it too. Ain't no two ways about it; who feels it, knows it. And Johnny knew that he couldn't take the sexual starvation any longer. If Lesley didn't give it to him soon, he'd have to dig up and find it outside.

Patrick Augustus

Unbelievably, even surprising himself, he had been totally faithful since the summer... In a manner of speaking. In other words, he had been celibate and apart from a little harmless slap and tickle with a couple of the women who came into the Book Shack, he hadn't been intimate with a woman. Even though he had been in situations where he was left in no doubt whatsoever that a particular woman wanted to get off with him, he had maintained his dignity. And that was no easy feat. One woman came to the Book Shack to buy BeBe Moore Cambell's *Brothers And Sisters* and departed only after leaving a less than ambiguous invite for him to come in her house anytime!

Not too long ago, he would have taken her up on the offer. But that was the old Johnny, he wasn't like that anymore. He rarely raved these days and hadn't been to a club in a long time. He uncharacteristically didn't go out that much at all and if anything, he would relax by chilling out at home with friends and cook for them.

After a quick breakfast of fruit and juice, he made his way to the Book Shack. It took a couple of bus rides to get there. The sun was shining, despite the cold November weather, and an icy breeze blowing in. Johnny shivered. Peckham as always seemed dismal. But he wasn't there to sightsee, he was there to earn his bread and butter.

The Book Shack was situated on the High Street, which was at times so lively that it seemed like one of the big Avenues in New York, rather than a working class area in London.

He soon opened up the shop. He hadn't been there a few minutes when a woman came in asking for a copy of *The Autobiography of Malcolm X*. Johnny didn't have to think to find that one. It was a good seller, always had been and always would be.

Much of the day was spent seeing reps from different publishing companies who came in by appointment. The little Book Shack in Peckham was a vital outlet for them, being the only bookshop in that area. For many of these larger publishing companies, the Book Shack served as a way to gauge which type of books the expanding market of black readers were buying.

It was difficult for Johnny to see his job in a glamourous way when it included packing and unpacking boxes and stock-taking, but a lot of black women did, particularly the more educated types. In their eyes, Johnny was an up-and-coming black 'publishing' magnate and several of them commented on how pleasurable it was to, "see a brother in a bookshop -- period." It made him swell-headed to be regarded by the fairer sex as being on the intellectual side and he had even considered wearing glasses to put the finishing touch to the image.

By midday, only a dozen or so paying customers had dropped into the Book Shack, but business picked up in the lunch hour as usual. There were a large number of conscious black secretaries in the area; women whose talents were really wasted in their jobs and who sought the comfort of books as a way to exercise their under-used intellectual talents. Sharon was such a woman. She worked as a secretary in the finance department of the council at the Town Hall just up the road. She came to The Book Shack nearly every day, stopping long enough to browse through the newly-arrived stock and to exchange a word or two with Johnny. She would always buy at least one book before leaving and had managed to build a considerable library of black literature in her living room. Johnny looked forward to her daily visits and not just because she was a reliable customer. He had grown to like her. She was broad-minded and he seemed to be able to discuss practically anything under the sun with her. When he got to know her a little better, he had learned that although she hadn't gone to university, she had three grade 'A' passes at A-Level, but due to the tragic death of her father, she had had to abandon her academic plans and get a job to make a financial contribution at home.

On this particular day, she came in as normal. She and

Johnny hadn't been chatting for more than a couple of minutes, when the phone rang.

"Hello, The Book Shack," he answered mechanically, unprepared for the torrent of abuse which followed.

"AND WHERE THE HELL HAVE YOU BEEN? UNGH! I'VE BEEN CALLING YOU AND LEAVING MESSAGES."

Johnny was taken aback. There was no need for introductions. The high-pitch stream of curses that sounded down the line could come from only one person. Baby mother Pauline. He was embarrassed, but wasn't able to butt in.

"WHERE THE HELL HAVE YOU BEEN?! JUDE'S BEEN SICK ALL WEEK AND WE AIN'T HEARD FROM YOU. HOW COME? YOU HAVE YOUR RESPONSIBILITIES, WHEN ARE YOU GOING TO REALISE THAT? AND ANOTHER THING, WE'VE RUN OUT OF MONEY... ARE YOU GOING TO LET YOUR SON STARVE? I CAN'T EVEN AFFORD TO BUY HIM CLOTHES... WHO DO YOU THINK IS GOING TO TAKE CARE OF YOUR SON FOR YOU, ENH?!"

"Look, hold one... just slow down," Johnny tried to be reasonable, but Pauline wasn't having it.

"DON'T GIMME THAT! THIS IS SERIOUS AND YOU'RE TALKING ABOUT SLOW DOWN. YOU BETTER GET YOUR BLACK ARSE DOWN HERE STRAIGHT AWAY AND SORT OUT THIS PROBLEM, BECAUSE I AIN'T SLOWING DOWN FOR ANYBODY!"

Embarrassed, Johnny looked up at Sharon. She had obviously heard Pauline's volley of abuse and aware that he was dealing with some difficult domestic situation, had tactfully moved away to the 'Women Writers' shelf where she was assiduously studying the back cover of a new novel. Johnny closed his eyes tight for a second. He wished he could simply disappear. He didn't need this kind of distress when he was at work.

"Please don't trouble me today," he pleaded softly down the phone. "Give my ears a break..."

He replaced the receiver and let out a long sigh.

"Boy, you're too girlie-girlie," Sharon called back, as she walked out the shop, slamming the door behind her.

Johnny had never been a betting man, but he was currently working seven days a week to stand still. He made money with one hand and handed it over to Pauline or Lesley with the other, it seemed. And the future didn't look any brighter either. Not until his kids were old enough to support themselves in any case. Despite its odds of several million to one, the National Lottery seemed like his best option and he had diligently spent a pound every week at his local post office in the hope that his lucky six numbers would come up, although if only five of them came up and he got the bonus number with the sixth, that would also do very nicely.

He had never thought of the The Isis Cup and didn't even know it was on until Mellow Yellow burst into The Book Shack one Saturday morning. The young albino seemed anxious. He said he had a certain tip for the Cup and that he would let Johnny in on it if he wanted. Johnny smiled. "There's no such thing as a certain tip," he said.

"Nah man, this one is a definite tip," Mellow declared. "Me have contacts, yuh know..."

Johnny didn't doubt that. He knew Mellow to be a man who came into contact with all kinds of people, both law-abiding and less so. Although he knew of no slight on Mellow's character, he was a talented local MC who was just waiting for that one big elusive break, the company he kept was much less than illustrious.

Mellow was surprised, no, alarmed, to discover that Johnny hadn't even entertained the thought of betting on the race. Mellow's view was that you had to bet on the Isis Cup because it was an institution. The whole country put a bet on that race. Even the Queen Mother. And by the same token, this relatively new annual horse race sponsored by a black newspaper had to be supported by all the black folks.

Mellow succeeded in convincing him, but not enough for

Johnny to risk more than ten pounds on the said horse named Longshot. It was good odds as well, 20-1. "Not that I'm going to win anything though," Johnny said, waving goodbye to his money and Mellow as he headed towards the bookies.

The store was so busy and there was so much to do on a Saturday, that Johnny would have forgotten about the money completely if it wasn't for the fact that he was reminded about the Isis Cup by several other customers who stopped for a moment to have a chat while buying books. By the time the kids had piled in for Saturday School in the store's back room, Johnny could think of nothing more than his ten pound investment. It would be so good if somehow Mellow's tip came through. After all, he could use the money. Two hundred quid would give him a breathing space from all his other financial commitments, only a brief one, but a breathing space nevertheless.

The Isis Cup was being run at 3pm. Bang in the middle of Saturday School. By ten to three, the suspense was too much for Johnny. He put one of the senior kids in charge of the class and pulled on his coat. Making great haste, he ran through the book shop and out into the street and round the corner in the direction of the bookies.

The atmosphere inside was already at fever pitch. The smoky room was packed with eager punters all staring at the large screen televisions secured in strategic positions above their heads. Everybody seemed to be smoking, everybody seemed to have a can of Tennants in their hand and everybody seemed to be shouting at the same time. After a moment, Johnny located Mellow on the other side of the large room and managed to attract his attention. Mellow gave him the 'everything okay' sign above the heads of the other punters. Up on the screen, the final horses were being coaxed to the start line and then suddenly a large roar erupted as the race was away.

To someone who wasn't familiar with the aesthetic of a bookies shop, the sight of grown men losing their mind over a horse race may have seemed alarming. Every punter was hot and driven wild with excitement, and hollered words of encouragement or abuse at the television screens.

"Giddyup....! Giddiyap! GIDDYAPPP!!" some were screaming. Others were shouting. "Come on number nine... come on my son..." and getting down on their haunches and rocking backwards and forwards with their hands in front of them holding the simulated 'reins' and calling, "Gwan my bwoy, gwan nuh...Ride the donkey! Ride him... Ride the donkey!" On the whole the atmosphere was tense but good-humoured, except for every now and then when someone got over-excited and started jumping in the air to the disapproval of those whose horses weren't doing so well. For the Isis Cup's unpredictability had seen some experienced punters tearing up their tickets after the first fence. At every fence there were more casualties and many of them thought they had already won their money because their horse was leading the race, only to see it fall at the next hurdle.

For Johnny, it was hard to follow the race, he could just about make out what the commentator was saying above all the commotion and after every fence, the fact that he could still hear the name "Longshot" in the TV announcer's ecstatic commentary, reassured him.

After a few more minutes the race was coming to its closing stages. The commentator was still whipping up emotion:

"And coming up to the last fence, it's Randy Andy from Arabian Nights...Arabian Nights is moving up on the inside and they're neck and neck...these two horses several furlongs ahead of the rest of the pack and in the lead it's Arabian Night..."

Johnny didn't need to be told that his horse had faded and was nowhere near the front. He was about to tear up his ticket when an amazing thing happened...

"And as we're coming up to the last bend in the race now," the

voice of the commentator sounded above the roar... *"And they're coming up to the last fence and yes, they're coming up and... Oh my word, they've both refused, this is incredible the two horses in the lead have refused to jump the fences and are still refusing...And the frustrated jockeys are trying for the third time to get their horses to jump and they're still refusing and oh my word, here comes Longshot, Longshot, the 20-1 outsider is coming up fast on the inside and approaching the last fence... AND he's jumped it.. and he's taken the lead and coming up to the last furlong now, it is Longshot in the lead, the winner of the Isis Cup... This is a victory that the punters will be talking about for years to come!"*

Despite himself, Johnny let out a shrill 'whoop' at the same time as the few other punters who had wisely backed the long shot.

The cashier was already counting the notes into Mellow's palm by the time Johnny managed to push his way through. She had been counting out a wad of £50 notes. There was almost eleven grand. Mellow clasped his hand around the money, peeled off the two hundred for Johnny and pocketed the rest.

"You made ten grand?!" Johnny exclaimed. "How much did you put down."

"Hundreds," Mellow answered with a smile. "When you've got a certain tip, you gotta sell your house to finance it if necessary."

Suddenly, Johnny's victory had lost its shine. The money he had made seemed like nothing compared to what Mellow had earned. Why hadn't he risked more money? He could have borrowed some money even. It would have been worth it. Ten grand would have sorted out all his problems. Five grand even. Why hadn't he listened to Mellow?

Before long, Johnny got the gambling bug. That first win had shown him that work was only one way to get money legally. He soon became a regular at the bookies and was inducted into the Peckham Punter's Association over a pint at the pub across the street late one afternoon. He had entered into the seedy world of easy money and began to believe that he could predict the future, not always, but he just needed that one big win and he would be safe. The winnings from the Isis Cup had helped replenish his funds after Pauline had cleaned him out, so he couldn't knock it. Meanwhile, it was important for him to divide his time expertly between his work at The Book Shack and the bookies.

It was early one Saturday morning a couple of weekends later, when he was standing outside the bookies studying the form at the back of the Daily Mirror, that he heard someone cry "Yush!" from the other side of the road. He looked up and saw the rastaman with the huge tam waving to him. He squinted. It didn't take him long to recognise the man, even though it had been years. Free-I the Rastaman. He waited for him to come over.

"Hail me idren!" Free-I greeted, recognising the man, "Love star." The dread observed Johnny closely. He did remember him from back in the day. "Yes me idren. Long time me no see the I!"

"I was about to say the same thing," Johnny agreed. "You still running a shop?"

"Well... yes an' no," the rastaman answered mysteriously. "Me jus' buy a house down Tulse Hill side ah t'ings an' t'rough the money well slow, me deh 'pon all kinds ah runnings. But right now, ah dis me a deal wid..."

He handed Johnny a leaflet, which was calling for the community to come together for a march of protest to Kennington Police Station, following the death of yet another black youth in police custody.

Johnny read the leaflet. He had heard about the unfortunate man who was stopped by U.S.-style baton-wielding constables the previous Saturday night.

"It's important that we get the whole ah we community backing dis one yah. Too many people been askin' Mista Prime Minister, 'How many more ah we haffe die...' Well, talking done. Ah time fe we get up an' fight, iya."

Johnny nodded, those were his exact same sentiments.

"So ah bookies you ah deal wid?" the rastaman asked, nodding towards Johnny's paper, with the scribbles on the racing pages.

"Well, er..." he stammered. He knew it wasn't the kind of thing Free-I would approve of and he was right.

"Yuh waan go easy with dat, y'know. Bookies affect your spiritual healt' ", Free-I warned.

Johnny joked that the bookies were like a mistress who wanted more from you than you were able to give and yet you weren't able to cut yourself off.

"So yuh ah run after 'ooman too?"

"Yeah man. You know how it go: Me have woman 'pon consignment."

If Johnny thought that that would impress the old rastaman, he was very much mistaken. He had forgotten that Free-I didn't joke when it came to slackness.

"So how old you are?" the rastaman asked, then continued without waiting for an answer. "Yuh cyaan run around after 'ooman all your life, you know. What, so you're going to be all forty years old or fifty and still running after 'ooman? Come on, man, where's your dignity? Ev'rybody ah go laugh at you, man."

As far as Free-I was concerned, Johnny was no longer a youth. It was time to grow up.

"Yuh waan see, iyah," Free-I continued slowly, "there are t'ree parts to the brain; the lower animalistic part, the mammalistic part which is the middle, an' the highest part, which is the most spiritual. Yuh see when you check a 'ooman an' say, 'Dis 'ooman's fit, I want to go to bed with her, it's the lowest animalistic part what's talkin, seen? Yuh haffe reach your higher spiritual side."

Feeling chastised, Johnny now remembered that Free-I had always fancied himself as an amateur psychologist.

UNRULY PICKNEY

Lacquan has become a real 'pickney with attitude' who tries his best to forget the meaning of 'respect'. He sloped into the house at about quarter to eight this morning after his paper round, wearing dark glasses and strutting the gangtsa style. I greeted him as usual when I came down the stairs and he replied "Sup!" only bothering to look up briefly from a comic strip he was studying.

"Take off those sunglasses!" Marcia shouted at him. She was more used to his attitude than me and rarely gave him an opportunity to express it. She watched her son with a frown as he ate his cornflakes. "You better not waste any of that food, young man," she said. "Eat up!"

Lacquan ignored his mother and continued eating his breakfast slowly. Marcia had no time for his games this morning for we were being summoned to his school to see the headmistress and had both taken time off work. Marcia said it was nothing new to her, in Lacquan's last year at primary school she had made several visits to see the head teacher. She had hoped that he would improve with a man in the house and was irritated that he was still misbehaving.

"Why is it that you're always getting in trouble?!" she demanded from him.

Lacquan simply continued eating and reading his comic. I should have said something, but I didn't know what to say. I still wasn't used to bringing up a kid, so I let Marcia deal with the matter. I needed to concentrate my mind on learning to be a father after all these years and trying to be Lacquan's best friend. It still amazed me how much he was growing up to be just like me –same smile and everything - - and soon he would be just as tall, if not taller.

After breakfast, we each went upstairs to get ready. I put on my one suit, the one I got married in and Marcia turned herself out quite businesslike. Lacquan, however, came down the stairs in his 'uniform' of baggy jeans tucked into his trainers, baggy T-shirt with a basketball motif and his head tied up with a bright red bandanna above which a baseball cap sat cocked at an angle. On seeing his 'uniform', his mother sent him back up as quickly as he had come down.

"Do you think we're going out raving or something?!" she called up the stairs.

"But Mum," he protested, "nobody wears school uniform anymore."

"I don't care," she replied. "I don't care if nobody wears clothes anymore, you are going to school in your correct uniform."

It was already eight forty-five when the cab arrived to drive us to the school. It was enough time. The letter said nine am. This was one day it wouldn't do to be late.

"You see all the trouble you're putting me through?" Marcia asked Lacquan stiffly as the driver ploughed his way through the rush hour traffic. "Do you think I've got time to keep coming up to your school to sort out your problems? What's wrong with you?"

Lacquan simply stared out of the window. Whatever was on his mind, he wasn't sharing it with us.

Marcia was frustrated. She had fought hard to get Lacquan into the school of her choice, because she didn't want him being registered at the local roughneck comprehensive where the pupils could wear whatever they liked and where the kids seemed to have no respect for the teachers or anyone else. There was no shortage of that type of school in south London, but she wanted Lacquan's education to enable him to do more than pack boxes in a warehouse or dig holes in the road with a pickaxe. He would only get a good education in a school with discipline and Marcia was determined to make sure her son kept his place at Brixton High's two-storey, brownstone, utilitarian building.

We arrived at the school just as a buzzer sounded for the start of the day's lessons. The teeming mob of schoolboys and girls of all shapes and sizes quickly cleared the playground and disappeared into the building through three main entrances. Lacquan pointed us to the headmistress' office, before making his way to his first class.

"Well Mr and Mrs Henry, I'm glad that you could both make it, because this is a most serious matter Lacquan has been involved in..."

Mrs Dutta, the Asian headmistress shook her head mournfully, as she flicked through what looked like several pages of reports on Lacquan.

"What exactly has he done?" I asked urgently. "Your letter said it was a matter which could affect the rest of Lacquan's education at this school."

"That's right. In the three months since your son started at this school in September, he has been involved in five physical fights. The latest last Friday, was outside the school gates, where he was reported to have punched a boy from a neighbouring school."

"Are you sure it was my son?" Marcia asked.

"I can assure you, Mrs Henry," the headmistress said, peering over the top of her glasses, "there were two school teachers there who have reported that Lacquan started the fight totally unprovoked. Now I see on his report from his junior school that he was in trouble there during his last year. I'm concerned that the move to a senior school hasn't matured him. When I spoke to you in the summer, Mrs Henry, you assured me that Lacquan was now going to have a much more stable family life and that you would keep a very close watch over him."

"Well, all that's happened just like I said, that's why I can't understand why my son seems to be getting the blame for every little thing that happens in the school."

"Please, Mrs Henry... You're suggesting that your son is being singled out for accusations and that is just not the case. We have given Lacquan a lot of leeway already and if you take a look at some of these comments from his teachers, I'm sure you'll agree. Read them, this one says, 'He seems to float in and out of daydreams while he is in class'... This one that, 'he would do very well at English if only he could look at literature with an eye other than that of Shabba Ranks...' And more worrying is this report from his form teacher that he spends his time in the company of a rough set of older pupils..."

"Look, fair enough," I interjected, "but what can we do?"

"You're his parents, so you know best. But if you're asking me, your son needs all the attention you both can give him at the moment. He needs to have love lavished on him like never before. Because Lacquan is not a stupid boy. In fact he's very intelligent. He knows exactly what he's doing. I think it's a cry for attention."

"Are you trying to say my son doesn't get enough love and attention at home? Is that it?" Marcia glared.

"No, not at all, just that he needs more. However much you're giving him, double it. Spend more time with him. Organise things for him to do and do them with him so that he doesn't have time to hang around with the wrong people, that kind of thing... Listen, Mrs Henry, I know how upsetting this can be, but I have to be honest with you. The situation at present is that if Lacquan gets into one more fight this term, I will have no choice but to exclude him from the school."

We left the school in silence, Marcia and I. What was there to say?

"Bwoy, it sounds like Lacquan is cruising for one rahtid lick upside the head," I offered.

Marcia grimaced.

"Honestly Linvall, sometimes I think you've gone deaf. Didn't you hear what the woman was saying?"

"Yeah, yeah, yeah...But what do they know about our son?"

"What do *you* know about your son, more like."

"Please Marcia, let's not get into that now. We've covered that ground 'nuff times already."

"I'm not getting into anything," she replied casually. "I'm just stressing the point, your son needs a lot of love and attention. This will give you an opportunity to spend more time with him and get to know him better."

I sighed. Wasn't I spending enough time with him already? How many more hours are there in a day? How come it was me that lost out whenever Lacquan needed extra parental attention?

"And another thing," Marcia added, as we walked down the hill towards the tube station, "you heard what the headmistress said about 'a rough set of older boys', those friends of his that are always coming around, I don't think you should encourage them so much."

"Encourage, like how?"

"You're always inviting them in when they come around to see Lacquan and letting them play music on your stereo."

"Aww come on, Marce. That can't do any harm, they're his friends."

"Yes, but are they the right friends? Haven't you wondered why all his friends seem much older than him?"

I conceded that I had, but I didn't think anything of it.

"Well, I just think that you're encouraging the wrong sort of friends."

"So what is all this apportioning blame business?" I asked, fed up. "As it goes, I think Quan's behaving badly because of all the fuckries you filled his head with when I was still pretending to be his 'uncle' rather than his father. He already told me how, when he was growing up, you would tell him that his father was in America and that he was a bastard. If you ask me, that's got something to do with everything that's going on now. When you then tell him that I'm really his father and not his uncle, he's thinking 'well, aren't you the one Mummy keeps describing as a bastard?' "

I had bottled that information up for several weeks and only brought it up as a form of defence. I had to hit back with something.

"But you were a bastard," Marcia answered, unphased. "And maybe you still are, I'm just giving you the benefit of the doubt to prove me wrong. That's why we got married isn't it...?"

Patrick Augustus

The message on the answering machine was clear and to the point:

"Linvall, whe' yuh deh? Daddy Kulcha speakin'... Me want a photograph for my new record cover, 'Reggae Smash - Volume 24', seen? Tek a picture of a 'criss' gal in red, green and gold sunglasses. Usual t'ing, yuh know..."

I had to smile. When you heard Daddy Kulcha's unsophisticated gravel voice, it was hard to conceive how he had built up such an impressive reggae music empire. But he had, and from his Kulcha Records headquarters in a newly-built warehouse in Harlesden, he was able to control most of the reggae runnings in the UK, (rumour has it that he works every day of the year, including Christmas Day).

It took him almost a year to get back to me after I took my portfolio up there for him to look at. When he finally called, I was desperate for work. It was in October. I had been married just over a month and to be honest, I had spent the time maxin' and relaxin' with my woman. Work couldn't have been further from my mind. In this business, if you're not out there chasing up the work, it eventually dries up. That's how most freelance photographers go under. Eventually the money stopped coming in altogether. It was then that Daddy Kulcha called me and gave me the three-cover job. It was a life saver. It wasn't well-paid, but it was bread and butter and right now I can't afford to be choosy. He must have liked the shots to call me up and give me more work on his various compilation albums. Well if Daddy Kulcha wanted a sexy photo, a sexy photo he was going to get. And I knew the perfect model for it.

I pulled out my Mercury One 2 One and went through the list of entries in its address book until I came to the one I was looking for. Marilyn... or Lady Marilyn as she was now calling herself. I pressed the call button and listened for a tone.

"Hello...?"

"Is that Marilyn?"

"Who's asking?"

"It's me, Linvall..."

There was a momentary silence.

"Oh Linvall... The photographer? Oh of course, how are you baby?"

I told her everything was cool. We exchanged pleasantries. It was a while since we had spoken, but I hadn't figured she would forget who I was so quickly. Anyways, I told her about the shoot. Was she available? We could shoot it the next morning if she was up for it.

"The sooner the better," she said. "I'm off to Morocco for a ten day shoot at the weekend."

"Ah so you ah get big time now," I teased. "Well don't bother with none of that: 'Won't get outta bed for less than ten grand' business with me. Remember, I knew you when you were small pickney. Seriously though, you know how Daddy Kulcha is, he hates to dig deep in his pockets so you'll be working for expenses mostly."

Marilyn sighed, but said it was cool. "Honestly Linvall, you could talk a woman into anything."

"That's why I'm a photographer," I said, as sensually as I could. She giggled.

That's the way it is sometimes with a lot of the models I photograph. We just tease each other, it's nothing serious. It's all part of building a relationship of trust between the subject and the photographer. When I take pictures of a beautiful woman, I've got to make her believe that I'm her best friend, to relax her.

"So what do you want me to wear?"

"Ragga clothing, you know batty riders and that type of thing. It's got to be sexy."

"Oh no, I gave all my ragga clothes to my younger sister... I thought all that was played out months ago. I didn't think that I'd need them anymore."

"Don't worry," I said reassuringly, "I'm sure you'll find something. For all I care you can come naked."

"Yes I'm sure you'd love that wouldn't you," she whispered in the receiver and blowing me a goodbye kiss, she ended the call.

Every schoolboy has a dream and long before I grew out of short trousers, mine was to become a fashion photographer. While the other boys bought football transfers and comics, my pocket money went on buying film and developing paper. On leaving school, I didn't have to consult with any careers adviser either. I got myself an apprenticeship with a freelance paparazzi, where I learned my trade. From there, I got my first fashion shoot for one of the women's magazines. I was at the right place at the right time and perhaps most importantly, I quoted the right price. Since then, I've always worked. I've had several covers and done the rounds of the mail order catalogues, advertising agencies, fashion and beauty houses. But photography is like anything else, if you're not out there touting for work, you quickly become yesterday's photographer. They say a lunch-break is a long time in the photographic world; the month I took off work after the wedding was like early retirement. Work has been picking up though. I've had a few calls this week and a few of my Bob Marley photographs, which I took when I was just an up and coming yout', have been chosen for an exhibition of 'Street Style' at the Victoria and Albert Museum. There won't be a huge amount of corn from it, but the kudos is priceless. In fact, even though work is nudging along, I've got more work than time at the moment. I didn't know that fatherhood could be so time consuming. I'm even considering getting a secretary to take care of all the administrative stuff in the studio.

Marilyn arrived at nine in the morning as we agreed. She stepped into the studio, looking as alluring as I had remembered her, shapely hips and breasts bursting out of a flimsy raincoat. At only 19-years-old, she was every bit a woman.

"I hear you got married," she said, shedding her outdoor clothes.

"Oh is that what they're saying," I said, slightly irritated. "You should know better than to listen to gossip."

We chatted a little over a cup of coffee. Marilyn filled me in on everything that had happened to her since I last saw her. Things had been going well and were looking promising. "I'm coming hot dis year, you cyaan do nut'n to cold me." She said she was hopeful that she'd be chosen for a high-profile ad campaign by a black hair care products manufacturer. She would know sometime next week.

"So what about you," she asked, "how've you been keeping?"

"Oh I've been in America."

"Oh really? What, working?"

"Yes you know, a bit of work and a bit of pleasure. All work and no play, makes Linvall a dull boy," I laughed.

I don't know why I lied. It just slipped out. I'm still not comfortable with the 'married man' tag and finding it difficult sometimes to admit it. Especially to women. But that's not why I slip off my wedding ring when I arrive at the studio every morning. As I've explained to Marcia, the reason I do that is because when I'm developing film, I have to dip my fingers in all kinds of chemicals which could end up rubbing the shine off the ring.

After coffee, we started setting up the shoot. I handed Marilyn the red, green and gold sunglasses and got down to fixing the lights. We continued our banter. Idle chat, but yet not so idle."

"So who are you seeing at the moment, Marilyn? Not that same idle jubie I saw you with when I bumped into you in Leicester Square that time?"

"Oh him...!" she spat out. "That done long time. That boy is history. You're not keeping up to date, Lin, that's two romances behind."

"Yeah, he seemed like a bwoy. When are you young gals going to realise that you need to check a mature thirtysomething to really know what good loving is?"

"When we realise how important it is to give mouth to mouth resuscitation after a heart attack!" Marilyn quipped.

I started taking the pictures. It was a pleasure to

photograph her. Marilyn knew exactly how to turn a man on with just a look, a smile, a jerk of her head. And dressed in the skimpiest of clothes, she was a real live wire. My eyes feasted on her huge pointed breasts. She breathed in deeply, nipples surging, dark rings discernible through the thin bra. Through the lens of my Hasselblad, I admired her taught stomach and her ample hips. They looked very inviting and for a moment I imagined how comfortable they would be. Without realising it, I licked my lips and unable to stop myself, I told her that she had the world's greatest hips.

Marilyn didn't catch my drift. Like most models, she was probably used to men passing the odd complimentary remark, but when a photographer tells a model how attractive she is, she only sees it in a professional sense. They imagine that a photographer studies their body with detachment. I don't know about other photographers, but me...? I'm a red-blooded Caribbean man, what can I say?

I couldn't concentrate on what I was doing. After a few more shots, I decided to release my tension. I peeped up from the camera, with my eyes fixed on Marilyn's behind as she posed erotically in a pair of designer wellies and little else. She had a workable rear, firm and girlish, exactly how I like it. I conjured up thoughts of my lips crushing hers and my hands traversing her luscious body. Without saying a word, I walked over to her, seized her by the hips and pulled her towards me, my blood singing with desire, her eyes studying me expectantly. At the same moment, my mobile phone rang. Shit! I flipped it open.

"Linvall? Marcia. I've just had a call from Brixton High, the headmistress... Lacquan's in trouble again. I can't believe it. After all I've told him...! She wants one of us to come down. I can't make it, I've got an urgent meeting at work."

"But I'm in the middle of a photo shoot," I protested.

"Well you'll have to cancel it. This is your son we're talking about," she said forcing her opinion through with volume. From the tone of her voice I knew it was no use arguing. I flipped the phone shut and kissed my teeth.

"Bad news?" Marilyn asked, with a twinkle in her eye.

"Yes...yes, bad news," I stuttered. "I've got to go somewhere for a while."

"That's got to be really bad news," she said, still smiling. "Will you leave me so unsatisfied?"

"Well I suppose I could go in ten minutes time," I said, slipping an arm around her waist and glancing at my watch.

Marilyn wasn't having any of it though. She threw my arm off. "I knew you couldn't last... You think ten minutes is satisfaction? That's what I was saying about you older men..."

The caretaker at Brixton High nodded his head as I stepped in the gates. "Watcha mate!" he called out. "How are you doing?" He recognised me from the last time. I was becoming a regular.

Mrs Dutta was shaking her head mournfully, as I was admitted into her office, wondering what I was doing back there again.

"Mr Henry, this time I have no choice... I have tried to be understanding, but your son has gone too far."

"Who's he been fighting this time?"

"Fight? No, he hasn't been fighting... Something totally different."

"So what as he done exactly?" I was expecting the worst and there was no point in prolonging the suspense.

Mrs Dutta pressed her intercom. "Mrs Bailey, would you mind sending Lacquan into my office."

We waited a few minutes with Mrs Dutta still shaking her head. Then there was a knock on the door and Lacquan stepped in. I almost fell about laughing when I saw him. Since I had seen him at breakfast time, his hair had disappeared. He now sported a shiny Michael Jordan style, which on his small, dark head was reminiscent of a black ball on a pool table. I couldn't stifle a giggle. Lacquan giggled also.

"Mr Henry!" Mrs Dutta exclaimed in a thick Asian accent. "I can see that you are not taking your son's behaviour with the seriousness that we view it here at the school."

"So what's the problem?" I asked. "You don't like his haircut?"

"It's not a question of whether or not I like his haircut. The rules of the school state clearly that pupils must fashion their hair in conservative styles. We can be flexible. We allowed him to have several lines and patterns in his hair. But this... Can you imagine how disruptive such a haircut is to the rest of his class?"

"No I can't," I said seriously. "So don't tell me that you're going to expel him because he hasn't got any hair on his head."

"We don't expel pupils," Mrs Dutta corrected, "we 'exclude' them."

"Same difference," I replied, shrugging my shoulders. By now I was fed up with the way the school was hounding 'Quan for every little thing. " 'Expel' or 'exclude', no way can you tell me that you're going to distress my son like that over a haircut."

"I've already made my decision Mr Henry," the headmistress said, raising a hand to cut me short. "I cannot allow Lacquan to return to school until his hair has grown to a minimum of two millimetres. So I am suspending him until such a time..."

Outside the school gates, I slapped Lacquan on his head playfully.

"Aooowww!" he cried out.

"If you don't like slaps on your neck-back, you shouldn't shave your head," I said, offering words of wisdom. Looking at my son, I had to smile. Despite the Kojak style he still looked innocent and sweet. And even though he had cost me an afternoon of pleasure, he was still my son.

Normally, Lacquan goes to school with his hair close-cropped and tidy, his mother sees to that. But this morning he'd taken a detour on his way to school and popped in on a friend who had just finished shaving another friend's head.

"It looked dope!" 'Quan explained that he just had to have his head shaven too. I smiled knowingly. It was the kind of thing I would have done when I was his age.

"So who's this friend of yours who cuts hair?"

"Oh, Tyrone."

"How comes he's not at school?"

"Oh, he got excluded and so he sits at home making money cutting people's hair."

"And you think that's a good thing?"

"It's alright," Lacquan said with a shrug of his shoulders.

"No, it's not," I countered. "That's not the kind of kid you wanna be hanging around with, 'Quan. Why do you think he got excluded? It was probably because he was hanging around other kids who got excluded."

"No it wasn't. It was because he kept clicking his teeth at the headmistress."

"I don't care what it was," I said exasperated. "You know what I mean."

Lacquan shrugged his shoulders again. It was nothing to do with him anyway, he said, pulling a baseball cap out of his jacket pocket and wearing it back to front on his smooth head.

"If you had a cap on you, why didn't you wear it in school? They probably wouldn't even have realised you had a shaved head and you wouldn't have got into all this trouble."

"I did wear it," he said smiling. "But when I got in class, the teacher told me to take it off."

"And then what happened?"

"I said, 'no'. And so he says 'Take off your hat', again, so I said, 'Okay, I'm going to take off my hat, but when I catch a cold and my mum comes up to school looking for me, don't say I didn't warn you'. So I took it off, and the whole class burst out with laughter and my teacher said I had to go and see the headmistress."

I sighed. However amusing it was, I didn't find it funny that the whole class was laughing at my son's expense. I warned him not to keep careless company and that if his rough friends were trying to pull him the wrong way, he didn't have to follow.

"What happened to all those other friends you used to hang out with at junior school?" I asked him. "You know, like that nice kid who used to be your best friend?"

"Oh he's a kid. I haven't got time for kids," Lacquan said, sounding grown up.

"Then why don't you go to army cadets any longer? You used to love all that."

"It was air cadets actually. And I stopped going, because I got a little more conscious."

"Stop chat foolishness," I said, pushing his head forward. "And start thinking about a good excuse for when your mother gets home."

"She ain't going to do nothing," he said confidently.

"Are you sure? What makes you think that?"

"Because like she used to say, I'm just like my 'no good father'."

He got another slap on his head for that. "I said stop chat foolishness!"

If Lacquan thought he was going to get off lightly, he had another thing coming. When Marcia got back from work, she was incensed. She didn't see the funny side with the haircut and she even backed the school.

"I would have suspended you too if I was the headmistress! " she bawled. "Why did you have to get suspended over a silly little thing like a haircut?! You know what the school rules are, so why did you do it? Why do you think I go through all the trouble of buying decent clothes for you to go dressed to school in? Enh?"

Lacquan wasn't listening to her. He lay sprawled out on the rug in front of the television with his hands on his cheeks and his elbows on the ground, watching a cartoon film and contemplating the fact that he had been grounded, his pocket money had been stopped with immediate effect and his mother had promised to give him "more maths and

English to study at home every day" of his suspension, than he would have ever had at school.

"And another thing," she said, turning off the television with a click, "there'll be no more television until you learn some manners, young man."

Patrick Augustus

MISTER MENTION

Courtney King was one of those guys Gussie had known from time. One of his homeboys from around the way when they were kids. He hadn't seen him for a long time until they bumped into each other in Brixton one Saturday afternoon in early November.

Saturday afternoon in Brixton is pure roadblock. It's shopping day. Everybody wants the freshest produce in the market. While Gussie manouevered his way through Atlantic Road to get to the Arcade, he saw Courtney across the road, reasoning with two sisters, trying to convince them of one thing or another.

"Yaowza!" Gussie called out. Courtney looked up.

"Gussie, ah you dat?" Courtney called back. He made his excuses to the two sisters and crossed the road, where the two men punched fists and slapped each other's backs.

"Long time."

"Well yuh know how it go," Courtney replied, "when the ducats ah run slow, you don't really have time for socialising."

"Well, it looks like business ah run all right, still," Gussie said, admiring Courtney's criss grey suit of quality wool. It had obviously been tailored by a master craftsman.

"Well, you got to look the part, innit?" Courtney replied.

Courtney King was small in stature, but what he lacked in height he always made up for in big talk. He graduated from street hustler to astute businessman when a few years ago, he backed a musical based on the lives of black heroes and heroines throughout history. It was the first time anybody had attempted such a thing and with Courtney's promotional strategy, the show had turned out to be a hit in every sense of the word. Since then, Courtney had gone into the promotions game and had become one of the largest players in the reggae promotion scene in London. Not bad for a Jamaican breddah whose shiny bronze skin and curly silk hair belied his Indian ancestry. From what Gussie had heard, Courtney even had shares in several of the pirate stations up and down the country.

"Hey, me hear seh yuh get married the other day!" Courtney remembered. "Yes, my yout', 'nuff respect, y'hear? You get official now, yuh is big man now. So wha', the gal ah breed fe yuh?"

Gussie kissed his teeth and looked away in disdain. It seemed like the whole world had heard about his marriage and try as hard as he might, he couldn't get away from it.

"That's finished long time, you know."

Courtney looked surprised, but he could see from his friend's face that Gussie didn't want to talk about it so he let it drop.

"So how's tricks? I hear you're in the broadcasting business nowadays," Gussie said.

"Cho' man, don't pay no mind to all that su-su business. Yuh know seh dem t'ings is illegal. And you know me – legal me legal." Courtney winked his eye and smiled a knowing smile. Then he continued. "Right now, me deh 'pon another runnings. Check this," he said, pulling a leaflet out of his breastpocket and handing it to Gussie. "Read that and tell me if I'm not the don."

Gussie glanced at the leaflet promoting a boxing match at a venue in Lewisham, between two middleweights. At the top of the leaflet was the legend, 'Courtney King Promotions'.

"Respect!" Gussie said, touching Courtney's fist with his again. "Maximum respect is due! Most definitely. No wonder you're modelling inna yuh t'ree piece suit an' t'ing. So when did you become a boxing promoter?"

"I can turn my hand to anyt'ing, yuh nah see't?" Courtney insisted. And then stressing his point, "ANY-T'ING!"

"So how did you start?" Gussie pressed again patiently.

"Well yuh see dis breddah on the leaflet..."

"Sugar Ray Williams?" Gussie remembered the boxer from his youth. At one time he was being tipped as one of the finest middleweight boxers in Britain and then suddenly he disappeared out of the news after losing one fight and you never really heard of him anymore.

"Yeah, well I met up with him. One of my spars brought him around my house one day, and you know how it is, we got to chatting, because he had retired by this time, you see, and I was asking him all kinds of questions about what it was like being a boxer, you know and he then said the one thing he regrets, the one thing he regrets is not having had a second chance at the title, so I say 'why not, why didn't you get another chance?' and he says nobody was prepared to back him. So, you know me, I just moved in and took over management and promotion and now a couple more fights and he'll be heading towards the title. Believe!"

Somebody tooted a horn from a passing car. Courtney turned and hailed up the driver before continuing.

"If we get a chance at the title, you'll be talking millions and yours truly is Mr Fifty Percent. Believe."

Gussie wanted to believe, he really did. But he couldn't help wondering whether his old mate was flogging a dead horse. Williams must be over 40 if he was a day. How could a boxer that age seriously consider being a challenger for a title?

"But that's the beauty of the whole thing!" Courtney insisted. "Here you have a boxer who nobody believes can still stand toe-to-toe with the best of them, so when he goes in the ring, there's always good odds against him. Every Sugar Ray fight I've made more money at the bookies than I've made from the ring."

"Sugar Ray is a dynamite boxer, I'm telling you, I've seen him take guys out. It's like he goes into the ring and then it's 'biff-baff' and the other guy's down. Believe. The other day he had this fight man, and bwoy, you shoulda seen the other guy by the end of the first round." Courtney chuckled, a big, hearty grin on his face as the memory came back to him.

"Yeah alright," Gussie conceded, " he can take guys out, but he's too old to be a serious challenger to any titles."

"Nah man, you crazy? You must be one of those ageist guys, innit? Didn't you see what happened with George Foreman. Oldest world heavyweight champion, man. You go an' tell George Foreman to leave the ring. Ol' man like him had to knock out a yout'man to win the title, you know. And that didn't trouble him too much. Most people think boxing is all about strength, but now me get to know a bit about it, I check seh it's about experience, and most times that counts for more than youth."

Gussie was still not convinced; he had seen the George Foreman fight where the 45-year-old champion won the title. As far as he was concerned it was a fluke. Fluke or no fluke, Courtney insisted, Foreman was sitting tight on a multi-million dollar sponsorship deal with McDonald's. If Foreman could earn that kind of money from making people believe that Big Macs keep you young and healthy, surely Williams could get a few hundred grand from Wimpy or Burger King to do the same?

"You see this fight yah," Courtney started, "this is a fight which takes my comeback kid to the next level, seen? After this fight, people will be saying 'Sugar Ray Williams is still a great fighter'. Because this white guy he's up against ain't just an ordinary fighter, you know. He's an ex-champ."

The two men chatted some more, taking in the breeze. Courtney was adamant that Sugar Ray would come through on the fight and before departing invited Gussie along to the rematch. He pulled out a couple of tickets from his breast pocket.

"Come and check it out, man. You won't be disappointed."

Then Courtney's phone rang. He pulled out a miniature mobile from his breast pocket and answered it. He chatted businesslike for a moment or two before slamming it shut.

"Gotta make tracks," he said, holding up his fist for Gussie to punch. "More time. Mek sure you come to the fight, you got front row tickets and t'ing. Bring your woman. The ladies love it. Believe."

Patrick Augustus

LIVING ON THE FRONTLINE

"The biggest talk of the day is the lottery. Everybody wants to win. All you need is one pound and six lucky numbers and, bingo you could be a millionaire. Everybody wants to be a millionaire..."

Beres was giving an economics lecture to the attentive Saturday School students assembled in the back room of the Book Shack. He had become a regular lecturer to the group of eager boys and girls who crowded into the tiny storage room for the support classes which Johnny organised to supplement the unsatisfactory state education offered to the local black kids.

"Fourteen million to one. Those are the odds in winning the jackpot. And if your parents have been playing it for a couple of weeks, they're probably thinking the computer is fixed, but they won't stop playing until they win the jackpot, because they want to buy a home and land and to set up a plan for their retirement. And after all, if an Asian guy can win £18 million, it means a black man could as well. Black people all over the country are going crazy about this National Lottery. They really will go crazy, because at fourteen million to one, most of them will be losers. Now some of the MPs have said that it is 'obscene' for people to win more than a couple of million... That shows you what hypocrites they are. Look how many of them have more than £18 million and I don't hear any of them complain yet...

"I'm not here to knock the Lottery, because when those black pensioners in Birmingham won a million each, I was overjoyed. But what I'm saying is, you've got better odds of becoming a millionaire by the fruits of your own hard work and sweat. I can't afford to live my life on odds of fourteen million to one, can you?

"So what's my point, I hear you ask? My point is this: education in Britain is not working. Not for black youth anyway. The school system today is educating us straight back into slavery, because it's not dealing with what you've got to deal with in society. The school system is teaching us to be able to get jobs when we leave school, but that's the old way and that's played out because there aren't many jobs out there to be had. Do you know the extent of unemployment amongst black youth in London between sixteen and twenty-four? It's over fifty percent. And it isn't getting any better, because this world doesn't owe you a living. That means that most of you will be twiddling your thumbs when you leave school, or college or university... Now what I'm saying is that school should be teaching us how to be businessmen, how to set up a little something of our own. But how many of you when you come out are going to be able to set up a business? How many of you are going to be able to conduct market research and study your market and your customers' habits, or understand the complex but essential tax laws? How many of you are going to be able to deal with distribution or spreadsheets or business plans? If you don't understand these things when you leave school, believe me, you're in trouble.

"And one more thing, when you hear people talk about the 'information superhighway', don't just let it go in one ear and out the other. Check it out, it means something. It means your future and it offers you opportunities to understand and develop business. All of you radical youths who want to be 'just like Malcolm X', check out the information superhighway, because that offers us a way to make the black nation rise. When we're all keyed up to it, we will take power away from our elected bodies. We'll all be able to link up and we won't just be talking about recycling that black pound. We'll set up a successful black economy. Look at the Asians and ask yourself why they're doing well. We've got to get our economy together too. And fast!"

Beres sat down to the resounding applause of the students. As always, they were impressed by Beres' confidence that they, each one of them, could be as successful as any of those big shots in *The Sunday Times* 'Richest 500', given half the chance.

Patrick Augustus

Johnny had now been running the Saturday school on a voluntary basis for eighteen months. Last year's crop of students had done him proud by scoring higher grades in their GCSEs than their secondary school teachers had thought possible. One of them was even now being considered for an Oxbridge entrance exam in a year's time. And of course, the parents were delighted at their youngsters' new-found enjoyment of academic studies and the improvement in their school work. Word had quickly got around the estates of Peckham that however badly your kids were doing, the Book Shack's Saturday School could sort them out. This year, the class was over-subscribed and Johnny was obliged to give Linvall an exceptional squeeze to get Lacquan into the class.

There was one more speaker to follow -- Free-I, the rastaman.

The previous day, during a quiet period in the Book Shack, Johnny had been listening to the local pirate station when he heard a teenage voice reading the following advert in the 'community information break':

"Ladies and gentlemen, mum's and dad's... For the best and freshest back-ah-yard produce at competitive prices, why not try Free-I's Mobile Supermarket. If it's callaloo you want - we have it, if it's sugar cane you want - we have it and even if a nice juicy coconut is your desire - we aim to please... So don't be Insanesburys an' leggo your Testicos, there's only one place to shop for the best in Caribbean foodstuffs and that's Free-I's Mobile Supermarket, parked up outside 86 Railton Road... We also deal with import and export of all kinds of herbs and spices..."

That was followed by a short musical interlude. The voice of Bob Marley sang:

Don't care what the world say
I and I gonna have things our way...

Then the stern voice of an older man which Johnny immediately recognised as Free-I's:

"Dis is Free-I, the rastaman... I'm not begging you, I'm just telling you, if yuh waan good food, check my mobile supermarket. But even if you don't, my people, look inna yuhself 'cause dis is the time we all must unite... For hundreds of years we have been here as a slave, now I an' I must find a way of not being enslaved. So whether you ah Smallie, or a Yardman, whether Yankee or African, live good, work hard an' love one another. Dis is Free-I, the rastaman, the dreadlocks, sent dung ah babylon to warn Jah nation an' tell dem 'bout Jah works. Seen?"

The unusual radio advertisement gave Johnny a thought, his head was buzzing. He was always looking for new speakers to inspire the students of his Saturday School. He had managed to get several television personalities as well as nearly every graduate he knew to give a short lecture. But none of them would be as animated and penetrating as Free-I was likely to be.

After closing up the Book Shack's early that evening, he made his way to Brixton and on Railton Road, he spotted a big van half parked up on the pavement with its rear shutter raised, revealing a dwindling stock of long sugar canes, large yams and other tropical produce. Standing at the tailgate was Free-I, the rastaman, chewing on a banana and listening to an agitated older man who was insisting that no way could the West Indies cricket team have lost to Australia in the Caribbean, in the days of the great Garfield Sobers. Meanwhile, on both sides of the road, workers hurried home to start the weekend or simply to pass out in front of the television after another hard week at the grind.

Johnny shook hands with his old friend and without further ado, explained his purpose. The rastaman listened intently, scratching his beard the whole time. He had heard about the Saturday School and heard that it was doing good things. "Ah your t'ing dat?" he asked impressed and pleased. And as it was his philosophy that you must always take time out to educate the youths, he would come the next day to 'reason' with the youths about their roots and culture. One of his sons, he explained, would be able to look after the 'supermarket' in his absence.

The Saturday School students observed the older man with the huge red, green and gold tam on his head with increasing curiosity. Somehow, they couldn't picture why he was there and what he had to offer. To many of these youngsters who identified with the hardcore 'by any means necessary' philosophy of rap music, rasta was pre-historic and rastamen considered to be at best 'quaint' figures. But something was about to happen to each and everyone of them...

Free-I got up to speak:

"Well, 'nuff respect to the man like Beres fe a conscious lecture. I hope all ah unuh was listenin' to the breddah... The first t'ing I want to say, is congratulations to unuh who passed your GGCs an' all dem sump'n deh. Yeah, respect. Me hear seh mos' ah unuh pass. Well, dat is a good t'ing. An' for unuh what nevah pass, don't cry yout, have no fear. An' yout.... try again. Yuh know how it go – one day fe you an' another fe s'maddy else... Try again an' mek sure yuh pass the second time around... Don't give up. The heights achieved by great men were not attained by sudden flight. Seen? Nevah stop. Endurance is the key my bredrin. So once again, congratulations if yuh pass, sorry if yuh failed... Must work harder, seen? Each disappointment is fe a reason. When almighty Jah decide fe pay yuh, your reward will be bountiful. Seen? Education is very important, because unuh are the men an' women an' leaders of tomorrow. Use your intelligence in life an' mek some money instead of working for the council for all two hundred an' ninety years with nut'n to show fe it but a lickle two up an' two down in Tooting. Eh, yuh see me, me waan all unuh to be billionaires. Nuh worry 'bout millionaire, ah *billionaire* we ah deal with...!

"Yeah, roots an' culture is my lecture fe the day... Me hear Barry White the other day on some radio show an' him seh, 'if black people knew their history they would succeed much more'. Yeah man, ah dat me waan fe show unuh. Or like Marcus Garvey seh, 'A man without his history, is like a tree without its roots'. Same t'ing, but different still. An' from Barry White seh dat, me personally love dat yout', yuh understand? 'Cause more musicians and players of instruments, more artists, boxers an' runners an' politicians shoulda seh dat.

" 'Cause when I first come ah Inglann, I was terrified ah Scotlann Yard because of their reputation an' all programmes like *The Sweeney* 'pon TV. I just thought 'bwoy these guys are serious'. But when I get to check my history, me know seh dem couldn't do me nut'n an' me get to realise dat my gran'fadda an' him fadda before dat and him mumma before dat, slave fe dis country widout no pay. Dat's why I an' I don't pay no bills what come from babylon. An' I won't pay no TV licence because black people contribute 'nuff money to TV an' there ain't nut'n there to represent us. An' then again, when black people pay tax the money goes to the Old Bill to come down an' harass us. We payin' dem to beat us. Yuh see me, how me live free? An' anyway, the Earth is the Lord's an' the fullness thereof, so when Scotlann Yard lock me inna jail, it's pure persecution. Our foreparents contribute blood, sweat an' tears to this country, others get compensation for their works, yet we receive only humiliation. Look how many rivers we've had to cross... Full time now fe we reap what is rightfully ours. So lissen keenly to wha' Barry White seh. Know your history... Unuh hear dat tune, *Practice What You Preach*? Me mus' send request out to all the selectors in an' around the capital to play this record, because whenever I go ah dance each an' every lady know the lyrics an' likes to sing to it. Me nuh know why, whether it's because it have a nice beat or sump'n..."

There was an eager buzz amongst the students. Most of them were familiar with the record and one or two even considered it amongst their favourites. Free-I continued:

"Yuh see music now, music is a very important part ah we struggle, seen? Back in Jamaica, I had the opportunity of being around the man – Bob Marley. 'Cause I come from Trenchtown, Jamaica. In those days, Trenchtown was a musical town, everybody sing. People talk less an' sing more. An' we used to mek guitars outta bamboo an' ol' sardine tins an' we would mek the strings from the copper in electric wires. We really had fun, y'know. In those days everyone passed t'rough Trenchtown. Bob used to hear me sing an' always try to encourage me to cut a record. Dat was before my madda send me fe come ah Inglann fe work get some money an' set meself up. Peter Tosh was livin' in Trenchtown as well. Peter now, he was a man who could play guitar an' organ an' all kinda instrument an' he was always singing ol' religious songs like, *"Go tell it on the mountain"*... Dem man deh, was heartical. We shared a bus to Port Antonio to do a show, but too much rain ah fall, so we nevah actually get to perform. But it was great talking with some good musicians an' learnin' 'bout harmony an' all dem sump'n deh. We drove back an' forth to Kingston with the breddahs dem an' I reasoned with the man. Bob was a man who knew his roots an' culture, an' who practice what him preach. When him seh 'I'll be forever loving Jah', ah so him stay. An' when him seh, him nevah shoot no sheriff ---- him nevah dweet! So 'nuff respect to the man fe the sounds an' the positivity. Yuh waan hear roots an' culture? The music he lef' behind was like an encyclopedia. When yuh inna situation, you check the songs an' you find a answer. Listen to *Redemption Song*. Dat one deh touch me mentally, spiritually an' physically. Music is very important, man. An' the roots of music is even more important. Ol' time somet'ing come back again...

"Know yuh history, youts. Know yuh history. When teacher seh Crucifer Cunnnilumbus discover Jamaica in 1492, tell him he's a dyaam blasted liar! Let me tell unuh, the only t'ing Cunnilumbus did in the Caribbean was spread venneral diseases all over the islands. Him nevah discover nut'n! Dyamn blasted liar! An' until unuh understan' dat, unuh cyaan understan' nut'n about unuh past or unuh future. Unuh dig? DYAM BLASTED LIAR!! There was 'nuff Arawak Indians there long before Cunnilumbus... an' one or two black man as well.

"An' another t'ing, when dem tell unuh in school dat some white man called Wilberforce abolish slavery, just laugh at dem. Him nevah abolish nut'n. Not a dyamn t'ing... It was black people like you an' me, ordinary people, who refused to take it any longer and fought the white man in every way dem could, until the man dem said, 'A'right, we cyaan win dis war, dem stronger than we. Let dem have dem freedom.' Ah wha' de raas nonsense was dat? We had already taken our freedom away from dem. Dem couldn't' gi' we nut'n! Unuh evah hear 'bout Nanny, Queen of the maroons? Read up on it, man! Because even though unuh is born ah foreign, all ah unuh is African, seen? But it's not just enough to have yuh skin colour an' seh, 'well there I am, I am African...' Unuh must know more than dat. Unuh must learn African history, politics, unuh must get to know the heroes from the zeros. Yuh must know where you're coming from an' where you're going. So in class, don't just sit back an' let dem tell lies. And don't let them tell you yuh mentally sick neither...

"Okay, me done with the 'roots', time to check yuh 'culture'. 'Cause culture come fe cure all ah unuh of the slackness which is spoiling up unuh minds..."

Johnny was impressed with the way Free-I managed to grab the students attention with his own mixture of streetwise talk and pow-wow pan-Africanism. They listened to him with a hush that was remarkable. There were no whispers among them, nobody shifted in their seats. Each and every one of them was held captive by the rastaman and listened in awe.

"Hol' up your han' if you love carrot juice... dumpling...?"

Patrick Augustus

Free-I scanned the room. The students looked at each other pulling faces of distaste. Free-I shook his head sadly:

"Why unuh pickney love rush inna Macadunnal' fe go nyam 'amburger an' fizzy drink when ackee an' rice an' dumplin' an' sour sop ah one good-good food? What happen to the yam an' banana? Milk shake look foolish nex' to pineapple juice, y'know. An' dem quarter pounder cyaan stand up to fried plantain. Yet still, ah whole heapa unuh black yout' boost it up, sayin' you cyan live widout the Big Muck. Me nevah eat no Big Muck from the day me born. Me prefer eat me food from a black man an strictly vegetarian.

"An another t'ing, why are all unuh black youts getting expelled all over the place? From what I hear, unuh is MISBEHAVIN! Enh? A lot of unuh t'ink yuh smart, because yuh goin' to school wearing the latest of everyt'ing. An' the teacher's laughin' because him know yuh not smart. Unuh black youts mustn't live up to the negative stereotypes..."

At this point, Linvall interjected on behalf of some of those kids such as his son who had fallen foul of the school authorities.

"But that's how the teachers see our kids anyway," he said. I remember when I was in school, even if we were well-behaved the teachers always felt uneasy and regarded the black pupils as a threat to their authority. They always found an excuse to say the black kids were noisy and disruptive. The teachers weren't interested in educating us, because they were occupied with the suspicion that the black kids were up to something and thinking that we were in a one to one battle with them. When I think about it, with the little education we had it was amazing that any of us emerged from there able to deal with the world. Education in this country's all culturally biased. Always has been..."

Free-I granted him that. Though he had preferred to educate his children himself instead of sending them to "babylon's univershitty", he had heard that black pupils generally got more than their fair share of distress. But Free-I didn't want to give his attentive young listeners any excuse.

"You rude bwoys must learn not to follow bad company. Seen? Education is too important," he stressed, "an' no matter wha', unuh must get t'rough, come what may, or suffer blood sweat and tears on these shores. Be a credit to the nation. Right now, Africa needs all ah her sons an' dawtas, at home an' abroad. Because the bottom drop outta the West the other day... Wha' dem call it? Black Monday or Tuesday. Anyway, black sump'n or other. When stock market ah crash an' all dem dignitaries inna dem criss suit ah bawl fe dem momma!"

The class roared with laughter at Free-I's undignified take of a dignitary bawling out for his mother. He continued:

"Yeah, dem all run up and down an' ah jump an' shout when them realise seh, Jack be nimble an' Jack be quick, but when Black Wednesday ah lick, Jack couldn't jump over no candlestick. The table is turning an' throughout the world everybody ah realise that all the lyin' an' cheatin' an' hustlin' is done. So now dem turnin' to Africa, to rape it an' bleed it dry. Dem show a programme the other day, on bi-o-technology an' genetic engineerin'... All these Western scientists go down to Africa, teefin' the knowledge of the local people, askin' dem which plants an' t'ings dem use when dem sick, then robbin' the seeds an' carryin' dem ah West fe come patent it. Then dem turn it into a chemical drug an' sell it back to Africans as a tablet. Las' year dem chemical highway robbers mek $30 billion dollars from Africa, widout paying one penny, an' because dem get patented, we cyaan even use the t'ings again. Africa's wealt' is being robbed, an when dem rob Africa, dem rob all ah we of we heritage. Seen?"

Free-I left the floor to rapturous applause. Johnny was proud. The students had listened with rapt attention. They wanted to know. Now none of them were sniggering at the dread. After Free-I's speech, the hunger for information in their eyes would increase as they tried to carve out their place in society.

Patrick Augustus

VOULEZ-VOUS COUCHEZ AVEC MOI, CE SOIR?

Marcia eased out of her T-shirt and bra, then climbed out of her skirt and panties. Lying naked on the bed, my blood was rushing hot. She knew I couldn't resist her little striptease. She joined me on the bed and breathed hot into my ear. The she let her hand wander deep down and grabbed hold of my cock. It went stiff like a rock.

"I'm going to make you feel alright tonight," she whispered. "Just lie back, relax, don't move a muscle. Tonight, you can ease up and take it easy," she breathed with raw passion. I did as I was told. I just lay my head back and watched the ride as Marcia fondled every part of my body. And then, when I least expected it, she was astride me, gently lowering herself down onto my upright wood.

"Ohhhh yeeeesss! Yesssssss! Yessssss!" I moaned, despite myself. "That's it, just like that. Don't stop, please don't stop!"

The smile on my face said it all. I was simply kicking back savouring every minute of it, every touch, every lick, every whisper of sweet nothings. I loved it all.

Marcia wined and twisted and wined as if she didn't need me there, she just needed my cock. I moaned some more as I felt her hand wandering up my back, scratching deeply. I closed my eyes to meditate on all the sensations tingling through my body and I felt her bite my ear, which excited me even more.

"Ohhh noooo! Oh nooooo!" I cried. "Oh no, I can't hold it any longer... oh no, it's coming...!!!"

Almost instinctively, Marcia quickened her pace, rocking up and down more frantically and she too began to moan. I felt like a volcano about to erupt. Any moment now, any moment now, any moment now... Somehow, I just managed to wait for her climax before allowing myself to relax and release in a gush of pleasure and ecstacy, not once but twice and yes, before I knew it I had scored a hat trick of orgasms. My first ever.

My eyes remained closed for several minutes afterwards, with Marcia sprawled, exhausted, on top of me. It had been a particularly torrid session of lovemaking, just the way I like it. Marcia may not be able to give me any new sex, but she's got the juice when it comes to good sex.

"What are you going to do about Lacquan?" Marcia asked suddenly.

We had been lying silently in exactly the same position for about half an hour, listening to each other's breathing as our heart beats slowed down in syncopation. Outside, the streets had gone quiet. It was the midnight hour when most couples in Brixton were lying arm in arm just as we were.

"What am *I* going to do?"

Hardly a night has passed in recent weeks, when we hadn't lain in bed for hours trying to answer the vexed question of where we were going wrong with Lacquan. This was much more than puberty pains, as he seemed to be getting into far more trouble than his classmates.

"Yes, I've already tried everything I know. For years I was bringing him up alone, remember? He needs the father's touch now."

"Why do you always have to bring that up? I know I wasn't around all those years. But we've been through it enough."

I wasn't angry, just weary of the same old argument. She was always bringing up the worst in me. "Why can't you say something positive about me for a change?"

"Because of what I've been through with you. As much as I want to, I can't just erase that from my memory. I brought my son up as best as I could on my own for eleven years. I taught him to do the right thing, so I can only assume that everything else he does is your fault."

All the shouting and blaming each other for Lacquan's behaviour hadn't gotten us anywhere. Marcia's 'absent father' card was wearing thin as were my reminders of the way she had dissed me to my son many times. I wasn't interested in laying blame. Lacquan was growing up fast and needed an example. We had to forget the past, and try to figure out why he was being a rebel without a pause. He was too grown up to be wet-nursed.

Even though he had been home for more than a week, there was yet no sign of hair on Lacquan's head. We figured that it would take another couple of weeks before it would reach 'regulation' length. Meanwhile, Marcia didn't want him staying at home on his own, believing that the moment he wasn't being chaperoned Lacquan would hit the streets to spend the day with his skylarking friends. She was probably right. Lacquan had discovered that staying at home was boring. Especially when he couldn't watch TV or go out and when all his friends were 'banned' from coming to visit him.

"You're treating me like I'm in prison!" he moaned.

But it was no use. His mother lectured him that prison was where he would be heading if he didn't start behaving himself, so he might as well get used to it. "When you were getting your head shaved, you weren't thinking about the consequences were you? Next time you'll think about what your mother can do to you before you decide to do the wrong thing."

The only leisure time Lacquan was allowed during his days suspended, was to blast one of the local junglist pirates from the stereo in his room, or to play with his Game Boy, and that was only depending on how well he had done in the taxing mathematics questions and essays his mother set him daily. Marcia set him enough school work for him to have to spend exactly seven hours every day on completing it. She also marked his papers. If he got things wrong, that was fine, but it meant that he would get some 'homework', which meant less time for leisure. But if he didn't at least attempt to complete all the academic tasks she set him, 'Quan wouldn't even get to talk to his friends on the phone at the weekend.

"We have to decide what we're going to do about someone being at home with him," Marcia said.

So far, she had stayed home with Lacquan. She took six

days off from her job in the advertising department of one of the national daily newspapers, but, she explained, she couldn't take any more time off. And I was adamant that I had to work. I had a few jobs that needed doing.

"You should be able to take more time off than me, because at least you're self-employed. If you don't go to work nobody sacks you."

"Yes, but if I lose the job I'm supposed to do, the company will probably never use me again."

"You see!" she cried triumphantly, "that's what I meant when I said that you need to get a corporate job. At least then you could take time off your leave every time you needed to stay at home with your son. And believe me, there'll be lots of times when you're going to need to be at home with him for one reason or another. I know. Being a photographer is fine when you're on your own, but when you've got a family to take care of, you need to have something more solid. Okay, I know you don't want to work in a bank or anything like that, but why not get a job on a picture desk with one of the national papers? That would still be creative wouldn't it? And I'm sure you'd have no problem getting a permanent position, considering all the experience you have of photography. I'll ask on our paper for you, if you like."

I should have figured that Marcia wasn't going to let up on this career business. I am a photographer and that's all there is to it. Why can't she have faith in me? Or maybe she's jealous, is that it? Maybe she still has a problem with me working in a job with scantily-clad women?

"No, it isn't that," she insisted, "but while we are on that subject anyway, don't you think it's out of order that you, a married man, leave your wife and son every morning to go off to take photographs of naked women?"

"Oh so it is about that," I said with a sigh. "Deny it as much as you want to, but if I was taking photographs of naked men, you wouldn't be bothered. Come on Marcia, you don't need to be jealous of those women. None of those models could give me what you can give me. I'm not interested in any of them." I tried to sound reassuring, but the look on Marcia's face told me she found that hard to believe. "Why don't you trust me, Marce?"

"Because your flesh is weak, Linvall. Your flesh is too raas claat weak!"

I sighed again. I didn't know what to say. At times like this, I ask myself the question, 'why did I get married?' Here I was giving her the best of me, one hundred percent of me. We had been married nearly three months and I hadn't had a single infidelity...

"At least I haven't caught you in one," she corrected.

"Awww come on, Marce. If I say I haven't been unfaithful, I haven't been unfaithful. As far as I can tell, I'm treating you right... aren't I?"

"Damn right!" she said. "If you weren't treating me right you'd have been out the door long time."

The way she was talking, I realised that this wasn't a good time to mention that I was thinking of employing a rather attractive secretary to help me with the administrative side of the business.

"Well if I can't stay with Lacquan and you can't stay with him, what are we going to do?" she asked.

I had to admit that I didn't know.

"What about your father?"

"What!"

"Your father. He's been phoning up telling me how much he wants to spend time with the grandson he didn't even know he had..."

"No, no way... I don't think that's a very good idea."

"Why not? I think it's a great idea."

"You don't know my old man like I do," I said defensively.

"What do you mean?"

"You just don't, that's all."

"Okay," Marcia said in a slight huff, "you come up with a better idea."

I searched my mind and came up with one before too

long.

" 'Quan can spend the day in the studio with me. He could take all his work with him and do it there."

"That's a ridiculous idea. How do you expect an eleven - year-old boy to keep his mind on any academic work when women in all states of undress are parading themselves in front of him?"

"He could sit in a quiet corner..."

"There are no quiet corners in your studio, Linvall. It's a loft, remember. It's just one big room. I mean, don't even try and convince me..."

"Okay, okay," I said. I would give it a bit more thought. I was sure I could come up with an arrangement that would suit the both of us.

"Why is it that I'm the only one disciplining him?" Marcia asked. "Whenever he does something, you just smile and leave it to me. Pretty soon, he'll be bigger than me and he won't have to listen to my orders, which means you're the only one he'll obey. You better start getting used to it. What's wrong, don't you know how to bring up an eleven-year-old?"

That was just it, I didn't. I didn't know how to bring up any child. How could I? I'm new at this game. All I know is that everything Lacquan's done, I've been through as well. It's not an excuse, it's just that in the old days, your parents gave you a good whack upside the head and you never repeated it. Today though, it's like before you can teach discipline, you have to learn child psychology.

"Try using your imagination," Marcia said yawning stiffly. "If you don't know how to bring up your own son, use your imagination."

The next morning was Saturday. I had agreed that I would spend the day with Lacquan. Just me and him, spending some 'quality time' together. He came downstairs for his breakfast dressed in a beige two piece with shorts and matching vest top and the dark hood of a sweatshirt covering the baldness of his head. On his feet were chunky sneakers. That was his favourite style.

"Seeing you like expressing yourself so much with haircuts and so on," I began, "I'm going to give you a chance to really express yourself today."

"Uh-ohh," Lacquan said. "It doesn't sound like I'm going to enjoy this."

He protested admirably but my mind was made up; we were going to spend the day together and we were going to express ourselves artistically. I got out a couple of sketch pads and some pencils and I found a couple of fold up stools. Lacquan's protests were even more vehement when he discovered where we were going to sit and draw.

Brixton Market is always packed to its seams on a Saturday morning, but in the run-up to Christmas it is truly a 'roadblock'. Especially the Arcade. I tried to reassure Lacquan that the bustling atmosphere would be good for what I wanted him to do. I just wanted him to draw what he saw, with as much skill as possible. "I used to love doing that when I was a kid," I told him. Lacquan sniffed, unimpressed.

"Everybody's going to laugh at us," he protested. "They'll think we're crazy. Suppose one of my friends sees me."

I echoed his mother's words and told him that next time, when faced with the option of being obedient or disobedient, he would first consider how embarrassed his father could make him feel before making his choice. Then I set up the folded chairs and sat him down in one and I sat down in the other one beside him. I thrust him a sketch pad and some pencils.

"You may as well start," I said reassuringly, "because the longer it takes you to draw this scene before you, the longer we'll have to sit here with everybody staring at us."

And people really were staring. It wasn't unheard of to see artists in one of the Arcade's many 'avenues', but nobody could remember seeing a young black man with his son. And from the look of anguish on Lacquan's face, they were probably wondering why the boy was being forced into it.

Lacquan pulled the hood of his sweatshirt low over his eyes, trying to hide himself as much as possible, but he quickly decided that, as he had no choice, it was better to get it over with as soon as possible. He picked up his pencil and began to draw as frantically as he could.

As I drew, memories of my own childhood came back to me. Those long, summer holidays when every day seemed to hold a new adventure. Something as mundane as going over to Brockwell Park with a few friends turned into an action-packed afternoon. In those days, it was the simple things in life which gave me pleasure, things like taking my sketch pad and a pencil and making illustrative records of everything I saw and every interesting looking person I came across. But when was the last time I sat down with a sketch pad? That was the sort of thing I just didn't have time for anymore and I couldn't help wondering whether I hadn't lost something along the way.

I lost myself in thoughts as the sounds and smells of the Arcade wafted around me and the crowds of shoppers pushing past. I looked beside me at my son as he lost himself in his task. He seemed to be really getting into it. I glanced over at his effort. It was really coming along fine. Very detailed and accurate, with the faces of shoppers and the fresh vegetables from the stalls in the foreground. I smiled, proud that my son probably enjoyed the same simple things as I did, given half the chance.

His enjoyment was rudely interrupted however, by a trio of slightly older boys who recognised him.

"Hey Troop, is that you?" the tallest of the three boys called out. Like Lacquan, he had a hood covering his head.

"Hahahahahaha!" roared the other two. "Bwoy you should be shamed of yourself, guy!"

Lacquan stood up to face them with a look of deep embarrassment on his face.

"So this is what you get up to when we turn our backs," said the tallest boy. "Ain't you got no shame sitting in the middle of a market like a crazy?"

Patrick Augustus

I could see that Lacquan felt like a dog. He looked across at me with miserable eyes and for a moment I considered giving him some support. I decided otherwise. He had to fight his own battles.

"I don't normally do this," he protested, turning back to the three boys, "my dad's just trying to teach me a lesson, he made me do this."

The three boys teased him some more before leaving. When they had departed, Lacquan threw me a cold stare. If looks could kill...

We sat there for maybe another hour or ninety minutes, with Lacquan sketching away as swiftly as he could as the crowds did their shopping and haggling with the stallholders. He finally stood up and announced that he was finished. I looked up, there was a big smile on his face as he showed me his effort.

"But wait, you never told me you could draw so good!" I really meant it. Lacquan's sketch was on the money. "Let's go and get it framed. There's an art shop in Camberwell Green. We'll frame it and hang it up on the wall at home..." I admired the sketch proudly. "Wicked picture!" I said, holding up my fist for him to touch with his.

MAMA SAID KNOCK YOU OUT

It used to be that when Gussie told women what the real deal was, they were cool about him being only interested in sex. But it was no longer like that. Lifestyles had changed. Whether it was because of the real threat of AIDS or whether it was because the women he tended to date now were older. Either way it meant that if you weren't offering something more durable than a one night stand, you were unlikely to get any action.

So it was with curiosity rather than sexual anticipation that Gussie rang the buzzer of Evelyn's luxury apartment in the Docklands. His sister was always trying to fix him up with dates and when she told him that she was inviting someone special over for dinner she wanted him to meet, he knew that it would be someone Evelyn saw as a 'potential'.

The bright light of the TV intercom dazzled him momentarily, then he heard a voice say, "Oh...it's you."

Gussie kissed his teeth. "Beckford, just open the door, nuh man!"

A moment later the glass entrance door buzzed open and Gussie stepped into the marble-floored entrance hall of the Riverview Apartments building and took a lift to the penthouse suite.

Gussie's sister could afford to live in the lap of luxury. Not only was her own solicitor's firm doing well, but her husband Beckford, was a rising barrister with an equally good salary. Gussie could also afford to live in a place like that, he mused to himself. But the area wasn't to his liking, despite all its panoramic views of the River Thames. For one thing, there weren't enough black people in the area and Gussie often wondered how his sister handled that situation. For another thing, as far as Gussie was concerned, Clapham Common was as far enough from his Brixton roots as he cared to go. Docklands just wasn't his scene.

"Uncle Gus! Uncle Gus!!"

Evelyn's three-year-old daughter Ebony came running

through the open front door to greet him, eyes wide open with excitement. Gussie scooped her up as she approached and threw her up in the air.

"Ebbie-Ebbie-Ebbie... How's my baby doing?"

"Okay" the little girl uttered between gasps of air. "Mummy took me for swimming today, and I did nearly drowned."

"You nearly drowned?" Gussie remarked in mock horror. "You're going to have to learn to swim then aren't you, so that you don't drown next time."

"So you've finally decided to stroll in..."

"Wha'..?"

Gussie looked up to see his sister standing in the doorway with her hands on her hips and her face in a scowl."

"You're ten minutes late..."

"Aww come on, Evelyn, give a man a break. I'm on time... Just on time."

Evelyn smiled. She was only teasing. Ten minutes late for Gussie really was like being on time. She knew him well enough to know that he was improving in the time keeping department although it would take a lot more teasing to wean him off Black Man's Time completely.

Evelyn Pottinger had grown up in the shadow of her elder brother. She, like everybody else in the family, was proud of the tall, handsome and clever Gussie who did well in sports and always had good reports from school. But sometime during their upbringing their positions were reversed. Suddenly, it was Evelyn who made the family proud with her excellent academic results and her maturity. She read law at Oxford, while her elder brother was flitting from one college course to another, and she went straight into the profession. Already, she was a senior partner in her own law firm. To top it all, she had married the perfect husband and was the perfect mother, as well as wife. Meanwhile, her elder brother got married for a night and his life was a shambles. It wasn't that Gussie resented his sister in any way, on the contrary he was proud of her. She had truly grown to be a successful, woman. The only thing was that he felt that she could have done better for herself than marry Beckford, the buppie barrister.

"I suppose you better come in then," Evelyn said. "I've got someone I want you to meet. And anyway the food will get cold."

"My food won't get cold!" Beckford called out from the dining room, " 'Cause my belly won't wait for a man who can't tell the time."

"Behave yourself!" Gussie called back as he followed his sister into the living room with Ebony hanging from his neck.

"Behave yourself both of you," Evelyn commanded when they were all in the dining room. "I'm sorry about this Winsome..."

Gussie turned to see his sister's surprise guest, sparkling at the dining table, next to his brother-in-law.

Like everybody else in the black community, Gussie recognised Winsome Scott. After all, she was the Channel 5 weather girl and could be seen on TV several times a day.

"Well, are you going to stand there all day or can we start eating now?" Beckford scowled.

Slightly embarrassed, Gussie stretched out his hand to Winsome. "Hi, I'm Gussie, Evelyn's brother, which unfortunately makes me related to her husband."

The weather girl smiled broadly, revealing a perfect set of glistening teeth which formed a symmetry with the pearls of the necklace around her neck. She was dressed in a figure-hugging tight black dress with tiny sequins, a far cry from the more sedate outfits for which she was famous for wearing, especially when she was about to announce a spell of cold weather.

"Hi," she said cheerfully. "I'm Winsome."

"Yes, I know, I've seen you on TV..."

"Hasn't everyone," she replied.

"That's it!" Beckford announced. "You'll have to excuse

me Winsome, it doesn't seem like my brother-in-law is hungry at all. He obviously prefers to chit chat than to eat, so if you don't mind, we'll start eating."

With that Beckford dipped into the salad bowl and passed a portion over to Winsome.

"Cho', you're too craven, man," Gussie said in disgust.

"I hope you two aren't going to carry on like this all evening," Evelyn warned, throwing her hands up in the air and steering Gussie into the seat opposite her special guest. "Honestly Winsome, sometimes I feel like I'm bringing up three children and not one."

"Which other two children are you bringing up, Mummy?" Ebony asked, dragging her chair to the corner of the table beside her uncle.

"Now you know you're not supposed to interrupt when big people are talking don't you, Ebbie?" her mother warned.

"But I'm not imper-upting, Mummy, I was only asking a question."

Evelyn couldn't argue with that. Winsome and Gussie laughed.

"I can't believe she's only three years old," Winsome said, as they settled into the meal. Evelyn had cooked Italian for the evening. Three different kinds of pasta with three different sauces on a large silver tray.

"I must admit, sometimes it feels like I've lived with Ebony ten years!" Evelyn laughed

"What does that mean, Mummy?"

"It means I love you very much," Evelyn retorted.

"So, I hear you've left the business to run itself," Beckford said, turning to Gussie between mouthfuls.

"What are you talking about?" Gussie asked with a scowl.

"The shop. The Mighty Diamond. What I hear is that the chief's gone A.W.O.L. and the lunatics are running the asylum."

"What is he on?" Gussie asked his sister, nodding to her

husband. "And can I have some?"

Winsome laughed. Evelyn sighed. Beckford kissed his teeth. And Ebony giggled. She didn't know what the grown-ups were talking about, but her uncle had made the special guest laugh and she too wanted to join in, even at her father's expense.

"Evelyn tells me that you run a diamond business in Hatton Garden," Winsome said, sounding impressed. "There can't be too many black men doing that."

"I'm one in a million," Gussie said proudly.

"Yeah, right," Beckford added.

"That's a fact!" Gussie stressed.

"But it's not a real job though is it?" Beckford continued.

"What do you know about that?"

"Well it's not is it, it's not a real profession."

"Why not?"

"You tell me what qualifications you needed to get that job?"

"What's that got to do with it?" Gussie asked throwing his hands up in exasperation.

Beckford continued coolly.

"You see that 's what I can't stand with you Gussie-Come-Latelys, you don't even know the difference between a fly by night job like your own and a real profession like law. I mean, selling diamonds is one thing, but anyone can call themselves a diamond merchant and you can't say otherwise, whereas with law, you can't say you're a barrister or a solicitor or even with medicine, you can't say you're a doctor, unless you can show the certain qualifications that make you one. That's a fundamental difference between what I do and what you do. In fact, you're not one in a million at all, you're just the one in a million that calls yourself a diamond merchant, anybody else could call themselves that if they wanted to."

A broad grin spread across Beckford's face. He felt that he had made his point succinctly and in the eternal battle of the wits between himself and his brother-in-law he felt as if he had scored a goal in the FA Cup final Ian Wright would have been proud of.

Gussie meanwhile was shaking his head solemnly. "Sis, you sure that you don't want the number of that shrink that I know?" he asked, "I really think you need to have your husband committed." He didn't mind the constant jousting with Beckford, because at the end of the day it was harmless. As he reasoned, it had started when Evelyn first met her future husband. Beckford was always trying to impress on Evelyn how bright and clever he was and he found it convenient to use her wayward elder brother as a beating stick. After all, Gussie couldn't even complete a degree whereas he had gone to Oxford. And while his brother-in-law's domestic life was in tatters, he at least knew where his duty lay with his wife and children and went out of his way to be a model husband. Gussie wondered if Beckford wasn't going out of his way to wind him up this evening, just to impress Winsome.

"So Sis, you never told me that you were brushing shoulders with media celebrities now..." Gussie said as Evelyn brought in the dessert.

"Brushing shoulders?" she laughed. "Well, I suppose you could call it that, Ms Scott is a client of mine."

"I see..." Gussie began, then turning to Winsome: "That at least answers one of my questions."

"What's that?" Winsome asked.

"They must be paying you well at that TV station, because I know Evelyn doesn't come cheap."

"Stop that!" Evelyn shrieked, slapping her brother's hand playfully. "I never invited you to dinner so that you could chase away my clients. Anyway, you know that solicitors as good as I am can't afford to undersell themselves."

"True, true," Beckford agreed.

"That's right," Ebony chipped in. "My Mummy's the best sociliter in the whole wide world, so there."

"Well I can't argue with that can I?" Gussie laughed, taking his niece's point. Then turning back to Winsome.

"What about your job?"

"Well I'm just a weather girl," Winsome laughed. "I'm sure Beckford wouldn't consider that a 'profession' either."

"On the contrary," Beckford spluttered as he tried to gulp down a mouthful of his wife's home made apple pie, "your job is of the highest profession. I don't know about you, but I see your job as more than just being a woman who tells the weather; you're a role model to the whole community."

Gussie nodded. That was one thing he and Beckford didn't have to argue over. "You brighten up my day when I switch on my TV and see you there," he said smiling.

"I should get you to do my P.R. for me," Winsome laughed shyly.

"No seriously," Gussie continued, "if they took you off the box, a lot of people I know would just switch off. If you don't mind the expression, I think you look 'criss' on TV and I haven't met a single black person who isn't proud that you're up there. I love your outfits, where do you get them from?"

Winsome explained that several of them had been given to her by designers who gladly supplied clothes for her to model. Like the outfit which she had on tonight was an original Wayne Smith, given to her by the young, black, up and coming rasta designer.

"My only criticism... and it's only a small one..." Gussie began cautiously, "is that you could improve your look in the jewellery department."

"Do you think so?" Winsome asked listening keenly.

"Most definitely. Jewellery is such a subtle thing and I'm not saying that what you wear isn't fine, it's just that you could be saying so much more with your jewellery. You could be wearing stuff that tells people who you are and where you're from."

"So, any suggestions?" Winsome asked intrigued.

"I'll tell you what, here's my office number." Gussie pulled out his business card and handed it to Winsome across the table. "Why don't you give me a call and I'll arrange a time for you to come in and I'll hook you up with some beautiful African jewellery."

Winsome shook her head. She had a better idea.

"Here's my cellular number," she said, handing him a card. "Why don't you give me a call when you're free?"

On hearing this, Beckford grunted. "Gussie's the last person on earth I'd give my mobile number to, especially if I was a woman."

"Darling, why don't you say something nice about my brother for a change, you know you love each other really."

"*Me* love *him?!*" both Gussie and Beckford cried out simultaneously.

"Sis, let me assure you, I don't love your husband. You love your husband – I suppose you haven't got much choice. But unless I end up marrying him, I'll never love Beckford."

"Well you know all about marriage, don't you Gus?" Beckford quipped quickly.

Gussie felt the blow. He glanced over at Winsome smiling sweetly across at him. Then he screwed his face at Beckford and kicked him under the table. Then he turned his attention to Winsome's plain, yet elegant business card and for a moment tried to memorise the mobile number, just in case he lost the card.

Things were to get better for Gussie, despite Beckford's chiding. After the meal they all sat down to play a game of charades before Ebony was packed off to bed against her wishes. While Beckford was showing off his new TV and stereo gadgets to Winsome, Gussie joined his sister in the kitchen.

"So what do you think of her?"

"Winsome? She's safe."

"I thought you'd like her?" Evelyn said with a wink.

"Yeah, you know my tastes."

Though it was sometimes irritating that his sister was always trying to fix him up with the right woman, Gussie couldn't argue with the fact that she always managed to find a high calibre of woman for him. He had dated several women she had introduced him to and although her choices weren't always the right ones, they were never totally the wrong type either. As she had reminded him several times over the last few months, Chantelle was totally his choice, she would never have introduced him to a woman who he would walk out on during their wedding night. Gus had to admit that this was probably true, even though he neglected to tell her the real reason why his marriage broke up on the first night of the honeymoon.

"Well you're in luck," Evelyn continued. "Winsome split up from her childhood sweetheart and is now footloose and fancy free."

"So she's on the rebound?" Gus enquired.

"No, she split up from him over a year ago and though she's been single ever since, she's over him now. And she's ready for the 'real thing', if you know what I mean."

Gussie chewed it over in his head. He had never considered dating a celebrity and he had to admit that there was something rather attractive about the prospect. And to be sure there was no arguing with the fact that she did look good. Then he remembered himself. Wasn't this how he got into the trouble of his marriage in the first place, by focusing his attention on a woman's attraction? Wasn't that why it had been so easy for Chantelle to deceive him? Who was it that said that it was a mark of prudence never to trust wholly in those things which have once deceived us? He'd be crazy to make the same mistake again. No, he resolved, it would take more than physical attraction to get him to consider Winsome Scott as anything more than a potential 'ting'.

"Oh, it's been such a wonderful evening Evelyn, but it's getting late and you know how it is for us working girls, gotta get up early. Have you got a cab number?"

Evelyn looked at her watch. It was midnight. They had spent the last two hours telling each other their best holiday stories. The minutes had whizzed by.

"Where are you going to?" Gussie asked.

"Why, are you driving?"

"Well, riding actually. I've got a motorbike. I'll drop you home if you like."

"Supposing I said I lived in Brighton, would your offer still be open?" Winsome asked.

Gussie thought about it for a second then answered, "yes".

"Being chauffeured home on a motorbike does sound like fun. I've never been on a bike before."

"I wouldn't advise it," Beckford butted in. "Not with Gussie up front. And it will be freezing on a bike at this time of year."

"I don't mind a bit of cold, but is he safe?" Winsome asked Evelyn playfully.

Evelyn answered that she personally wouldn't get on a bike for love or money, but her reluctance had nothing to do with riding pillion with her brother. That seemed to reassure Winsome, who was more than keen for the experience. She said she lived in Highbury. Gussie said that it was no problem. He was really getting into her, she seemed like fun.

A few minutes later, Gussie astride the Harley and Winsome on the pillion behind him were waving goodbye to their hosts. Then with a roar, the bike pulled away. Luckily it wasn't too cold, despite the time of year. And fortunately Winsome had a thick outer coat with her. Gussie felt good. The whole thing was like a dream. He had Winsome Scott riding pillion on his bike! Who would believe it?

They breezed through Aldgate. At first, Winsome held onto the grip behind the pillion seat, but by the time they arrived at her apartment in a huge Victorian house on Highbury Fields, Gussie had teased the throttle so many times that he she was gripping tight to him with her arms around his waist. Gussie had a satisfied smile on his face as he pulled in at the kerb.

Winsome climbed off first, then he followed. She pulled the helmet off her head and touched up her hair.

"Thanks for the experience," she said with a smile. "It was really good fun. I hope we'll get a chance to do it again."

"I don't doubt that," said Gussie. "I'll call you."

"You do that," Winsome said with a smile. "Anytime." Then handing Gussie her helmet turned with a skip to run up the path to her front door.

"Well, if it's like that," Gussie called, "I may as well come up for a coffee now?"

Winsome turned her head briefly and waved a negative finger at him.

"What kind of a girl do you take me for?" In a moment, she had unlocked the front door and stepped in, closing the door quickly behind her.

Even as Gussie drove home, he had resolved to call Winsome the next day. He couldn't wait. She wasn't like all the women he had met before, she really wasn't. He remembered his deliberations at the cottage in Wales, but convinced himself that Winsome fell within his guidelines. After all he wasn't checking her for her beauty. He wanted to check her because she was an intelligent black woman, who seemed conscious and was generally a lot of fun. That she looked criss was just an extra really. The fact that she was already a success in her career, with her own independent means was more important.

Gussie drove home to Clapham, wondering all the time whether Winsome Scott would be the woman he would spend the rest of his life with. It was of course, too early to tell.

The next morning, he got up early. He was feeling great. He had decided that he would be going into work that day. He had been loafing a lot and there was too much work to be done at the Mighty Diamond.

The great thing about having a motorcycle, is that you can always find somewhere to park, even if you work in the city. There was a free motorcycle parking spot just around from his Hatton Garden store, so door to door the journey usually only took Gussie twenty minutes, and that in rush hour traffic.

"Oh my goodness, it's a ghost!" Brenda called out as her

boss stepped into his store for the first time in several days. She was a well-dressed browning who looked as elegant as any of the celebrity customers who frequented the store.

"Yeah, yeah, yeah, Brenda," Gussie answered. "I do the jokes here, you sell the diamonds, that's what you're paid for."

Brenda smiled curtly. Gussie was right that was what she was paid for and she did her job well. She knew everything there was to know about gold and diamonds. She had studied jewellery-making at college and had used this to the advantage of the Mighty Diamond. That's why Gussie had made her Manager. He knew that she was more than capable of taking care of the shop while he was away on his meditation. Yes, he had been at a really low ebb in his life, but now the sun was shining in his heart and he was back and in control of himself and his emotions.

He spent the morning going through the books with Brenda. He was pleased to see that business had picked up over the last few weeks. Leading up to Christmas, he hoped, they would do even better. Afterwards, while relaxing in his little office in the back room, he pulled out Winsome's card. He studied it for a moment before picking up the phone.

"Hi...how ya doin'? It's Gus, your motorcycle escort. Listen, I've got a couple of tickets for a boxing match... That's right, boxing... You've never been to one? Then you'll love it, most definitely. No, not that violent, not that violent at all. That's just the media blowing everything out of proportion again. Yeah, it's tomorrow night. Lewisham. Yeah, yeah, that's right, on the motorcycle. Of course I'll pick you up from the TV studio and of course I'll drop you home. Gimme the name of that bar again...?"

With a broad smile on his face, he replaced the receiver. For the rest of the day he was in a glow. Brenda saw it, but she didn't say anything. After all, she was payed to sell diamonds, that was what she was there for.

Winsome floated into their appointed saloon at six on the nose. Dressed from head to toe in appropriate leathers, she was a living, walking dream with shapely curves and pert breasts swelling under the jacket. Gus was at the bar talking with the bartender and didn't see her enter, but the barman did and looked up. Gus turned on the stool, following the man's eyes. She was a beauty, he thought. But he was not going to allow himself to be influenced by that. He had to stick to what he had decided. All that meditation wasn't for nothing.

They stayed at the bar for a couple more drinks before making their way south on the Harley. The Civic Centre in Lewisham seemed to be packed with eager punters and a good number of well-known faces all waiting expectantly for the Sugar Ray Williams fight. *Good old Courtney*, Gussie thought as he proceeded with his date, behind other formally dressed couples into the auditorium. Dressed in his dinner suit and Winsome in her designer-styled leather jeans and jacket, they had turned heads as soon as they rolled up. *Good old Courtney*, Gussie thought again, as he escorted Winsome to her seat. His old friend had managed to get them the best seats in the house, front row and in the centre too. The only thing wrong with the seats was the old guy who sat next to Gussie and kept asking him if he was sure he wasn't Lennox Lewis' brother.

Winsome was excited at the prospect of her first boxing match. But it didn't take long before her excitement waned. It was in the middle of one of the warm up fights, when one of the boxer's collapsed on the ring just in front of her after a particularly severe upper cut.

"Oh my God!" she screamed, jumping up. "He's dead!"

"Sit down," Gussie said, restraining her. "He's not really hurt. He's just a bit dizzy. These boxers are trained to take the blows. Most definitely."

Winsome wasn't convinced, but whether because of curiosity or addiction, she sat through the entire evening, sometimes with her eyes closed tight, but she sat through, nevertheless.

By the time the main fight came on, the crowd was at

fever pitch. There were journalists, TV crews and more importantly, there were eager punters who had staked a lot of money on seeing the 'great white hope' knock out Williams. But their wishes were not to be granted, not on this night anyway. For, though Williams looked heavier and slower than his younger opponent, his greater experience was going to count for more.

It was 'high noon'. The two fighters eyed each other up in the centre of the ring like gunfighters in the Wild West. Two hard men each with his own cruel scowl, and the diminutive referee between them, duelling to discover who was the fastest and toughest. The winner would carve another notch on his record, while the loser would fade into the lower ranks of the sport or disappear altogether. Neither wanted that.

The first four rounds were pretty even between the fighters. The white boxer perhaps just having the edge. In the fifth round, what seemed like tragedy struck. An accidental butt over his left eye caused blood to gush down Williams' face. The ref studied it closely, but finally allowed the fight to continue, for now. Somehow, Williams managed to keep the other boxer off his face over the next four rounds. The white boxer should have played it safe for the remaining rounds, because he was way ahead on points by now, but he would have none of that. He had a gunfighter mentality and wanted K.O. notches on his gun handle.

It was in the tenth round. To the raucous cheers of his fans, the boxer had Williams up against the ropes and was pumping everything he had into the older man's chest and kidneys. It looked like Williams was going down, but the wily older boxer was only feigning. In his eagerness to step in for the kill, the boxer walked into a gloved sledgehammer blow to the chin. Williams put everything but the referee in that punch and his opponent's legs gave way. The boxer went down and stayed down.

"So what did you think of the fight?" Courtney was asking Winsome back in Williams's dressing room afterwards. Gussie had spotted his spar in the ring after the fight, lifting his fighter up high and had motioned to him. Courtney had ushered his guests through to the winner's dressing room, which was already packed with friends, family, well-wishers and hangers-on of the middle-aged fighter.

"Oh I couldn't watch most of it," Winsome said. "It is very brutal... You don't really get the true sense of how violent it is when you watch it on your TV at home."

Courtney shook his head. "No, that's what you don't understand. It's not that brutal at all. Most people don't get hurt from it. Ask Sugar Ray. Some people say he's over fifty and it hasn't done him any harm. They're all trained boxers, you know. You expect to get knocked about a bit, but no, it's not violent."

"So why don't you get in the ring and fight then?" Winsome asked.

Courtney had to throw up his hands in defence. "Ouch! That one went straight to my head. And I always thought you were a nice woman when I saw you on the television."

Courtney introduced Gussie and Winsome to Sugar Ray. Close up, they could see all the cuts on his face, but the boxer seemed to be taking his bruises stoically.

"I'm not the baddest super middleweight in the world," he told his admirers, "I'm the baddest fighter in the world. I'll take everybody on. I want them all, light-heavyweights, cruiserweights, heavyweights and Tyson. When I get going, nobody is safe. I'm gonna crack their heads like eggs."

"Yeah, when you've got a minute," Courtney whispered in Gussie's ear as Winsome quizzed Sugar Ray on the Marquis of Queensberry's rules.

"What about right now?"

"Okay right." Courtney pulled his friend to one side almost conspiratorially. "It's like this, man," he began. "Sugar Ray's got a chance for a really big fight now against Pata Moreno, you remember him, Puerto Rican fighter. He was the WBC champ a couple of years back. This is the big one, Gus, that's why I'm offering you this business opportunity. You're going to be grateful for it. You're going to thank me for it. You'll be practically stealing from me, but you're my mate and well, what are mates for...?"

Gussie looked at his friend quizzically. What did Courtney mean exactly?

"I'm going to give you a slice of the action, man. The Pata Moreno fight is in Las Vegas, one of the big hotels out there. It's going to have cable coverage. You know what that means, you're opening up the American market, man. They'd love Sugar Ray over there, just see the way they went crazy over George Foreman and his comeback? It could end boxing's slump. It could also make us both very wealthy young men. So what do you say, star? You wanna step on the money-go-round?"

Gussie thought about it for a minute. Boxing wasn't really his thing and he wasn't too happy about investing in someone who some reports had suggested was anything from forty years old to sixty. Williams would probably be eligible for free bus travel in a few years. There wouldn't be enough time to get a return on his investment.

"And anyway, how much exactly will it cost to ride on this 'money-go-round'?"

"Not much," Courtney insisted, "not much at all. I'm practically offering it to you for nothing. Just say the word, Gus."

"How much is 'nothing'?" Gus repeated.

"Fifty Gs," Courtney said, but hurriedly corrected himself when he saw the negative expression on Gussie's face, "but I'll let you on for twenty – and that's practically nothing."

"That's not practically nothing," Gus corrected, "that's some serious ducats and I don't know if I've got that much. Anyway, I'll have to think about it. What am I going to get for my money anyway?"

"Well here's what I propose," Courtney said, sounding like he had already worked things out in his head. "You and

I go into joint promotion. We split everything fifty-fifty."

"So how much are you putting in then?" Gussie asked suspiciously.

"You ask me that?!" Courtney cried in mock horror. "Think of all the money I've already spent on Sugar Ray, think of all the time I''ve already spent? I've been doing the work on my own up to now, remember that."

"Well, if and only if, I did consider it, I wouldn't have time to devote to the day to day running of his management."

"But that's alright Gus, don't worry about a thing. I'll take care of all that. You'll be the silent partner. Don't worry about a thing, all you'll have to do is sit down with your feet up watching the money roll in. And it will be good promotion for your shop and all. Believe me Gus, when people know that you're a boxing promoter, it will do your status some good. Believe!"

"Yes... Most definitely. So what's all the money going to be spent on?"

"The expenses, Gus, they're killing me. Everything costs these days. There's training, sparring partners, gyms, equipment...You name it. Look at that old bathrobe he's wearing. If he goes to the States he's going to need a new dressing gown. Look at those baggy blue trunks. He's boxed in those for twenty years! We've got to get him some new gear, pardner."

"Look man, it's too much for me to take in all in one go," Gussie said. "But we'll speak tomorrow."

Courtney was cool about that. "I'll give you a call. We can go and get a couple of cold beers somewhere."

"That sounds just fine by me."

"Here," said Courtney, pulling out a couple of large tickets out of his breast pocket, "while you're thinking about it, take your lady and go out and have a nice evening with her. These are invites to a party tonight down at Moonlighting. I'll see you up there later if you go."

Gussie took the tickets, thanking him. It was up to

Winsome, but if she was cool with that maybe they'd see each other later.

Shortly after, Winsome and Gussie left the boxing venue. Before climbing onto the Harley, Gussie ran through the options.

"Well it's still relatively early," he said, glancing at his new Cartier. "We could catch a bite to eat in town if you want, or else we could go to a party at Moonlighting. I've got a couple of invites."

"I got an invite to that too," Winsome said cheerfully.

"Or..." Gussie continued, "we could go back to your place or mine..."

It was wishful thinking on his part and Winsome told him so with a disarming smile.

"Let's go to the party," she said.

So it was agreed. They climbed on the Harley and roared off westward towards Soho.

For those who haven't been there, Moonlighting is a tight squeeze at the best of times. When they hold one of their regular black functions, the place is rammed to the maximum. This party was such a function and celebrity or no celebrity, Winsome had to ease her way through the narrow gaps in the basement venue, before she and Gussie found a corner to hold as their own. Some of the ravers who recognised her, came up to say a word or two of praise. Gussie was proud of her. It was the first time he had been out with a TV star.

The music was firing. The Prezedent was on the wire, easing and teasing his public with a haul and pull up style that showed that he was in control of the wheels of steel, in fact he was in control of the dance, period. The entire massive seemed to be following him, moving to the rhythm like it was stuck to them. Gus and Winsome even got a chance to do their thing on the packed dancefloor when the pace of the music settled for a while. She couldn't resist Barry White at the best of times, she explained, and *Practice What You Preach* was her favourite. Gus held her close to him as they moved as one to White's sensuous vocals mouthing the refrain to each other playfully.

They were probably there for an hour, before Gussie whispered in Winsome's ear, suggesting that they should go somewhere a little quieter. He could feel that things were going right for him tonight and he had already started imagining what her bedroom looked like.

Winsome agreed. They forced their way towards the exit. They may have had enough, but the crowd hadn't and the Prezedent was still bigging up all the "supes" in the house, while dropping that needle for just a little snatch of the latest groove. Gussie led the way, up the stairs and back up to street level when someone called out, "Hey Winsome, baby. What are *you* doing here?!"

Gussie spun round. He saw a tall, slim, elegantly-dressed and heavily made-up woman that he thought he recognised. It was Yasmine. Gussie recognised her. He had even had occasion to catch her 'agony aunt' show on television once or twice. Most people in the black community knew Yasmine. She didn't need a surname, because her *The Yasmine Show* on one of the black cable stations was the most talked about black programme for years. Large numbers of African and Caribbean people went out of their way to get their homes cabled-up so that they could watch *The Yasmine Show*, with it's steamy mix of sexy topics.

"I thought you weren't coming," Yasmine called up to Winsome from the bottom of the stairs.

"I wasn't," Winsome said cheerfully, walking back down to her friend, "but we just ended up here."

They embraced briefly and kissed each other on both cheeks affectionately.

"So who's this?" Yasmine asked, indicating Gussie, who had also walked back down the stairs and was now standing directly beside his date.

Winsome introduced them.

"You didn't tell me that you had such a charming date," Yasmine said, playfully, tossing back her long weave out of habit. "So you keep these things quiet from your best friend, do you? So where did you find this hunk, girlfriend? And has he got a brother?"

Yasmine and Winsome talked for a while. They exchanged a few private jokes and both agreed that it had been a good do.

"Look, I'm off to my private club on Frith Street. Why don't you two come along and we'll make it a threesome," Yasmine said with a mischievous smile.

Winsome said that she was tired and had an early start in the morning. "I really need to be getting back."

"You want to talk to me about hard work," said Yasmine, "don't forget, I've got a show to do tomorrow."

"Why don't you take Gussie along to the club?" Winsome offered. "I can always catch a cab home."

For a moment, Gussie considered the suggestion. It was tempting, but even he knew that it was bad form, whether Winsome was agreeable or not. He decided against it and made some feeble excuse, to Yasmine's exaggerated regret.

They said their goodbyes and allowing Gussie to kiss her once on either cheek, Yasmine added that she was sure that she would see him again. Gussie smiled and added that he hoped so.

"So you want me to take you home?" Gussie asked Winsome as they pulled on their helmets again.

Winsome nodded. "You want to come up for a coffee?"

Gussie didn't need to be asked twice.

"Okay, but no funny stuff," she added, playfully wagging her finger.

There wasn't much traffic on the road and with his hand firmly on that throttle, they made it to Highbury Fields in minutes.

Winsome's ground floor flat was a revelation, a real designer's pad. For the first thing, it was huge. Only two rooms, but each one the size of most people's flats and with an amazing mirrored bathroom. From the entrance, you stepped into a hallway the size of a living room and tiled with marble.

"Take off your shoes," Winsome commanded as they entered. Gussie complied and in his socks, followed her through double doors into the living room. "Wow!" he exclaimed as he entered. Everything was sparkling. A huge chandelier hung in the centre of the room above their heads, illuminating brightly the white walls of the ballroom size living room with its high ceiling. Now Gussie understood why he had to take off his shoes. The new parquet flooring didn't have a mark on it.

"This is really something, this place is beautiful," he commented as he flopped himself down on the khaki sofa. He picked a magazine up from the smoked-glass coffee table in front of him. It was *Interior Design*. "I see you take this stuff seriously," he said, holding up the magazine.

Winsome explained that working in the media, she was accustomed to a certain lifestyle. Her flat was commensurate to that.

"Well you know what they say about a black woman's home being her castle... I want to be queen of some place that looks nice."

"You are a queen," Gussie agreed. "I bet the Queen of England doesn't live this good."

He considered the statement for a moment. Maybe that was an exaggeration, but Winsome's home really was the best designed place he had ever been into.

She brought in some coffee, while Gussie was working the multi-deck CD with a remote, trying to find a particular Al Green track.

The time slipped by unobtrusively as Gussie sipped on his coffee and listened to Winsome telling him the story of her life, or at least a brief sketch of it.

"I didn't plan to become a weather girl," she said. "the job kinda found me, you could say. I'm an actress really. I was head-hunted while I was the lead in a play at the Tricycle Theatre a couple of years ago. The TV company made me an offer I couldn't refuse, so I thought, yeah, why not."

Gussie told her about himself. It was an even briefer account.

"My parents have gone back home. My father still owns the business really, but I suppose I'm the managing director... Diamonds are most definitely a growth industry.

He told her about his relationship with Evelyn. Being his younger sister, he often tried to be protective of her, but it always turned out that she ended up having to look after him. Or at least she felt she did.

"I have a problem with that," he admitted, "or at least I used to. We're cool now, but you should have seen what it was like before. I still have a problem opening up totally with her and I can sense that she sometimes feels uncomfortable with me too. And the strange thing is that we're very alike in certain ways, everybody says so."

The conversation eased naturally into more intimate things. Why was Gussie still single, Winsome wanted to know. He asked her the same question back. He couldn't believe his luck that he had met such a gorgeous and intelligent woman and she didn't have a man; there had to be someone somewhere.

"Oh I want to get married at some point, but at the moment my work comes first," she answered. Then after a pause, "Of course I have to find the right man first."

Gussie's eyes lit up. She described herself as selfishly independent and very set in her ways. At the moment she wasn't interested in being swept off her feet. Gussie simply smiled. That didn't bother him. If anything, it would be a challenge.

"I'm tired of dating second-best," she continued. "I've dated so many of the eligible black men in the media and to be honest, they're not saying much. Anyway, that's where I'm at right now and I don't know when I'll change. I know I don't want to be alone for the rest of my life, so I'll have to change at some point, but at the moment I just can't take men seriously when they say they want to marry me, because I know they're not being sincere. I don't have time for games.

When I find that somebody special, I'll be ready to start dating again."

Gussie said it was the same for him. Wasn't that a coincidence? Maybe this really was the right woman. Six months earlier he would have proposed to her there and then, but now he was more restrained. Instead, he teased her and she teased him back.

As the time ticked on, his interest sharpened even more. Gussie soon managed to get the conversation down to an even more intimate subject.

"A good sex life is absolutely essential to a good relationship," he said slightly pompously.

"You just can't have sex without soul, the two go hand in hand," she replied swiftly.

Gussie smiled. She had a point there. Again, Winsome asked him how much longer he intended to stay single. He said he never stopped looking for the right woman, and when he found her, he would marry her. He considered every woman he met in the light of what she could offer a single man looking for a good wife. He wanted the right mother for his children.

She smiled sweetly with a twinkle in her eye.

"I hope you're not including me in your plans," she said between sips of wine. "I'm not ready to give up my career for a child. Financial security comes before starting a family and I am just not ready to be responsible for another human being."

Gussie insisted that wouldn't rule her out.

"The woman I marry won't have to give up her career. I have a successful business and can afford to pay a nanny plenty of money to take care of our baby. How does that sound?"

Frankly, it didn't. Not for Winsome. "I'm not the maternal type anyway. Never have been and probably never will be."

That was too bad, Gussie thought. Because joking apart, he was looking for the maternal kind.

They continued chatting, the atmosphere still very

mellow and relaxing. She started talking more openly and personal. He was highly interested in what he was hearing. For he still held a hope that Winsome had invited him back to her flat for some other reason than for them to chat about each other's love life, or lack of it. His throat screamed for something wet and sexy. Like his coffee, he liked his women black and boiling hot. Winsome in every aspect, was his cup of coffee with those kissable lips. He could hardly wait to get her into bed. It felt like love had come again for him. Why should he wait? He fancied her and he could tell that she fancied him. He finally plucked up the courage to slip his arm around her waist. She stiffened, but didn't say anything, not that is, until he let his hand wander to her breast.

"You promised." she said, pushing his hand away.

Gussie tried to shrug it off with a grin. "I forgot," he said, realising that he needed to ease a little more loving out of her. Or was she simply playing hard to get?

STRICTLY BUSINESS

Sunday was my regular time with Lara. Her mother and I had agreed on it, so everything was convenient and hassle-free when I came to pick her up at noon to spend the rest of the day with me. The stipulation was that I had to return her by six pm in the evening. That didn't leave me much 'quality time' with my daughter and I wasn't totally happy with the arrangement. But as Caroline advised me, it was better to just accept it for the moment and deal with it.

Sonia was now living in our house. The house we lived in as a married couple until she left me. The house which I was still paying the mortgage for. She was living there with her girlfriend and our daughter. It wasn't a situation that I was at all happy about, but then again, as Caroline had advised me several times, there was nothing I could do about it. The house was part of the divorce settlement.

I know my responsibilities and I was happy to pay my parental contribution before being asked anyway. Because whatever's happened between me and her mother, Lara's still my daughter. I support mothers who go out and stand up for their rights and hunt absent fathers down for child support. That's simply going out and getting what's right for the child. But all I'm saying is that the CSA have gone too far with me. They tried to suck my blood like a vampire and wanted to leave me with £1.90 a week! In effect what they were asking me to do, was not only to pay for my daughter, but also my ex-wife *and* her girlfriend! So I had to come up with a better idea. Fortunately, Sonia agreed to take the house and that I should pay Lara's school fees. It still hurts me to go to the old place every Sunday, knowing how they are living.

I didn't need to enter. As usual Sonia had Lara ready when I arrived, and met me at the door.

"Daddy, Daddy, Daddy!"

Lara raced up to me and jumped in my arms. I scooped her up and embraced her tightly.

"I made this at school for you," she said proudly handing me a watercolour of me driving in my car. It was quite good actually. For a seven-year-old Lara had an eye for detail which was impressive. I told her it was beautiful and she replied that she had made it beautiful, because I was beautiful. I thanked her and kissed her on the cheek. She kissed me back on both my cheeks because, "French people do it that way," she explained.

"If you're going to take her out to lunch, could you make sure that it's vegetarian. Lara doesn't eat meat anymore."

"Wha'...?"

"She's a vegetarian now," Sonia repeated as she stood at the half-open front door with her arms crossed. "We're all vegetarians now."

I looked at my daughter.

"When did you stop eating meat, Lara?" I asked.

"On Wednesday. That was when Mummy told me that meat is bad for you and that if you eat meat it means that you're a murderer and you're eating a dead animal. And I don't want to do that anymore, Daddy."

I looked hard at Sonia. "Don't you think we could have discussed this first?"

"We did discuss it. Me, Lara and Grace..."

"I meant with her father. Don't you think something as important as changing your daughter's diet should be discussed with her father?"

"Well you know how it is, Beres, me and Grace are mother and father to her. We take care of everything she needs."

I kissed my teeth. I wasn't angry about my daughter not eating meat, that was fine. I'm sure it will do her good. But I was angry at another erosion of my role in her life. It wasn't the first. My daughter who used to be so lady-like was now becoming a tomboy. Her mother and 'father' have decided that she shouldn't wear skirts or dresses anymore, so now she wears jeans. There's nothing wrong in the way Lara dresses, it's just that it isn't the way I want her to. And it's affecting her generally also. It's more than a coincidence that Lara no longer seems bothered if she comes home from school with dirt under her fingernails or not.

I gave Sonia a final angry glare, before turning my back on her and carrying my daughter to the car.

It was hard for me to reconcile the mother of my daughter now with the Sonia I first met eight years ago. Sonia was born beautiful and in those days spent much of her time in front of a mirror to make herself even more attractive. She would never have answered the door to anyone with her hair uncombed and without make-up on as she does now.

We had a real good thing going when we married. There was the material wealth, with a big house on Streatham Common, as well as our beautiful daughter, and we were in love. I provided well for my family and was proud to send my daughter to a private school and of giving her the best start in life I could afford. But Sonia was too hot for me, I couldn't control her. It all came crashing down when I came home one day to find my wife gone after seven years of marriage.

As for my estranged wife's sexual preferences, I haven't mentioned that to anybody and I'm still hoping it will stay a dark secret.

"So where are we going, Daddy?" Lara asked as I slipped the car into gear and pulled away.

"Where do you want to go?"

"Erm... Could we go to a football match?" Lara asked eagerly.

I couldn't believe what I was hearing. "Football match?" I repeated.

"Yes, football match. That's what I'd like to do."

Lara explained that she was now an avid football fan. 'Auntie' Grace had introduced her to the game. She always watched the football on the TV and had even taken Lara to a couple of Arsenal games. Now Lara was mad about Ian Wright and, she said, would love to meet him. She even said she'd like to be a footballer when she grows up!

Patrick Augustus

"Wouldn't you rather go to McDonald's?"

"I don't eat McDonald's anymore, Daddy. Mummy says that kind of food is not healthy. And 'Auntie' Grace taught me a song: Old McDonalds got some shops eeyay eeyay oh, but I don't eat from there no more, eeyay eeyay oh, with a big mac here and a big mac there..."

" '*Any*more'..." I interrupted.

"What did you say, Daddy?"

" '*Any*more'. 'I don't eat from there anymore'..."

"Why, are you a vegetarian as well, Daddy?"

I glanced at my daughter and began to realise that pretty soon she wouldn't be my daughter anymore. Not if 'Auntie' Grace had anything to do with it. I wanted my daughter to some day grow from a girl into a woman. But the way her mother was bringing her up, she wasn't being prepared for womanhood. I had to do something about that and soon. That was when I started planning on a way to get her back.

When Lara realised that she wasn't going to get to go to a football match, she suggested a boxing match. Boxing was another favourite of 'Auntie' Grace's apparently. And she added that 'Auntie' Grace felt that, "Tyson should stay in prison because, after all, all men are rapists..." I was boiling under the collar, but decided to contain my anger. What I was hearing had made me even more resolved to get my daughter back.

To Lara's dismay, there wasn't going to be any boxing either. At first we went to the park to feed the ducks. Lara dragged me across to the children's play area. "I need somebody to push my swing," she said. I must have done my job too well, because she kept me pushing for a good half an hour before I got her permission to take a rest. We ended up spending the rest of the day in the West End, shopping for Christmas presents. Of course we ended up in Hamleys, Lara's favourite store, where she wanted to try out some of the latest toys and insisted that I should try some out too, though she had an easier time figuring how to work some of the video games than I did.

With her new dietary regime, it wasn't easy finding somewhere to eat with Lara. Not fast food anyway. We did find a little Arab restaurant in Covent Garden which was open and which was vegetarian, or as good as. Afterwards we took in a seasonal cartoon film which Lara showed an interest in.

Time is so short when you have to see your daughter by appointment, and before long it was already evening and my time was up. I drove Lara back to Streatham Common. Sonia was waiting at the door when we arrived. I looked at my watch. I was exactly on time.

"So did you have a good time?" Sonia asked.

"Yes thank you, Mummy," said Lara, struggling with her parcels of Christmas presents. "But Daddy says he won't get me any more presents if I start playing football."

Sonia turned to me and sighed. "Yes dear, it's probably because he's afraid that you'll end up being a better footballer than him."

Lara kissed me goodbye until next week. I waited until she had gone inside before addressing Sonia.

"I don't like how you're bringing her up," I said in hushed tones.

"That's too bad."

"I mean it, Sonia. I don't want my daughter to end up all mixed up. I don't care what you get up to with that woman in your private life, but when it starts affecting my daughter, it affects me."

"Is that it?" Sonia asked unimpressed. "Can I get along with my life now?"

With that she slammed the door shut.

Working from home became easier once Colin had decided to take a rest from his vigil at our house. After a week of squatting in our living room, he decided that he had made his point and, besides, he had to get back to work. I was able then to concentrate on my work and building up my business.

I had always possessed an edge for business, but the

extra financial burden of my alimony payments had sharpened my instincts. Who dares wins, and I knew how to win. I was determined to work twenty-four sevens if that was the only way to feed my two families.

I became a member of various black contact organisations for like-minded professionals and businessmen and women, for the social life as much as anything else. 'Networking' was a buzz word which every upwardly mobile black man and woman understood. With a community that evolves so fast, you need to know what's going on in every aspect if you don't want to be left out in the dark. As a good friend said just the other day, "the community has moved on from where it was yesterday." I was proud and impressed to meet so many forward-thinking and hard-working people who knew that they weren't in the struggle by themselves and that because of the 'handicap' of race, the only way their businesses could survive was to link-up as a community and help each other. For, just as the rain falls on everyone's head, when the sun comes shining through for you, you need to make sure it's shining for others too. Men and women coming together making connections. Men and women involved in every type of business, from a pin to an anchor, and who lived, breathed and talked commerce.

There were even one or two hustlers who juggled their way through life, yet the philosophy of 'united we stand, divided we fall' ran through the veins of these business people and the slogan 'Recycle the Black £!' was their battle-cry, even if one or two men were there specifically because they had a penchant for an attractive, middle class, single black female.

I had decided to use my redundancy money from Dan Oliver's to start trading in new cars for myself. My plan was simple really. Knowing enough about dealers and the margins they make, I could just go up to them and say, 'Look, I'm going to buy a dozen Volkswagen Golfs off you over the next month, what discount are you going to give me?' That way, I can knock down the prices much more than an ordinary customer gets to. What I do then, is put a two-line advert in the Evening Standard, saying, 'NEW GOLFS: CHEAPER THAN THE DEALERS. That in effect is it. I can make a few hundred pounds from every sale and I'm currently up to three sales a week. All of it at the end of a phone line from home, with little overheads, no commuting, and a lot of free time.

Anyway, some guy smashed into the back of one of the Volkswagens, as it was parked outside our house waiting to be delivered to a customer. I heard the crash and rushed out in time. The old guy in the Merc, said he was in a hurry and wrote down his number before speeding away. Of course it was a false number. But fortunately, I had the registration number. The police tried to trace it only to find that the vehicle owner was no longer at that address. When Caroline next came home from Belgium for the weekend, she suggested that I get hold of a private detective.

Amos Butler was recommended to me by Gussie, who had had occasion to use him in collecting evidence to prove that he hadn't consummated his marriage. I don't know how you go about doing that, and Gussie wouldn't elaborate. Anyway, whatever it was that Butler collected, it convinced the judge that he could safely annul the marriage. And it was in expecting equal efficiency that I went in search of 'Butler & Associates, Detective Agency'.

There were no 'associates' in the tiny office above the Pizza Hut on the corner of Brixton and Coldharbour Roads. Only a shabily-dressed middle-aged Caribbean man, who looked like he was desperate to get back to the pub. He reeked of whisky.

"I'm looking for Mr Butler...?"

"Yes man, come in. Come in, man!" he cried. "I've been expecting you. Tek a seat. Mr Dunkley, isn't it? Pleased to meet you. I'm Amos Butler."

The fact that the man before me wasn't exactly how I had imagined a private detective, was evident from the expression of surprise on my face. Butler noticed, but it didn't seem to bother him.

"So what can I do for you? I take it this isn't a social call and if it is, it's your round."

He sat himself down on a chair, with his back to the window. Beyond him, the busiest junction in south London was visible with the hustle and bustle of the afternoon rush hour, where a traffic jam had formed as cars waited for a defective red light.

I smiled and sat down on the only other available chair. Butler swivelled on his chair absent-mindedly and stared beyond the big window across the busy Brixton Road. Then he swivelled back to face me.

That was my cue. I explained my problem. Butler said it wasn't a problem at all. The police had given me the name of the vehicle owner and Butler assured me that there were only a finite number of Adam Stephenson's in the age group I had described.

"The guy must have paid a bill or signed a cheque in the last year. If he has, me mus' find him."

I wasn't as convinced as Butler, but sure enough, he managed to track the man down and gave me an address. I drove down there one morning and caught the man just as he was stepping out of his house, into his newly-repaired Mercedes out front. The man almost had a heart-attack when I approached him. He couldn't believe it. He tried to bluff and say that he must have given me the wrong number by accident. I told him that I was even passing the £200 bill for my private detective to his insurers. Insurance was a sore point with Stephenson, who assured me that, he would rather avoid going through his insurers. I knew what he was trying to say, but decided that it was his business if he drove without insurance. All I wanted was £1700 in my hand. £1,000 for the repairs to the Golf, £500 for the inconvenience and Butler's £200 bill. I had no sympathy for Stephenson as he drove me around to his bank to literally empty his account of every penny in there.

Butler's efficiency got me to thinking. Gussie told me that

despite his appearance, Butler was actually a former police officer who had attained the rank of Detective Sergeant, before deciding to go into business for himself. The day after I got the money from Stephenson, I paid my second visit to Butler's office.

This time his office was locked. There was a note on the door informing clients that 'Detective' Amos Butler was at lunch at Dickie's on Railton Road. I studied the directions and took my leave.

Dickie's turned out not to be a restaurant at all, but an off licence on the seedier end of Railton Road, the part which in the old days used to be known as the 'frontline'. From the outside, you couldn't even tell it was an off licence. Because most of the window to the street was boarded up and there was no sign anywhere to suggest that it was anything other than an abandoned building. I walked past the place three times, before I noticed the word 'Dickies' scrawled in thick red paint on the boards that covered the entrance.

Inside, a trio of middle aged Jamaican men were enjoying a game of dominoes and laughing and shouting loudly. In the middle was Amos, concentrating his mind on the next play. Nobody paid attention to me and I felt as if it was rude to interrupt, so I stood in the background while they played. I looked around the place. Sure it was an off licence, but the shelves were all empty. In fact the only drinks in the place were in the hands of the domino players.

Finally, the game came to a resounding end, though an argument between two of the players continued long after. I coughed and Amos turned around to greet me.

"Oh, it's you," he said, looking at me through bloodshot eyes.

I wondered for a moment if I hadn't made the wrong decision by coming there. Then he said something strange.

"I was expecting you."

"What? How?"

"I knew you had something more on your mind... I didn't know what, but I knew that your car wasn't your only problem. I used to be a police officer, remember? I can always tell when someone's withholding information."

We walked back to his office, with Butler chatting amiably about how Brixton was changing with every day.

Back in his office, a few official looking letters were lying in the letterbox for him. Butler tossed them aside disdainfully. I guessed they were bills.

"So what's your problem?"

It was a very confidential matter, I explained in hushed tones. Butler assured me that he was the very embodiment of discretion and that his client's cases were treated in the strictest confidentiality.

I didn't know where to start and Butler asked me why I thought it was that people always say that, "What's the point of starting anywhere but at the beginning?" he asked. I took his point and told him all about my marriage and what had happened. That my wife had left me and had custody of my kid and she wasn't bringing her up right and I needed the evidence to prove it.

Butler pulled out a pen and a note pad and took some notes. Then he started asking questions:

"What's your wife's name...? Where does she live...? Who does she live with...? What's her lover's name? Grace?!"

"Yes," I repeated, too embarrassed to look the man in the eye. Yes, my wife is having an affair with another woman. I'm not concerned about that, I just want my daughter back."

REWIND SELECTOR, AN' COME AGAIN...

The last person I wanted to see when I got home with Lacquan, was my father. But there he was, making himself comfortable in the living room, with a glass of rum at his side and engaging Marcia in a game of dominoes.

"Linvall, whe' yuh been so long? I've been waiting fe you, yuh know. Whe' me gran'pickney deh?"

Lacquan popped up from behind me and fell into his grandfather's open arms.

"Wha'? Lacquan? I haven't seen you in two months and you've grown another few inches. Lawd, me cyaan believe it!"

"Hello Dad," I said. "What are you doing here?"

My father turned to me with a look of surprise.

"What am I doing here? Is that the way to greet your father when I come all the way across London to see you?"

Catford wasn't all the way across London, but the old man had a tendency to exaggeration. I turned to Marcia.

"Your Dad just happened to phone up after you went out. I mentioned that we needed someone to supervise Lacquan while we're at work and he offered..."

I flashed her a vexed look. She knew my answer to that.

"Yes," Dad concurred. "It will benefit my grandson to have a man around."

I looked at my father, screwing my face up. What was that supposed to mean? But he didn't catch the drift.

"Grandad, do you want to see my drawing? We've just got it framed. Dad's going to put it up on the wall."

My father took the framed picture from Lacquan and studied it briefly before exclaiming:

"My grandson drew this?! But this is lovely, this is wonderful. This is boonoonoonoos!"

Lacquan laughed at the word and asked his grandfather what it meant. It was a Jamaican expression for 'perfectly lovely', and a word my father loved to use.

"So why are you misbehavin'?" Dad changed the subject.

"Dunno," 'Quan answered, shrugging his shoulder.

"You don't know? Well, the first t'ing you do, is tek a pen an' paper up to your room an' write down everyt'ing which has got you into trouble at school. We'll soon find out why."

"Awwwww, why do I always have to do something I don't want to do?!" Lacquan cried out.

"Hush up, hush up!" Dad hollered, raising his hand with a finger pointing skywards. "You rude bwoys don't cry, that's what I hear. Just go up to your room and write an essay on how you got into all this trouble. I want to see you writing not listening to music on your walkerman or walkerwoman."

Lacquan went up sulkily. Once he was out of sight and out of earshot, my father turned to me, staring deep into my eyes.

"I hope you haven't been smoking some of that ganja?"

I looked at him puzzled.

"Come of it, Dad, you know I don't deal with dem t'ings."

"So how come your eyes so red-up?"

I shrugged my shoulders.

"Well anyway" he continued, "now that you're here, the first thing you can do is take my luggage up to the spare room." He pointed to two heavy-looking suitcases behind the door.

There were several reasons why I didn't want my father around. I know how he stays. He blames me for not telling him that I had a son all these years and worse, he has still not got used to the idea that I'm not in his charge anymore and that I now have a son of my own to bring up. With the ladies though, Dad's a charmer. To my embarrassment, he entertained Marcia for over an hour with stories of how I was as a child.

"I used to have to give Linvall some blouse an' skirt licks when he was a teenager though," he chuckled, "because he was always getting in trouble with the police... Did I tell you about how he used to wet the bed when he was just a small pickney...?"

Marcia said he could tell her that later but first, before she forgot her manners, she had to offer him some food.

"Oh that's so thoughtful of you," Dad praised her. "You are such a wonderful girl, Marcia.. You're the best thing that ever happened to Linvall."

Marcia looked across at me with a big smile on her face and a look that said, 'I told you so... You don't know how lucky you are.' When I saw that look, I knew it wasn't the last I had seen of it.

As soon as she had disappeared into the kitchen, the old man turned to me and started lecturing.

"Linvall, don't have no outside 'ooman, yuh hear me? NO OUTSIDE 'OOMAN! 'Cause this outside 'ooman is a bad t'ing, yuh know. It could break up your family... So boy, no outside 'ooman. Marcia is a good wife an' mother, mek sure you don't lose her. You don't have more pickney by any other woman, that you haven't told me about, do you?"

I shook my head, how could he ask me that?

"Well, you didn't tell me about Lacquan until he was eleven-years-old, did you? So you cyaan blame me for asking. An' Lacquan now, you cyaan blame the yout' for getting in trouble, when he never had a father he could turn to all these years. And you cyaan blame him for misbehaving at school when all they teach dem nowadays is 'the cow jump over the moon and the dish run away with the spoon'. So you cyaan blame the yout'..."

At that point, Marcia returned with a plate of rice and peas and chicken on a tray, with a glass of fizzy mineral water beside it. The old man received the food happily and tucked in. He said that the food was "boonoonoonoos" and that he could understand why "Linvall is putting on a bit of weight at last. Linvall, you must leggo the takeaway mentality an' stay at home more to enjoy your wife's cooking. Eat well to stay strong, boy!" Within minutes, there was nothing left on the plate but bones. But Dad wasn't finished yet. His favourite part of a chicken meal was still to come. It gave him an opportunity to continue his lecture as he tackled the ancient art of sucking every bit of juice out of a chicken bone. When he was finished finally, he remembered that he had brought some gifts and briefly went upstairs to his suitcase. He returned a short while later, with a jar of Blue Mountain coffee in one hand and a bottle of Wray & Nephew Jamaican rum. One of his friends had been back home and returned with them, he said, presenting them to Marcia.

"It's probably the best coffee in the world. Drink it and dream of sun-drenched beaches."

Marcia rustled up a decanter full of the coffee and we sat down to drink it. The Old Man was right, it really was good.

"I know it's difficult for you young people today," he said, addressing both Marcia and myself. "After all, I have personal experience of what it was like to start a family at a very young age and once you start off young, everything is an uphill struggle..."

Dad sucked on a thigh bone, as he cast his mind back to the old days. He assured us that the grey hair on his head and the wrinkles on his brow only told part of the story of the struggle of keeping a child fed and maintaining a roof over his family's head.

"We didn't have much money when Linvall was born. My parents weren't able to help me out. Me and Mrs Henry had to just get by as best we could." He fiddled nervously with the wedding ring on his left hand as the black and white memories of those early days in the sixties flowed through his veins again.

I knew he was thinking of Mum. Since she passed away the previous year, we had avoided talking about her. He wasn't ready, so we each kept our thoughts about her to ourselves. I was thinking of her too. How she held the family together financially and otherwise in those early years. How I got everything in terms of the love I needed; how I used to enjoy going to the park with my father on a Sunday to play cricket. I felt guilty, because I knew that Lacquan had never had my love in the same way.

My memories of growing up in the sixties and seventies are filled with flashbacks of carefree innocent days and of Dual floor cleaning liquid, paraffin heaters, Long Life beer, Mackeston stout, football pools, the Daily Mirror, the pubs for the dads, bingo for mums and Saturday morning pictures for the kids. My parents came to this country, not because they wanted to, but with the intention of making money, because of the circumstances back home. They never stopped missing the sunshine they had left behind them. I remember my mum carrying heavy shopping bags through Brixton, through snow, on the buses, getting verbal abuse from teddy boys and looking forward to the day when she would be able to go back home to the beautiful Caribbean. My dad used to keep blues dances to help out with the housekeeping money. There was really nowhere else for the ravers to go after the pubs shut at eleven so all his friends would come to let their hair down at our place. In those days, neighbours were quick to call the police at the slightest sound of a dance, even if they lived up the road and round the corner. It just wasn't the Englishman's way of life to have late night parties with the drum and the bass blasting down the house. But apart from the complaining neighbours, things were sweet. We used to have a big old gramophone with a cabinet, which had a heavy bass in it and could rock dancehall and party, even though you needed a two shilling piece on the turntable arm to keep the needle on the record. For some reason I have a vivid memory of all the popular record labels of the day like Bluebeat, Studio One, Trojan with the horse logo and Treasure Isle. I remember the Pioneers had a song out called *Long Shot Kick The Bucket*. I used to love dancing to that tune anytime it played and my dad's friends would see me and call out "drop foot bwai!" That was the command for me to do the fastest shuffle anyone had seen, or the mashed potato or funky chicken. When the song was finished, they would throw money on the floor for me and I would see from my dad's expression that he was so proud of me. He would even give me a sip of his Long Life and let me stay up late. My dad would wait until my mother had gone to bed before throwing down some heavy 'wining' on some of the women revellers. That gave me the opportunity to go round tasting all the drinks while his back was turned. By the time I was in secondary school, I had tasted Bacardi, brandy, Guinness and my favourite at the time, scotch whisky and orange.

In those days, we lived in a three-storey house, with a different family on each floor, but more time we would all cook together, especially on Saturdays when one pot would do for the whole family. From morning you could smell Irish moss on the fire, alongside fish soup, cow-foot soup, cow-cod soup or red pea soup. In the afternoon, Mum would drag me along to the laundry, which we used to call 'bagwash'. But we would only wash the clothes there. The spin drier was too expensive. Instead we took the heavy wet washing home to dry in front of the fire. Back then, mothers needed a degree in financial management and economics to make ends meet. Somehow, they managed nevertheless. It's no surprise that black women have achieved more than black men, when they had to strive to survive in those days. Mum was always knitting or sewing curtains or holding tupperware parties for extra cash. There never seemed to be enough money in the house and if it wasn't because of the 'pardner system' of loaning money from one member of the community to the next, we would have starved, many times, for in those days banks weren't too keen on lending money.

Before he went to bed that evening, Lacquan came down to hand his grandfather the story of his school yard exploits. He had completed the essay, *How I Keep Getting Into Trouble* and, he said, "I hope I don't have to write any more essays tomorrow, because after all it is Sunday!" he stressed before going back upstairs.

My father put on his glasses and quickly glanced at the essay. Then he held the note pad up, and read 'Quan's essay aloud:

It all started on a Monday, when a new pupil called Nathan started in my class. By Wednesday, he knew everybody. His attitude to people in the class was very rude. He called me a 'bitch' and he kept on doing it. Then on Friday, in the first lesson which was computers, he called me 'bitch' again and to get back at him I told him to take a look at his own peppergrain head. He came over to me and punched me at the side of my arm where I got my injection and he saw that it hurt, so he laughed and did it again. After that I waited for the pain to cool down, because it was still sore, before going over to him and putting him in a headlock. But he just laughed and said, "So, was that meant to hurt?" After that I just went to my seat and sat down, because it wasn't worth it. I did not want to kill him, I just wanted to teach him a lesson. I didn't see Nathan at break time, but the next lesson was history. We had a supply teacher who wasn't strict, so Nathan carried on calling me 'bitch'. All the teacher said when she heard him was that he was a "very rude child indeed." By this time Nathan was getting on my nerves. I just had enough and I decided to teach him a proper lesson. Because he wasn't supposed to laugh. I didn't want to make him cry either, he was just supposed to stop calling me a bitch. So when I saw him looking for his next lesson which was French, I punched him in his mouth. I didn't mean to knock out his teeth. When Nathan saw the blood from his mouth, he started crying and saw Mr Thomas walking by. He went to him and told him what happened, but because Nathan had on his trainers which he wasn't supposed to wear in school, Mr Thomas didn't want to know. So Nathan got told off and I went back to my class. After that I didn't see Nathan for a week but that same day I bumped into Mr Thomas and he said to me, "You better think of what's going to happen to you after knocking out three of Nathaniel's grown-up teeth."

It was just before registration when I went up to my teacher and told her I needed to speak to her about the situation and then she said to me, "I want to speak to you too." But I never told her the full story. When Nathan came back to school, he said to me, "I hear you've been telling everybody that you punched my teeth out." And I said, "I haven't told anybody anything." "Well, that is not what I've heard," Nathan replied. "Well, you've heard wrong, haven't you?" I said. "He said, "I've got friends in this school, you know." And I said, "I've got friends in this school too." And then he said, "I'm ready to fight you now, you know." I just kissed my teeth and carried on talking to my friends. So then he said, "I'll kick you so hard, you'll cry to Ethiopia." So then I just ignored him and carried on talking. So he said that he would kick me so hard that the prints on his trainer would stay on my face. So I said to him, "You better shut up before I punch out your teeth again!" So he said, "Come nuh, if yuh ah bad bwoy." So I just ignored him and then he went back into the corner. After that I had to go and see Mr Thomas about football. But then a woman came in who was Nathan's mum and she said to Mr Thomas that she would like to see him ----"Now!" So he dismissed everybody apart from me and another boy and then he went upstairs to see my teacher and then Mr Thomas said to me, "Do you know who that lady was?" I said, "No." And then he said that was Nathaniel's mother. "So go upstairs until I sort out this other boy and wait for me." So as I reached to the top of the stairs and turned a corner, I saw Nathan's mum talking to my teacher. When I saw her and my teacher, I ran down to Mr Thomas in a flash and he was still there talking to the other boy. So I interrupted him while speaking to the boy and said, "She's up there, Sir." Sir said, "Who's up there?" "Nathan's mum." So he said "Okay, wait down here for me and then I'll take you up." So then we went upstairs. On the way up Mr Thomas and I planned that if she was still up there to act like we never know what was going on and hope that Miss wouldn't say "Oh Lacquan!" and call out my name in front of Nathan's mum, who was very angry and looking for a Lacquan. After registration Miss asked me to come and see her after school, because she is going to write a letter home. At home time when I went up to my class my teacher said to me, that I just don't know when to keep my mouth shut...

Then there was the time I got in trouble when the teacher turned around and saw that someone drew a big willie with two big balls on the blackboard. I didn't do anything, but because I laughed *he told me to stand in the back of the class and see him afterwards. Whenever there's any trouble, they just blame me.*

My father sighed after he had read out the essay. I had to laugh, Lacquan hadn't even attempted to answer the title of the essay, but had instead diverted the issue to one where he could not be held responsible. I could have added that there were times when he was totally responsible. Like the time when he got hold of the school tannoy in the headmistress' office and started sending out 'special requests' to all his friends in the school, without realising that his voice could be identified. From the way she recounted the story the other day, the headmistress still hadn't recovered from that prank.

"You think this is funny Linvall?" my father asked sombrely.

"Well, you've got to laugh haven't you," I answered jovially. "That Nathan boy deserved the kuff, if you ask me. This isn't just about Lacquan, you have some feisty pupils at his school."

"I don't care if all the pupils are feisty, I don't care if all the teachers are feisty too, it's my grandson that is getting in trouble and that's what concerns me."

"Well don't worry about that Dad, I'm sorting him out. He ain't going to get into that kind of trouble again. Hell no!"

"I notice you gwan like you smart..." my father said. "What bad ah mornin' cyaan turn good ah evenin'. You understand that part deh? If you stop and think for one minute about this essay, you'll understand that Lacquan's problems are all your fault."

I slapped my head in wonder. "How do you work that out?"

At this point, Marcia took her leave. She said she had something important to do. It was going to be an argument between father and son and she didn't want any part of it.

"This essay is a cry for help," my father continued. He looked about him to see if Marcia was gone before adding in a conspiratorial whisper, "You made the first mistake, because for years you lied to the boy about not being his real father. And after telling him the truth that his 'Uncle' is really his father, and giving him the biggest shock, you're surprised when he's behaving badly in school. You should never have pretended that you weren't Lacquan's father for so many years. Do you really need me to come and tell you that wasn't a smart move?"

My father went on about this for some time, turning the argument this way and that way and making sure that whichever way he turned it, I ended up getting the blame, and reminding me of his oft-quoted saying, "Lie an' teef walk same way!"

"If you were listening to me when you were a yout' you would never have gone wrong. Didn't I used to tell you not to get any girl pregnant unless you're married? Didn't I? In life, you start off as you mean to continue and you started off badly, that's why you have an eleven-year-old son but not the requirements to be a proper father and now you've had to call me in to come and help you."

"Wait a minute, I didn't call you. I don't know what Marcia's been saying, but everything's under control."

"If everything's under control, why isn't my grandson at school like all the other children?"

I shrugged and looked away. I really didn't need any of this. I couldn't win any which way. My dad must have sensed my discomfort and tried to reassure me.

"You think I'd be here if you were having an affair with another woman? I wouldn't approve, but I wouldn't leave my house to come and be concerned with your problems. But this is my grandson. Think of your mother Linvall, all she ever wanted was a grandchild. She died not knowing that she had a beautiful grandson. She would turn in her grave if she knew that her grandson was suspended from school. So now it's up to me to see that Lacquan succeeds in life. That he is a credit to his grandmother."

When he put it like that, there wasn't much I could say, except "Daddy, I really am trying my best with 'Quan. I really am trying to make up for the lost years."

"I know you are son," he said, "I know you are. But there are only twenty-four hours in the day, aren't there?"

So anyway, it was settled, the Old Man was staying. I got to realise just how big the mistake was from that very first evening of his visit. He had offered to stay in and babysit while Marcia and I went out and enjoyed ourselves. Marcia said she would take the opportunity to see one of her sisters over in the Hackney side of things. To be honest, that wasn't how I wanted to spend a Saturday evening. So I said if she didn't mind, I might go out with my spars for a few drinks. She said it was cool. Now I didn't come back that late— remember I'm a big man now and five in the morning is a simple sump'n – but when I got back, my father was still up, reading a book in the living room, with his feet up on the couch.

"So what time do you call this to be coming home?"

"Wh-whaat?" I couldn't believe the question, it sounded like Marcia confronting me. She had tried to ask me the same question many times before without getting an answer. But I had to answer my father, however big I thought I was.

"I... I was out with some friends..."

"You have a wife and family and you're out all night long with your friends? No wonder your son is misbehaving... How do you expect to get up for work early if you've been out all night long...? From now on, things are going to be different. While I'm here, I don't care who is in the house, if them is not in by 11.30pm, I'll lock the door an' let dog nyam your supper and you can sleep ah street!"

I let out a deep sigh. This was the father I remembered from my youth and though I had grown, he hadn't changed one bit. There was nothing much I could do about that. I knew better than to argue with my father. I was brought up the old fashioned way and knew better than to disrespect the man who brought me into the world, the man who didn't stop short of reminding me that as old as he was, he could take me out of the world as easily as he brought me in. And the hundred push-ups he did in the living room every morning to keep his belly hard, was proof of this.

Things had been different enough already in the house since the old man arrived. My father believes you must be up by seven o'clock in the morning – everyone. He expects me to jog to the corner shop and get his newspapers first thing in the morning and then to come back and make his breakfast. While I was at it, he'd ask Marcia what she wanted to eat.

"It's a long time me nuh taste Linvall's breakfast," he would say, "me miss it actually... An' when you done Linvall, just clean up my shoes. Put some black polish 'pon dem... What did you say you want for breakfast, Marcia, some eggs an' bacon? Yuh hear dat, Linvall?"

And I had to go through an informal inspection every morning. If I tried to leave for work without my shirt ironed, the old man would be calling out of the window before I made it to the bottom of the garden path, "Get back in the house, fix up your clothes... We don't dress like dat here!" I should have remembered that he didn't business about embarrassing me in front of people passing on the street.

I was feeling miserable the whole time the old man was visiting, but Marcia loved it. Because he sided with her in everything and she marvelled at the way he was able to get me to do the things she had asked me to do for so long. He got me to cut my funki dreds, or more precisely he pulled out a pair of scissors and cut them off for me. Marcia was pleased about that, as she was about all the little chores I was doing. Before my dad came, she had tried to get me to climb on to the roof to fix some loose tiles. I tried everything to get out of that without admitting my basic fear of rooftops. We discussed it for weeks. Surprise, surprise, the old man got me on the rooftop within a few days of his arrival. And when I came down the ladder, I heard his voice below me saying, "Alright now, go in the kitchen and do the dishes!" Of course I obeyed without answering back. I wasn't brought up to answer back.

All in all, my father's visit has changed the runnings in our house. Marcia basically runs my life. It's a skank of course. For example she'll complain of a bellyache and enjoy watching me jump when my father orders me to get her something for it.

Lacquan also enjoyed his grandfather's stay with us. They had only known of each other's existence for a few months and were best friends. Lacquan especially liked it when his grandfather would tell him stories. If there was one thing my father was good at, it was telling stories and he seemed to enjoy telling them as much as people enjoyed hearing them.

"You're gal friend is 'boonoonoonoo'!" Dad declared when Lacquan invited the girl next door round. "She's perfectly lovely. So my dear, come mek me hold your hand..."

Rosie from next door giggled, but gave him her hand.

"Now you see," the old man continued, "dat is the Jamaican welcome – come mek me hol' your hand."

He took her hand and proceeded to sing, to the youngsters' delight:

Long time gal me nevah see you, come mek me hol' your hand
It is a long time gal me nevah see you, come mek me hol' your hand
Peel head jancrow, sit dung 'pon tree top, pick off the blossom
Mek me hol' your hand, gal, mek me hol' your hand.

It's a long time gal me nevah see you, come mek we wheel an' tu'n
It's a long time gal me nevah see you, come mek we wheel an' tu'n
Peel head jancrow, sit dung 'pon tree top, pick off the blossom
Mek me wheel an' t'un, gal, mek we wheel an' t'un.

It's long time gal me nevah see you, come mek we walk an' talk
Long time gal me nevah see you, come mek we walk an' talk

Patrick Augustus

Peel head jancrow, sit dung 'pon tree top, pick off the blossom
Mek we walk an' talk, gal, mek we walk an' talk
Mek we wheel and tu'n till we tumble down, mek me hol' your
hand, gal,
Mek me wheel an' t'un till we tumble down, mek me hol' your
hand, gal...

KINKY REGGAE

It was like this: a cold afternoon at the Mighty Diamond shop. Gussie was in the back room, sorting some jewellery into the safe, when Brenda came in all hot around the collar.

"Guess who's just stepped into the shop?" she said excitedly.

Gussie, less excitedly, asked who.

"It's her... you know, Yasmine..."

"The TV agony aunt?" Suddenly Gussie's ears pricked up.

Brenda confirmed that it was that very same one.

Gussie stood up. Brenda noticed how he was suddenly interested. He stepped out into the shop. Yasmine was being shown a selection of gold necklaces by the junior salesman.

Gussie stood behind her silently for a moment, before coughing affectedly.

Yasmine spun around.

"Oh... it's you!" she blurted, surprised. "What are you doing here? Oh, I remember, you're a diamond merchant, aren't you? Is this your store?"

They exchanged pleasantries. Yasmine said that she was in a hurry, she had a show to tape, but she needed to buy some new jewellery. Gussie helped her choose a moderately-priced selection. She thanked him and began to rush out, but before leaving turned around as if she suddenly remembered something.

"By the way, I'm having a party later on tonight at my place. I'd love you to come if you can make it."

She scribbled down her address hurriedly on the back of her calling card and handed it to him. "I'm not begging you, I'm just giving you the number. Come some time after nine."

Gussie thanked her and said he might just do that.

"My oh my, we are popular aren't we?" Brenda teased after Yasmine had gone her way. "We're dating TV stars now!"

Gussie told her to behave herself and keep her mind on

what he was paying her for. He studied the address on the back of the card. It was a West-Two address in Westbourne Park. Yeah, he thought, it was about time he started going to celebrity parties. He was looking forward to it.

"Oh you must be Gussie?" said the girl who opened the door when he arrived at Yasmine's place.

"Yes, that's right."

"Hi, I'm Angela..."

"I know you," Gussie was saying, trying to put a name to the face. "You present that programme... what's it called?..."

"Black to Black," the woman filled in.

"Yes, that's right," said Gussie excitedly, stepping in. "You're Angela Braithwaite."

They shook hands, Gussie more eagerly than she. This was getting better all the time. The house would probably be packed wall to wall with celebrities.

"I'm Yasmine's flat mate," she explained, leading him through. "Take your shoes off and go into the lounge. Make yourself at home," she said pointing him through. "You'll find drinks and food and things in there... Yazz'll be down in a minute."

Gussie smiled as he watched Angela disappear into one of the other rooms. The lounge was completely empty. Embarrassingly he was the first to arrive. It probably seemed like he was desperate. He made a point to remember next time that these celebrities always arrive late. When they tell you to arrive at nine, they probably don't expect anyone to come before ten.

Winsome's flat in Highbury was fantastic, but this ground and first floor maisonette on Westbourne Park Road was just as good. It was set back from the road by a large front garden and inside, boasted newly-decorated rooms of enormous proportions and elegant furniture. There were many similarities with Winsome's flat, which wasn't so surprising seeing they were friends.

He poured himself a beer from the bar in the corner of the room and crossed over to the small charcoal-grey stereo unit to turn up the Billie Holiday playing softly in the background.

"Oh you've made yourself comfortable, I see," said Yasmine as she stepped into the room.

Gussie spun around to admire the woman. Yasmine was dressed flimsily in what seemed like a nightie, her well-proportioned body shimmering through. Gussie almost spilled the beer over his trousers.

"Oh don't worry about all this," she said, pointing to her attire. "I'll go up and change later."

"So where is everybody else?" Gussie asked. "What time's everybody supposed to be here?"

"Who?" she asked.

"The party, remember?"

"Oh," Yasmine said innocently, "you are the party. Didn't I tell you? I'm famous for my small parties, there's just me and you..."

She looked at Gussie playfully. He knew the score. Fortunately he had a condom with him, just in case. Well, here he was, and he was up for anything. As long as it didn't mean marriage, he was down with whatever Yasmine felt like.

She didn't bother to go up and change, but instead fixed herself a drink. She felt totally relaxed as they got to chatting. Before long, they were both lying down on the rug in front of the open fireplace, telling each other funny stories..

Just like her job, Yasmine tended to be a bit of an agony aunt in private too and was curious to find out as much of Gussie's personal details as she could. But she seemed fun-loving and pretty normal nevertheless. After what he had been through in the last few months, if he needed anything right now in a woman, it was normality. She was soon asking him all his intimate secrets and trying to give solutions to all the mistakes that he had made in his life. Of course, he didn't mention Chantelle. That would have been unbearable. It was then, as they lay on the floor getting cosy that she revealed her passion for hot sex. "I'm not the monogamous type," she said, then challenged him to lay his cards on the table. Gussie confessed to being a sexaholic.

"Oh is that all," Yasmine said, almost disappointed. "Big deal!"

She said she didn't expect any different, after all he was a man and "all men are dogs". Gussie tried to protest, but it did no good. She always got her own way, she said, that's why she wrote her diary a month in advance. She told him not to worry however, being a woman of the nineties she was indifferent to all the romantic stuff. She preferred men who were direct.

"Women today don't have time to spend looking for that special someone and those who do are finding that they are making mistakes anyway. You think you know your partner until you discover you've been having a relationship with a complete stranger. It's much better to be honest and direct. Men should carry identity cards which detail personal characteristics such as 'sexaholic', 'workaholic', 'alcoholic', 'bore' 'idiot'. That way women would know exactly who you are, what interests you have as well as what you look like and there'll be more chance for real chemistry. So if you're looking for an educated, down-to-earth, commitment-minded guy, you simply ask to see his ID card, instead of wasting time reading between the lines, because men always try and make out that they're someone they're not. So men suffer when they break up in a relationship...? Good!"

The more Gussie talked to her, the more he enjoyed himself. He found Yasmine entertaining if nothing else!

They had been drinking and talking for so long that Gussie had forgotten all about Yasmine's flatmate. But now, with the lights dimmed in the lounge and with them both lying on the rug under a blanket, Angela Braithwaite stepped into the room unannounced carrying a candle and wearing a pair of expensive-looking drop earrings but nothing else. Without saying a word, she joined Gussie and Yasmine under the blanket. Before long, Angela and Yasmine were locked in a tender embrace and caressing each other passionately. Beside them, Gussie watched with a hungry look. He didn't feel left out for long however. He reached across and let his hand wander across Angela's smooth behind and a moment later he was in the thick of things.

"You better be at your best tonight," Yasmine said, with a twinkle in her eye.

"What about Winsome?" Gussie asked breathlessly, as if he cared.

"Oh don't worry about that. This is just between the three of us," Angela promised. "No one will ever know."

It's every man's dream to be the only male in a love triangle. Once in his youth, Gussie had experienced a three-in-a-bed situation, where he and a friend shared one woman. That wasn't so enjoyable. His time had come to be the one man in the bed.

Angela and Yasmine were divine. As if it came naturally to them, one of them attended to his face while the other worked his penis like it was a plunger. All he had to do was kick back and enjoy. Then they swapped over. Angela sat on his face as Yasmine performed fellatio, and in between they kissed and caressed each other for Gussie's benefit. All three of them moaning together. Gussie's smile would make a Cheshire cat seem miserable. His only anxiety was that it would all end with his bedroom lumber still rock hard. That should have been the least of his worries. By the time both Angela and Yasmine were satisfied, it would be mid-afternoon the next day and it would be he who was praying for it to come to an end. They just wanted more and more and more, and then an encore. "We *deserve* an encore!" they demanded. Gussie had to agree. He had never made love like this before. It hurt so good he had to pinch himself to be sure. And he made it through. It was exhausting, but he made it through. He was still a worker man. A stamina daddy. The nagging fears about his own sexuality after his marriage to a woman who used to be a man, were now banished forever. He had given his two celebrities the performance of a lifetime! To get over this would take him several days of lying in the darkness of his bedroom with his eyes open, reliving the memories of their love-making.

Brenda commented about his health when Gussie staggered into the shop late that afternoon. He was too mashed up to respond, beyond murmuring, "Fe real, fe real," in agreement.

BUSINESS AS USUAL

I refused to be torn apart from Caroline, but as much as I wanted to 'stand by my woman', I was getting increasingly impatient with all the time she was spending in Belgium on her landmark case. It's hard work trying to conduct a part-time relationship and I had started to feel the stress of packing a week's relationship into a weekend. Caroline was also becoming stressed from all the work she was doing and on a couple of weekends she didn't have the energy to do more than sleep when she came home. I wasn't feeling married at all. All I could look forward to was the day when the case would finally come to an end and we could live as man and wife again.

This morning was another occasion when time came between us. We had got into the habit of making love first thing on Sunday morning, just in case we didn't get another chance before Caroline's flight was due to leave in the afternoon. Even though we had the house to ourselves and several hours to spare, the sex was tense. Performing to order is hard at the best of times. When you realise that you have to deliver because this is probably the last time you'll be making love to your partner for a week, it is even more difficult to relax. I wasn't relaxed, and neither was Caroline. And though she moaned for me to love her gently, I never quite got in the mood of things. It was still enjoyable sex, but far from being the best.

We lay in bed for a couple of hours, our bodies still entwined, listening to *Letter From America* and the Morning Service on the radio and whispering sweet nothings to one another.

Before we knew it, time had rushed by. Isn't it funny how you feel like making love just when you realise you've run out of time? We were both still feeling sexy, but time was of the essence. Sipping at a hot cup of coffee and with a sandwich in her hand, Caroline glanced at her wrist watch. "I really have to run, darling," she said. "If I didn't need to get back by early evening to prepare some briefs for next week's hearing, I could take a later flight. But my legal team is expecting me back this evening. Don't worry darling, we'll make up the lost time next weekend."

She quickly got herself ready, slipping into a neat, grey suit which complemented her gorgeous figure. She then spent a moment viewing herself carefully in the full-length mirror in our bedroom, twisting first this way then that, to check that she looked immaculate. Finally it was time to go. I helped her with her bags and drove the few miles to City Airport.

"Thank you, sweetheart," Caroline said when we arrived there less than an hour later. "You better rush off to pick up Lara, or you won't have much time to spend with her today."

"Are you sure you don't want me to help you with your luggage?" I offered.

Caroline said that she could manage alright by herself.

"You just go off and do your baby father duties," she joked. "And I'll see you at the weekend."

The less I saw of Caroline, the more I thought about my daughter Lara, and my ex-wife, her mother. Thinking about Sonia still bothered me. How had things turned out badly between us?

The vexed issue of my ex-wife's sexual orientation was uppermost in my mind as I pulled up outside my former Streatham home.

"Oh Beres, I've been trying to call you, but there was no answer at your place," Sonia said when she opened the door. "I was going to tell you to come and pick Lara up later, because she's gone off with Grace to a football match. It was a spur of the moment decision. And I knew you wouldn't mind."

I simply grunted.

"Is that the best you can do, Beres? At least show some emotion. Is it okay with you?"

I shrugged my shoulders. It was too late anyway. There

was nothing more I could do. I made a note to mention it when the inevitable court case for custody of Lara came up. Oh, I was definitely still going for custody of my daughter as soon as my detective managed to get enough evidence.

Sonia invited me in, which surprised me, as I was usually kept standing on the doorstep whenever I came to collect or bring Lara back home. It felt strange to be in my house again after all this time, even if I was only in the hallway.

"How goes your love life?" Sonia asked suddenly.

I thought she was being funny. "Why do you want to know?"

"Just asking... I want to make sure that it's still as enjoyable as when we were together."

Sonia winked at me. I made the mistake of winking back.

That was like a green light for her to go ahead with what she had on her mind. Again she smiled sweetly, seductively. In the next moment, she was unbuttoning my shirt slowly. I felt my temperature rise as her hands probed my hair, my ears, my neck, my chest and, finally, came to rest, gently, on my manhood. Before I knew it, my lips found hers.

With temptation staring me in the face, the world outside seemed so far away. The kiss was long, warm, sweet and slow. My hand went down and cupped her bottom, which seemed to bring back a flood of happy memories of our marriage. Flashbacks of our honeymoon flicked through my mind, of running breathlessly along the beach playing 'catch me if you can' and lying on the sand watching the sunset together. Those memories seemed far away from Sonia and her present lifestyle.

"I thought you were gay...?" I asked as an afterthought.

"Whatever made you think that?" she replied innocently.

"But you are, you co-habit with Grace, don't you?"

"I love Grace... that's different from being homosexual."

"But you sleep with her, don't you?"

"That's none of your business," she said, tickling me under my chin. Then she took me by the hand and led me into the living room. "We've just got enough time for a quick one before Grace and Lara get back. You do want to sleep with me, don't you?"

I couldn't deny that that was my desire, but I was so terrified, I couldn't move a muscle.

"We shouldn't be doing this," I tried vainly as Sonia pulled me down onto the couch.

"But we are, Beres."

She had taken off her sweater and her breasts were now jutting upwards towards me, cupped in a white bra. The softness of her body with her naked curves, like velvet to my touch, made it so easy for me to throw aside all discretion, all caution.

"I've missed you, Beres," she said almost solemnly.

I was surprised to hear this. As far as I knew, my ex-wife saw me only as a good meal ticket.

"Oh, it's been so long, I've wanted you so bad!" she groaned.

Before I knew it, my trousers were on the floor and my briefs were being pulled down also.

I was suddenly very jittery. I was new to this game after all. I had never been unfaithful while married, neither with Sonia nor with Caroline. And although I knew what I was doing was wrong and had unforetold consequences, I was gripped by a mad kind of hunger, an uncontrollable craving for warmth between Sonia's legs and the pleasure awaiting there. With trembling fingers I fumbled for the last of my shirt buttons.

Suddenly, Sonia stopped as if a thought had crossed her mind. "You seem to be holding back," she said.

"Me? No... nothing. Not me."

"But you are Beres, I can see it in your eyes."

I couldn't figure out what she meant. After having led me on Sonia was now apparently retreating. She studied me for a moment through narrow eyes. Then just as suddenly, she reached behind her and loosened her bra. She shrugged out of the shoulder straps and threw the bra on the floor. Her breasts jutted upward, the dark nipples pointing at me.

Again, I thought of my present wife and again I tried to shake her spirit loose. Pushing Caroline from my mind was as far as I got. In the next instant, both Sonia and I heard the distinct sound of a key turning in the front door lock. We exchanged only the briefest of looks, before both jumping up and in the same movement pulling on as much clothing as we could. I managed to pull my trousers back on – just, and was hurriedly zipping up my fly when Grace stepped in, followed by Lara.

Talk about shame! Grace didn't need three guesses to figure out what was taking place. Though Sonia had managed to pull on her sweater in time to hide her modesty, her bra still lay on the floor as a testament to our careless passion.

When I think about it, I'm glad Grace interrupted us, before I made a fool of myself, but I felt like an embarrassed child. Sonia straightened her skirt as best as she could. She too was embarrassed. Her girlfriend simply stood there, looking none too pleased. Fortunately, Lara didn't understand what was going on

I felt guilty during the short car ride from Streatham to Tooting. What had I done? Why had I done it? It wasn't even worth it. How would I be able to face Caroline when she came back at the weekend? Surely she would know I was lying if I tried to cover things up, she is a lawyer after all and used to catching liars out. But I had a greater fear of doing the right thing and owning up to my infidelity. Now I knew how Johnny Dollar often felt. I mean, it wasn't exactly as if I was actually unfaithful. I know the intention was there, but when nothing occurred, it was just as easy to forget it. Yes, I decided, that was what I would do. By the time I pulled up outside our house, I had resolved to never mention my encounter with Sonia to anyone.

To my surprise, the front door stood ajar when I entered. The first thing that entered my mind was that we'd been broken into. My fears were soon laid to rest however, by the sound of Caroline's voice on the telephone in the living room.

"What are you doing here?" I asked with a worried look. She was supposed to be on her way to Belgium by now.

"Damn!" Caroline retorted, replacing the telephone receiver in its cradle. "That was the airline. All the rest of the flights are booked for this evening. I won't be able to fly until the morning."

"But what are you doing back here?" I asked again.

"My ticket..." she said. "Can you believe it, I forgot it. I always have it in my handbag, but I forgot that I switched bags at the last minute and took the navy one instead of the black one. I didn't even find out until I got to the check-in desk."

"So what about your case and your legal partners, aren't they going to be expecting you?"

"Oh, I'll call them in a while, we'll have to work something out. It's not the end of the world... So how comes you're back so early? I thought you were going to be with your daughter until the evening as usual."

The question took me by surprise and I ended up saying the first thing that came into my head. I lied and said I had gone to pick Lara up directly after I had dropped Caroline at the airport and that me and my daughter had gone out together briefly. "But she wasn't feeling too well so I took her home. I'm coming straight from there now."

I was worried that Caroline would detect some quivering hint of untruth in my voice, but she merely stifled a yawn. She seemed not to notice my first ever lie to her.

"Oh honey," I said sympathetically. "You know, you're working too hard. That's what all this is about." I embraced. "Before you took this case you would never have forgotten something as important as your ticket. You must be exhausted. Well, I hope all this hard work you're putting in pays off at the end. I suppose forgetting your ticket is a blessing in disguise, it'll give you a chance to catch up on an extra night's sleep at home."

"Not a chance!" Caroline smiled cheekily as she stroked my chest playfully. "The blessing in disguise is that we'll be able to make some beautiful love for an extra evening. It's like an early Christmas present. Come on!"

Before I could say otherwise, Caroline was tugging at my zip and reaching down into my pants. The slightest touch from her managed to set me going. As always, as her tongue explored every crevice of my chest and stomach, I found my wife irresistible.

We didn't waste any time. Caroline wanted me to take her right there and then, on the living room floor, and I wasn't arguing. She pulled down my trousers in a hurry, eager for me to enter her and then reached for my pants also.

"What's this...?" she said suddenly, stopping in mid-passion.

"Don't stop," I breathed heavily. "Just go on, don't stop..."

"I SAID, WHAT'S THIS?!!!"

This time I paid attention. Those four words and Caroline's tone of voice, shriveled my manhood. I looked down, Caroline was tugging at my briefs. I still didn't understand.

"How comes your pants are back to front?!" she demanded. "When I left you this morning, they were the right way around. How comes they're back to front now, enh?!"

"I... I... I..."

I was trying hard to think up a good excuse.

Patrick Augustus

INDECENT PROPOSAL

Gussie got a call from Winsome Scott the very next day as he was musing over a VAT demand he had forgotten about.

"I thought you'd fallen off the face off the earth," she said.

At first he was a little nervous. Why had she called just today? Had Yasmine said anything? Or had she spoken to Angela Braithwaite about their night of fun? If the three women were such good friends, surely they would discuss things like that? That was up to them, he didn't owe Winsome anything. He sounded her out for a few seconds, trying to illicit what she knew and what she didn't know. She seemed ignorant of his adventures the night before. If she had spoken to her friends about it, Winsome was keeping it close to her chest.

"So do you want to come around sometime?"

Hang on, what was all of this? Why was she so inviting?

"I didn't think you wanted me around your place again... after the last time. I thought you were pissed off."

"Oh Gus, you are silly," she said with a laugh. "Look, you're not the first man to try to get off with me who got rejected. I'm old enough to be able to take it in my stride now, trust me."

He trusted her, but he still wasn't sure. Nevertheless, he agreed to drop in to see her later that evening.

"And bring me a present," she said, "that's what gentlemen are supposed to do when they ask a woman to forgive them."

Gussie arrived at her place late. He was in no rush. He had several things to do that evening and wasn't counting on anything special. He'd hang at Winsome's for a short time. If she wanted to go somewhere that was cool and if she didn't that was cool too. She opened the door, with a look on her face he hadn't seen before. She was dressed in what seemed like pyjamas and a sultry fragrance followed her back into the flat. Gussie handed her the gift. It was a plant for her living room. She said it was beautiful and placed it in a corner over by the window.

"I'm so glad to see you again," Winsome confessed.

She said she had been thinking things over. About how she rejected him the last time. She concluded that on balance she was losing out by cutting herself off from her desires. Yes, she had wanted to go to bed with him.

They had been drinking for a while. Winsome refilled Gussie's glass at every opportunity as well as her own. Slightly merry, they ended up recounting romance stories to each other. She asked him what his last girlfriend was like.

"Why do you want to know?"

"I don't know... Maybe you've still got plans to be with her?"

Gussie told her that she didn't know just how wrong she was. "But my love life won't interest you."

"No really," she replied, "it does interest me. Really, go on..."

Gussie began to yearn for Winsome. He felt an urge to tell her how he felt and yet, he couldn't understand the way he was feeling. At a time when he should be at his poetic best, when it was inevitable that they would end up making love, Gussie was struggling to make sense.

Before either could stop what was happening, they were kissing. Tentatively to begin with. She seemed to hypnotise him with her eyes. He couldn't resist it and began to caress her tenderly. She felt his tongue meandering on her chest, then just as it got lower, she slipped out from under him, giggling playfully. But he was bursting with longing and excitement.

"Ease up!" she begged, as Gussie tried to push his way in. Winsome was still not ready. She needed another moment. With ripples of joy pumping through him, he lay on top of her and kissed her full on the mouth. His tongue deep within her mouth, as the kiss went on forever. He felt for the hem of her silk pyjamas then interrupting the mouth to mouth resuscitation, he lifted the top swiftly over her head and threw it somewhere on the ground. For a moment, he stopped admiring her perfect breasts. Then he laid her gently on her back and managed to undo his fly before it popped open, revealing a huge erect penis. "Trust me," he whispered softly in her ear as he pushed deeper and deeper into her until she could accommodate him no more.

"I know you'll be gentle," she moaned quietly.

"I've waited too long to rush things. I'll make love to you slowly, pleasurably."

As he eased delicately in and out of her, Gussie felt the adrenaline rush to his head making him queasy. It was that good. After what seemed like forever, Winsome pulled back.

"I'm going to show you how much I want you," she said with a wink and then turning Gussie on his back, she kissed his belly button gently, probed it with her tongue, then wandered down to his stiff manhood and teased it gently with her mouth. Then she took him into her mouth, deeper than Gussie had thought possible. He cried with pain and pleasure as he felt her dental fillings scrape lightly across the shaft of his pulsating lumber, and her fingers tickling his balls gently. He had to admit one thing—she knew the tricks. "Yes, that's right!" It was just right. It was perfect! This is what going downtown was all about. This was what sex was all about... "Yes! Yes!! YES!!!"

But before Gussie could holler that final word of approval which would take him beyond the point of no return, Winsome drew back again, leaving him unsatisfied. But not for long. In the same movement, she eased her hips down on top of him and buried him deep within her. Inside her, he moved slowly at first, gradually building up pace. She could feel every inch of him. "Play it again, Gus?" she teased with a smile.

It was the most beautiful lovemaking and it felt like he was losing his virginity all over again. When he was finally exhausted in the middle of the night panting, she went into the fridge and got him some ice cream. Try eating some of this she said. Gussie wolfed down a spoonful hungrily... It took only seconds rather than minutes, but suddenly, his manhood was erect again and once more he itched to enter deep inside her.

"You still haven't had enough?" she asked.

"I love you... I love you... I love you!" he heard himself saying as his third orgasm that night consumed him

Though he would later claim that those weren't his exact words, in the heat of passion he uttered the words, "Winsome, will you marry me?" Not once but twice. And Winsome replied over and over again, "Yes, yes, yes, yes, yes, YES...!!!"

The next day, Gussie got a call from Angela, early.

"You dirty dog you," she teased, "I've got a bone to pick with you. No, not 'boning'..." Her 'bone', she explained, was a proposition. Gussie was intrigued. If the proposition was anything like the last time, he was definitely interested. She said she'd explain it all over lunch. He could hardly wait.

They met up at a little pub which served up nice lunches just around the corner on Farringdon Road. Angela, sporting a new bobbed hairstyle, was already there when he arrived, looking as delectable with clothes on as he remembered her without them. He kissed her affectionately on either cheek.

"Have you recovered from the other night?" Gussie asked with a cheeky grin.

"Well I should ask you the same question. The odds were against you, after all."

He smiled. He always liked talking dirty with a woman.

Angela gave him a rundown of where she was coming from. Of late she had become obsessed with conceiving. She put it down to her thirtysomething panic. She said that she dated quite often and had only good things to say about her experiences, but the men weren't quite up to scratch. And she usually knew by the end of the first date whether the man was right for her or not. As they ate their lunches, she started summing things up for Gussie.

"The good news is that I think you're pretty nice and I

feel your niceness is genuine. The bad news is that the sparks didn't really ignite for me the other night. And that's not your fault, nobody's lit my fire in a long while, though I remain optimistic."

She said she was optimistic about Gussie too. That was why she was going to put this proposition to him. The other night was just meant to be a fun thing, but the more she thought about it, the more she wanted to see him again. She flattered him with more words and talked about how special and wonderful he was.

"Let's face it, Gus, men like you are in short supply and you know it. You've got the looks, the intelligence, the charm and the ambition. I knew that as soon as I opened the door to you the other night. And I daresay, you've got a little hint of danger about you. I find that attractive."

He thanked her for her kind words.

"In short, you're the sort of man I've been looking for."

Gussie gulped.

"Take it easy, I'm not going to eat you, I just need your sperm."

Gussie almost choked on his baked potato. He looked about him nervously. Fortunately, nobody had heard her.

"It's simple," she continued. "I want a baby. And I've been looking for the right man to have one with. A surrogate father of course. I wouldn't want anything from you and you can continue living your bachelor life for all I care. Do you agree?"

Gussie was still reeling from the proposition, he couldn't say anything. Angela wasn't kidding when she said she was straightforward. She had no qualms about wanting a baby this way either. "I want to share my life with a child, but not with a man at the moment. I won't insult your intelligence by offering you money. I know you probably have more than enough money to be getting on with, but I am prepared to pay."

All Gussie could do was shake his head.

"It's not about the money. Most definitely not. That's the

last thing on my mind. It's just that I've never had to consider such a proposition before. I'll have to think about it. I need time..."

"Well don't think about it too long," she added. "I'm not getting any younger."

He smiled and promised that he would decide before she got her first grey hair.

There were two messages for him when he returned to the Mighty Diamond. Winsome had left her number and wanted him to call her and Courtney had called from a hotel in Las Vegas and wanted him to call back - URGENT!

Gussie's heart pumped. He had wanted to talk to Courtney for a week now to find out how things were going with the big eliminator fight in the States. Courtney was just as anxious to speak to Gussie. His voice came down the transatlantic line in hurried tones.

"You'll never believe what's happened."

What? What?" Gussie asked impatiently.

"You'll never believe what happened," Courtney repeated. "You know Danny Madhatter?"

Gussie said he did. Of course he did. Everybody knew the American impresario who was the world's biggest black boxing promoter.

"He's trying to skank us on Williams..."

"What?!"

"He's pulling a sly one, guy. He knows that Sugar Ray could win the fight and that it will mean a million-dollar sponsorship deal if he does. So now Madhatter's trying to teef him off us!"

It was beginning to make sense for Gussie. "But how?"

"He's told Williams and every other fighter, that they won't get a shot at the title unless he's managing them."

Gussie listened in silence and felt his heart sink. "And what does Williams say?"

"I've talked to him and he's laid his cards on the table. He's getting old, this could be his last shot at the title... He's done a lot of training... He's as fit as a fiddle and he's up for the scrap. But he can't let any 'technicalities' stand in his way..."

It was as Gussie feared. The worst.

"I can't blame Sugar Ray, because after all, he has his life to live. But what about our investment? We've got to get our money back."

"It's all gone, man. Every penny. I've had to pay for training and everything... I've spent every penny. You know how our deal was with Williams, it was a gentleman's agreement..."

"No, don't tell me this," Gussie began. "You said you had a deal with him."

"Yeah, but you know I couldn't have a proper management deal, because I haven't got a licence have I?"

"Okay, just give it to me straight Courtney, am I going to see any of my investment back?"

"That was what I was phoning about," said Courtney nervously, "I was hoping that you could send me a couple of hundred quid to fly back home with..."

GUESS WHO'S COMING TO XMAS DINNER?

The closer it got to Christmas, the more Pauline terrorised Johnny's telephone. He was trying to keep a distance from her, because of the seasonal commitments he had with his Number 1 family, but it was becoming difficult. Personally, he didn't celebrate Christmas or 'Kiss-Me-Raas!' as he preferred to call it, because he didn't want to tell his children lies. "You can't tell your children not to lie and then you start lying to them about "kiss-me-raas", he told anyone who would listen. "You gotta practice what you preach." He would much rather that he Lesley, Winnie and the baby celebrated Kwanzaa together. That would have been more conscious. They would have given each other more meaningful presents, not just toys and expensive goods. Besides, he figured that he worked very hard to buy presents and he didn't intend to give the credit to a fat guy who comes down the chimney. "After all, I don't remember Jesus Christ mentioning 'santa claws'!" The way Johnny saw it, the whole season of goodwill was just a money-making business. In fact, he knew 'nuff man who claimed that the actual 'kiss-me-raas' day was a pagan worship day, the day when Nimrod in the Bible, who worshiped false gods, would celebrate. "Blessed be the man that walketh not in the council of the ungodly," he would tell shopkeepers trying to sell him Christmas cards. And when people who didn't know him very well sent him Christmas cards, he would open them then put them in the bin. He understood the vibes and on one level, it's the thought that counts. But he just wasn't into the cards business. Normally, he wouldn't even open those envelopes, because Christmas cards always came in envelopes with the queen's head the right way up, whereas his friends always stuck the stamp upside down. Johnny was the kind of guy who liked to reason that the way a person stuck the queen's head on an envelope told you a lot about where that person was coming from.

And another thing, Johnny's diet was becoming

increasingly vegetarian and he didn't agree with turkey at Christmas and doubted if the turkey would agree with him. The turkey loved its life as much as Johnny loved his, "I don't want to have to eat all that flesh and bones and the batty and all the isms and schisms," he explained to Lesley, "me nuh inna it..." If anything, he would eat fish, but the way he was thinking at the moment, he would rather fast on Christmas Day. Why? "Why not?" Because Christmas was a day when everybody else was scoffing their faces and it would be an appropriately symbolic day to fast. "It would be a way of saying to God that we don't get involved with this heathen business. Me personally would prefer reading my Bible that day and you and Winnie should get involved too."

Lesley ignored him. She had heard the same thing every year for several years, but she always got her way in the end.

To Johnny, Kwanzaa was an altogether preferable way to celebrate. After all, it was a black holiday. It was a more meaningful tradition, related to the harvest season. Kwanzaa meant 'first fruits' and reflected the ancient times when Africans offered the first fruits of their harvest unto God and gave thanks. The descendants of those ancient men and women and children were now, in increasing numbers, giving up their offerings same way. That made more sense to Johnny. And the seven candles of Kwanzaa representing the light of our ancestors made more sense to him too. To Johnny, Kwanzaa would have brought his family together as Africans. Discussing the seven principles would have given him the opportunity to tell Lesley what he really felt about her and would, he was sure, open her heart to him. But it wasn't to be Kwanzaa. Lesley didn't see anything wrong with celebrating Christmas. Winnie especially, wasn't too keen on not enjoying Christmas just like all her friends at school did.

The first time Pauline called, it was about 4.a.m. Luckily Johnny was woken by the ring of the phone, which in his deep slumber sounded like a trumpet blowing in his ear. He jumped up reflexively and, still half-asleep, mumbled something into the mouthpiece. What came back in the earpiece was loud and clear:

"I've run out of money. I need some. When are you going to give it to me?"

Johnny tried to shake the sleep out of his eyes. The room was dark and everybody else in the house was asleep. Why was he standing with the phone at his ear? Was he sleepwalking? What was going on? He heard Pauline's voice, and he heard the words, but he couldn't make sense of it all. But he was waking slowly and wasn't too happy about how the situation was adding up. He tried to feel his way around in the pitch darkness of the living room. Even though he didn't smoke, it seemed like a good time to have a cigarette and he was sure he had seen a packet lying around earlier.

"Didn't I tell you not to call me here?" was all he could manage in a soft tone.

"So how the hell am I supposed to get in contact with you when the baby needs his father, enh? You live there, don't you?"

"But I told you not to call me here," he repeated forcefully.

"I SAID I NEED SOME BLASTED MONEY AND I NEED IT NOW!!"

That message got through loud and clear. He was awake now.

"What's it got to do with me," he croaked softly in reply.

"WHATDDYA MEAN WHAT'S IT GOT TO DO WITH YOU?!!"

Pauline's voice roared. Johnny winced and held the receiver three inches out.

"Okay... Okay. Fine. I'll sort something out in the morning."

"What's wrong with right now?"

"WHAT'S WRONG WITH RIGHT NOW!" Johnny found himself raising his voice despite himself. Then he

183

remembered where he was and the last thing he wanted to do was wake Lesley up. "Look," he continued quietly, "I was sleeping... I'm really tired. I need a few hours more sleep... Busy day tomorrow..."

"Yeah, yeah, yeah. Excuses, excuses. Look Johnny, I'm warning you... If you're not here by nine in the morning with at least sixty quid, you're in trouble. And you know what I mean!"

Yeah, yeah, yeah, he knew what she meant. It was the same threat everytime. If he stepped out of line, she'd report him to the CSA, give them his home address, his work telephone number and everything. She had him by the balls and knew exactly how to squeeze them to cause maximum pain.

The money that he got out the next morning, was his special savings account money. Basically, it was money to cover the extra cost of Christmas, the Christmas he didn't even want to celebrate. How was he going to get the money to pay for the Christmas tree and the decorations and the Christmas dinner and all the presents he was going to have to get? So without thinking about it he went to the bank drew out the money and sent it by minicab to Pauline's address, before he had time to change his mind.

Sometimes he felt like that. Sometimes he really felt like telling her to go and stuff herself. Because the way she was going on was far too distressing for him. If it wasn't for the fact that she was the mother of his son, he would have gone to see an obeah man by now and got him to put some spell on her to make her cross-eyed or something.

Johnny's mind wasn't on his work for the rest of that day. His mind was on money and how to make a little more. He had already been down to the bookies to place a combination bet. He had tipped five horses to finish first or second in their races. Three races were gone and he was on course for a large sum of money to cover his £10 stake.

When he laid himself down to sleep on the living room sofa that night, the last thing Johnny expected was to be awakened yet again in the wee hours by his errant baby mother. As he drifted into a deep slumber, somewhere in the back of his consciousness the incessant purr of the telephone triggered a reaction. Once again, Johnny jumped up in the early morning darkness, still not awake. Sleepwalking, he picked up the phone before it woke the whole house up and answered, "Yeah, hello," mechanically. Down the earpiece came a stream of distress which jolted him quickly into the here and now. It was Pauline.

"That money's done, you know," came the sour tone down the line. "I need some more."

"WHAT??!!"

"I said the money you sent me this morning, it's all gone. What's wrong with you, you nevah clean out your ears?"

"But how...? I sent sixty quid in the cab."

"Sixty quid, how far do you think that's going to get me? I had to buy your son a Christmas present with that money..."

"Christmas present for sixty pounds! The kid's not even a year old! What kind of a present does he get for sixty pounds?"

"Well, a push chair actually... It's a present that he's needed for some time now, if you even bothered to find out."

Johnny sighed.

"So how much do you need now?" he asked coldly.

"At least a hundred," Pauline replied, equally coldly.

"A HUN...!" he caught his voice just as it was about to erupt and wake the whole house. "A hundred?!" he said more softly. "A hundred quid?!" He just couldn't believe what he was hearing.

"I SAID I AIN'T GOT NO BLASTED MONEY!" Pauline exploded down the line. "WHAT DO YOU THINK YOUR SON'S GOING TO HAVE FOR CHRISTMAS IF I HAVEN'T GOT ANY MONEY?!"

"Yeah, but a hundred pounds..." Johnny tried to be reasonable now.

"This is your son's first Christmas," Pauline spat out. "I

want him to be a normal child. I want him to be able, later on in life, to look back at the photos and see that he had a huge Christmas tree on his first Christmas and turkey and pudding and everything else. So, I need to get a camera."

Johnny sighed. He knew what her game was, but what could he do. She was going to keep bleeding him dry...

"Okay, I gotta go," he said in a whisper. Pauline yelled down the phone some more, cussing him. "I said, I gotta go," Johnny repeated more hoarsely. He thought he heard a sound upstairs. He said that he would make sure she got the money the next day. She warned him that he better. He put down the phone and almost jumped out of his skin when he felt a hand touch his shoulder from behind. But it wasn't a duppie that frightened him. In the darkness of the living room, he heard Lesley's voice.

"Who were you whispering to?"

"Wha...? Oh Lesley, you scared the life out of me, I didn't see you coming up behind me like that." He could just make out her form in the darkness now. There was an eeriness about her and her cold voice sent a chill down his back. He was deliberating fast. He didn't know how long she had been standing behind him. Maybe she hadn't heard much. Lying was the only option he could think of because Lesley wouldn't appreciate Pauline calling up.

"You didn't answer my question..."

"What was that? Oh, the phone... I was talking to my mother."

"So how comes you were whispering to your mum at four in the morning, you never usually do that..."

"Well erm... I didn't want to wake the whole house up... She rang... She was worried about me... She had had a bad dream."

"Oh, I see..." Lesley said in a tone that said that she didn't believe a word of it. It was too dark for Johnny to see the expression on her face, but he knew she didn't believe him.

"Oh well I'm going back to bed," Lesley said with a yawn, turning to go. "And one more thing, if that baby mother of yours ever calls this house again, you're out. I don't want that bitch phoning my house at this time of night or any other time for that matter. Johnny, I don't care what foolishness you've got your life in, but I don't want that woman phoning my house... MAKE SURE!!! I don't want your problems affecting my children."

With that, Johnny heard Lesley's footsteps disappear out of the room and up the stairs. It was crazy. Why had he lied? Was he man or mouse? According to the King James version of the Bible, God gave man dominion over all things, why could he not have dominion within his own home? He tasted salt water on his upper lip. Why was he sweating?

Whether he liked to celebrate it or not, Christmas time was an extremely busy time for Johnny. Books were flying out of the Book Shack as quickly as he could ring up the till. One of the things Johnny liked especially about Kwanzaa was it's 'Recycle The Black £' philosophy, which obliged you to buy only from black stores for a month. That was a squeeze that he and every small black businessman needed to carry them through for the rest of the year, just as even smaller black traders relied on the Carnival to inject much needed capital into their funds until the next Carnival. It made Johnny feel proud that black people were prepared to support "dem one another." Books were the natural Kwanzaa and Christmas gift, you couldn't go wrong and if you were on the conscious tip, it had to be a black book. So the customers were in and out buying £50 worth of books and sometimes more. It was crazy, they kept running out of stock of certain books and Johnny had to re-order one particular novel three times in one week. There was more money in the till than he knew what to do with. Some of it he banked, some of it he never banked. That which went in his pocket, often ended up in the bookie's till, as Johnny tried to predict the future with the gee-gees. He was looking for that big win, the one that had to come because all the punters had told him he should be expecting a big win round about now... Mellow had promised him as much and with all the distress that Pauline was giving him recently with wanting money every other day, he was finding it hard to keep up with only his salary

Christmas Day came around. Johnny had managed to buy all the presents and trimmings. He still maintained that he wasn't going to partake in the turkey runnings, so Lesley had to deal with that. But she was pleased to see that he had taken his duties well-enough to not only buy his daughter a stereo for her room, but had even bought his woman a two-year-old Volkswagen Golf so that she wouldn't have to keep juggling on the bus with the baby. It was the kind of surprise that she wasn't expecting. He was already awake on the sofa in the living room when she came down early on Christmas morning. He had a big cheeky grin on his face and she knew something was up. He asked her if she wanted her present now or later. She said later would do, but he was so eager, he convinced her to have it now. Then he blindfolded her, led her to her own bedroom window upstairs, took off the blindfold and pointed to a new model grey Golf outside.

"You and the baby get to share a Christmas present this year," he said with a smile, "one that you both could use."

Lesley forgot herself for a moment and cried out excitedly and jumped up and hugged him around his neck. The noise brought a sleepy Winnie to the room, wondering what was going on. Her mother told her and Winnie hugged her father around the waist. With a grin, Johnny said that she could save her hugs for her own present. Now Winnie was excited. If Mum got a car, what was she going to get? She wanted her present now, she couldn't wait. But her father made her wait. Or at least another five minutes of torture anyway. When Winnie finally unwrapped the 'boom box', she couldn't believe it either. She jumped up onto her father, hanging from his neck and knocking him back on the double bed and kissing him all over his face and hugging him even tighter. Here they all were, or at least nearly all. Baby Jacob was still in his cot, sleeping soundly, unaware of all the fuss in the room. But to Johnny this was the most pleasant time he had had with his family for a long, long time. Both his women, one either side of him, just kicking back, close to each other. They really were a family. Maybe Christmas wasn't all that bad after all, he considered.

The whole day seemed to be perfect. Johnny still kept his vow to spend some of the time reading his Bible, but by lunchtime, they came together at the table and talked of the good times and their hopes for the future and the New Year. Everything had been going so sweet, that when the phone rang, Johnny was without a care in the world.

"SO HOW COMES YOU HAVEN'T BEEN ROUND?!"

In seven short words, Johnny's bliss was shattered.

"Whh...wha..?" He looked back at Lesley at the dining table. She smiled back at him sweetly. He was caught. He couldn't say anything.

"ARE YOU DEAF? I SAID, WHY HAVEN'T YOU BEEN ROUND?!"

"Bbb-but..." Lesley was still smiling sweetly. Johnny tried to mask what he was saying by turning his back to her but he could still feel her smiling sweetly and it made him uncomfortable. So he decided to play it a little way different.

"Oh hi Gussie... Yeah, wassup?!" he said loudly.

Pauline at the other end of the line was asking him what the raas he was talking about 'Gussie' for, she wanted to know why he wasn't around at her yard seeing his son on Christmas Day.

"Oh but Gussie, I thought you had other plans for today," Johnny continued loudly. He turned to Lesley and winked at her, then covering the mouthpiece, whispered to her, "It's Gussie... all alone on Christmas Day... you know how it is."

"Well tell him to come round," Lesley said.

"No... he doesn't want to come round... he's asking me whether I want to come out... I told him of course not, it's Christmas Day and I'm here with my family..."

He returned to the conversation on the phone.

"Yeah, you were saying Gussie...?"

Pauline repeated in no uncertain terms what she was saying. Yes, she had plans for Christmas Day but that didn't get Johnny out of his responsibilities to come and see his son... Johnny had better come by or else...!

Johnny's ears were still ringing from Pauline's mouthful when he turned to the dining table for the rest of Christmas lunch.

"Gussie... you know," he said to Lesley apologetically. "That's what comes from being a bachelor and not having a family of your own... He doesn't realise that most people are at home spending time with their loved ones. He thinks Christmas is just another day to go raving."

"You can go out with him if you want to, you know," Lesley said.

"No don't be stupid... I wouldn't dream of it."

"No really," Lesley insisted. "I know he must be feeling left out of things and you are friends after all. Me and the kids can go by to my mum's. She wanted us to drop by some time today anyway, so that she could see the kids. Now that I've got the car, I wouldn't mind taking it for a spin, anyway."

"Well, if you really think so..." Johnny said. And he joked, "You know your mother would probably prefer to see you and the kids without me...."

"Yeah," Lesley agreed, "you're probably right."

So it was arranged, and a half an hour later, Johnny took his leave and said he wouldn't be too long. He'd just go and keep Gussie company for a while and return.

It was difficult getting a cab on Christmas Day and when he finally got one, the driver said that no way was he going from Brixton to North London for less than a nifty, in other words a fifty. Johnny tried to reason with him, but it did no good. The man explained that he was giving up his Christmas with his family to be able to do a public service. "That doesn't come cheap. How would you like to spend the whole of Christmas Day driving a cab, eh?"

Johnny agreed that he wouldn't and that he had to make

it worthwhile for the driver.

Because it was Christmas Day, the London streets were more or less empty, even at this time of the afternoon. It only took half an hour for them to drive all the way from Brixton to Pauline's flat in Edmonton. Johnny paid the man and made his way up in the lift.

Pauline opened the door and for a moment, just stood there, squinting her eyes at him and blocking his way.

He held up the palm of his hands to her as if to ask, 'Wassup?'

'Wha'ppen, yuh nuh buy me no Chrismuss card, enh?"

Johnny had to admit that he hadn't. And no present either. Pauline kissed her teeth and looked to the heavens as if to say 'God, give me strength'. She finally relented and stepped aside to let him in.

As he stepped into her house, a delicious waft of Caribbean cooking floated out and tickled his nostrils, wet his appetite and twisted a pang of hunger in his stomach, but however hungry it made him, Johnny knew better than to eat food off of Pauline's plate. He had refused to eat any food at her house since the day he caught her sprinkling some 'Oil of Love' in his dinner. He had never liked her cooking anyway. She was the kind of woman whose cooking depended on a pressure cooker, yet she still managed to burn everything.

She led him into the living room from where a reggae record was bouncing loudly. Johnny recognised the song as one by a Jamaican female deejay who sang a long moan about a good man being hard to find. Whether those were Pauline's sentiments or not, it didn't take long for recriminations to start to fly about the place. Even before he had managed to take a seat on the sofa, she stated in no uncertain terms that she considered Johnny worthless, or more precisely, 'wotless'.

"I don't want my son to be like you, you're no flipping role model!"

Johnny could have said the same thing but vice versa. He

certainly didn't want Jude to be like his mother.

"You send fifty pounds every week for your son, how long do you think that's going to last? You're crazy. That won't even last for the nappies. How about food, eh? Or did you forget that Jude needs to eat? Or did you think because I was breastfeeding him, the food was free? And then what about clothes and transport? What about all the taxis I have to take when I go out anywhere? Or do you expect me to carry a child and a pushchair on a bus? Fifty pounds a week?! You're joking aren't you? And then after all that you start talking some nonsense about not being able to make it to see your son on Christmas Day, because you've got some other family somewhere else. You should have thought about all that before you got me pregnant, shouldn't you."

Johnny threw up his hands frustrated. She had wanted to see him and he was here. He was here to reason not to fight.

"That's what pisses me off about you," he told her, "sometimes you don't have no understanding."

She laughed out loud in his face. What did he want her to understand? Wasn't it him that needed the understanding? "You should just slow down for a moment and take a look at yourself," she said. "You think you can just go about having children all about the place, but have you ever sat down to count the cost?" It was a challenge as much as anything else.

If she only knew how many times he had counted the cost, Johnny sighed. But right now, the question of how much contribution he should be making to Jude's upkeep wasn't one that he could enter into. He was paying as much as he could afford to pay. He wasn't Gussie, he didn't have money coming out of his ears. How was he going to be able to afford more than he could afford? If he didn't tread carefully, she'd get onto that old CSA argument and his goose would be cooked so for the moment, she had him over a barrel. The only thing to do was pacify her. He moved closer to the other side of the sofa where she sat and put a reassuring arm around her.

"Don't touch me!" she hissed, shrugging him off. "Don't

touch me... and I mean it...! I don't even know what you're doing here."

By this point Johnny could see that he was on a hiding to nothing. However reasonable he tried to be it seemed it would do no good, not when the woman was in this kind of mood. She had her war paint on and she was ready for battle.

"Do you want me to leave?" he asked eventually. "Is that it? Do you want me to leave?"

"That's up to you. If you leave, that's probably what you wanted to do in the first place. If you really cared about your responsibilities you wouldn't leave. Not on Christmas Day. You would stay and sort them out."

What the hell did all this mean? He could leave but he couldn't? Every which way he turned there seemed to be nothing waiting for him but pure frustration.

"You see Johnny, this isn't about money, whatever you may think. This is about responsibility. It's time for you to grow up and take care of your responsibilities. Jude is your responsibility and he costs."

"He's not my only responsibility, you know. You're forgetting that I do have other responsibilities. Two other pickneys that need feeding. They cost money too."

"That's your problem," Pauline replied coldly. "All I'm concerned about is my son. And I'm going to make sure that you pay for him."

"Correction, that we both pay for him."

"Oh no, you can't get me on that. Not unless you want to pay for the cost of a full-time nanny. Because I'm paying my part already by looking after him. I paid more than enough by giving birth to him. Did you ever consider that, Johnny?" From the look on his face, he obviously hadn't, or if he had, he didn't think it was that big a deal. "No, you're not able to comprehend things like that. You see, all you were good for was sex and stress."

Now it was her turn to distress him.

"I'll need a long-deserved vacation very soon," she

suggested, "and it would be a good idea if you started saving for it from now on. I'll need to go by February, to get away from the cold. I want to go somewhere warm otherwise I'll get depressed."

Johnny held his head in grief. Pauline simply continued: "You've got to understand, Johnny, that it is really hard work bringing up a child on your own. If you had to do it, you'd also need a break. It can't be good for Jude if I'm stressed all the time..."

"Alright, alright...yeah yeah yeah...Alright alright..."

That was all Johnny could say. Any other comment would have elicited a response from her such as: "Wha' you ah deal wid... you're not taking care of your yout and the 'let off sump'n' runnings well soft."

"You ought to know that if I had corn you would get it, but as it is the bottom's run down on the one pair of shoes I own!"

That didn't impress Pauline too tough. Their relationship had gone one step beyond her harassing him for money. She now regarded him as a credit card.

Johnny said he wanted to see his son. Pauline led him to the nursery, where little Jude was asleep in his cot. Jude was still a tiny baby. Even though he was exactly the same age as his brother Jacob, Jude was only half the size. But he was healthy, that was the main thing. Johnny lived to see his son's lop-sided grin, which marked him as a true Lindo. And he would still laugh happily when little Jude wrinkled his nose in that same way he did.

While Johnny cradled his little son gently in the living room, Pauline explained that she wanted to go back to her job as a salesperson for a large pharmaceutical company, but that the more she worked it out, the more unlikely it seemed. She had been on extended maternity leave for more than a year now and she was tired of sitting at home bringing up baby. But going back to work would mean getting up at six in the morning to get Jude ready to take him to a nanny and it would mean picking him up at 8.00 in the evening and then feeding him and taking care of him until he went to sleep and then falling asleep herself for a few hours before the whole process would start again.

"I would be working almost non-stop. I would be on auto pilot most of the time."

No that definitely couldn't work. And the fact that Johnny offered to take care of Jude at weekends didn't help either.

"You really need to spend all the time with your son to understand what it means to have a child," Pauline said, "what it means to have him wake up every twenty minutes when he can't sleep very much. You've got to live with him full-time to understand that a child is someone demanding all your time and energy without giving anything back."

For all of her sexual attraction, Pauline was only supposed to have been a one night stand. Johnny met her at one of Gussie's buppie parties She was an engineering graduate from Birmingham who had moved down to London when she got the job with the pharmaceutical company. She was single and said she didn't have time for a serious relationship because she was dedicated to her job. And that all she required from a man was that his wood was long and satisfied her three or four times a day. When she made her interest in Johnny obvious, he found it too good to resist. She certainly knew what to do with her body and told Johnny not to waste "good grinding time" with compliments.

It was nice, but to Johnny, not half as nice as when he made love with Lesley.

That one night of hot passion was to cost him dearly however. Too dearly, some would say. For shortly after, Pauline presented him with the news that she was pregnant with his child.

The birth affected her health. At first she tried to juggle motherhood and her pharmaceutical career, but she soon discovered that 'Superwoman' is a myth.

Before the baby, her life was carefree and contented, she

visited a health club three times a week and was never off sick from work and just as she was beginning to look and feel wonderful, she got pregnant.

Her immediate reaction was excitement. The older you get, the more children become an essential part of your ego. Everybody else your age has them and that's all they talk about. But then as she realised that she had a baby but no father to share in his upbringing, her health began to fail. As a result she nearly lost Jude in the 14th week and had to be hospitalised for a couple of weeks. She had fibroids which were growing quicker than the baby, yet she was determined to go through with the pregnancy.

The months of worry were phenomenal. But Johnny was rarely around to share them with her. Instead, she was getting unwelcome advice from everybody else. She didn't return to work straight away after Jacob was born because she wanted to enjoy some time with him first. The pregnancy was too painful for her and when she recovered afterwards, decided she was not a natural mother and would never go through it again. People might say her son would be lonely as an only child, but he would have to cope with it. And though she loved Jude more than anything in the world, the baby had totally disrupted her life and she was still not used to it. Sometimes she would imagine that he didn't exist, only to come to her senses and realise that she really appreciated him. She had no regrets. He was a bright, bubbly child and often cheered her up when she was feeling miserable. When she was bemoaning the fact that she no longer had time for her friends and their problems. She hardly went out anymore, except when her African boyfriend offered to babysit for her. Inviting a friend around for dinner was nearly all the social life she got.

Johnny didn't like to hear that the African boy that Pauline was shacked up with was being left alone with his son. But what could he do? Still cradling his son, Johnny offered to contribute for the cost of a part-time nanny if Pauline wanted to go back to work. All in all, it would make the financial burden on him lighter if she could bring home some corn as well.

"You're damn right, you'll contribute, you're paying all of it. It would be letting you off the hook otherwise."

Johnny had had enough.

"There's one thing you've got to get straight, Pauline. You cyaan keep skinning me financially. I'm not your boops, you know. I do have another family somewhere else to support as well."

Pauline was silent for a while and just stared at Johnny with fire in her eyes. Finally she said slowly:

"So you're going to leave me aren't you?"

"What? Leave you? What's there to leave?"

"Whether you like it or not, we are together... Jude binds us together, like an umbilical cord."

"Wha'..?!"

That wasn't what Johnny wanted to hear. He had thought that Pauline had got beyond that long time. He decided to spell it out to her once and for all.

"Look, my life isn't here with you Pauline, it's down in Brixton with Lesley. And if everything works out, I think you should know, I intend to marry her."

Pauline broke down in tears unexpectedly. Johnny wouldn't have said that if he could have anticipated Pauline's reaction. But how was he to know that she had always hoped that despite everything, he would one day be a proper father to her son? How was he to know how much she feared that married to another woman, Johnny would withdraw more and more from Jude. How was he to know that Pauline couldn't bear to hear Lesley's name mentioned, refused to hear it. He tried his best to comfort her and embraced her reassuringly. But he didn't know what to say.

"I'm thirty-years-old, Johnny," Pauline sobbed, "and I'm not getting any younger. I'm too old to be the 'other woman'. And it's unfair on Jude to be the 'illegitimate' child..."

He tried to tell her that it wasn't like that.

"You've got your own life to lead, Pauline. What about

your African bwoy? He's there for you. You don't have to think of yourself as 'the other woman' to anybody. And as far as I'm concerned, Jude is as much my child as any of my other pickney. It's just that my other family needs me more, because they've always had me there for them. Whereas you and Jude haven't always had me, so what you haven't had you won't miss."

That didn't go down too well with Pauline either. Johnny had to hug her some more to stop the sobbing. Eventually she calmed down and looked up at him through tearful eyes.

"You've always treated me worse than you treated her... You never did say you love me. Not once. You've never bothered to fuss over me or to try to make me feel special. You've just treated me like I was nothing more than a baby mother. And the way you talk to me sometimes... I hate you when you try and talk down to me as if I haven't got brains of my own... You told me to have the kid, so I didn't dash 'way the belly. I carried your son for nine months and gave birth to him and now you treat me like it wasn't anything..."

Pauline was deep in moody thought, feeling dejected and rejected. Johnny wanted to make her feel better but he still didn't know what he could say without committing himself to something that he didn't want to. He didn't want to feel guilty, but at the same time he had to make it clear, that it was out of order calling him at Lesley's house. Lesley didn't appreciate it. How would Pauline like it, if Lesley called her flat to speak to him?

"So how am I supposed to get hold of you when I need to?" Pauline asked seething.

"Well you can always call me at The Book Shack, you've got the number, what's wrong with calling me there?"

"But you're not always there, are you?" Pauline spelled it out for him. "What do I do when something happens and there's an emergency, say Jude is ill in the evening or on a Sunday when you're not at your book shop? What do I do when I need to speak to you and you're not there...?"

Johnny had an answer for that one.... He had been

considering it over the last few days. Now that he was flush with money he could afford to get a mobile phone.

"Every Tom Dick and Harry has one now. Even young pickney of all thirteen and fourteen are walking up and down Peckham High Street with their mobile phones. It looks foolish when all big man like me still never have one."

Pauline excused herself a minute, she had to wash the tears off her face. With a sashay of her hips, she hurried out to the bathroom. Meanwhile, Johnny went and laid the sleeping Jude in his cot. He had to make a move back to his yard, before it got too late.

To his surprise, Pauline returned having slipped out of her white dress and was now wrapped in a bathrobe. He glimpsed lovely thighs and the margins of tight panties as she walked up to him. "I've got to go," he said quickly, looking deep into her dark eyes.

"That's alright," she said," wiping a final tear from her eye. "You go... Thanks for coming... Call me, let me know your mobile number when you get it."

She embraced him briefly. He could feel the heave of her breasts.

"Take care," she said, whispering in his ear, "I wouldn't want anything to happen to you. Jude needs his father alive."

Pauline's voice dripped sweetness. It had a rough, sex-heavy tone to it. She continued:

"You know what's funny about all of this? There's nothing she can do for you that I can't do for you..."

A wet tongue darted in Johnny's ear. He felt himself stiffen below the waistline, but there was nothing he could do. She felt it too and recoiled slightly. Then, without warning, she undid the belt that held the bathrobe around her together and let it fall to the ground. The robe parted. Like a man who was seeing a naked woman for the first time in years, Johnny's tongue hung out. He gazed down at her breasts, inches away, with the nipples perked up. Johnny found himself thinking that nature hadn't given her a heavy-

Patrick Augustus

busted body for nothing. Suddenly her arms circled his neck, pulling down his head and whispering that she was going to thrill him with it. His lips pressed hard and willingly against hers. Her body writhed under his hard kiss.

What was he doing? He had sworn never to sleep with Pauline again. Pauline was a vixen with a bitch's mind. An unpredictable woman who could really mess up his life. Why was he allowing himself to enjoy this deep, passionate kiss? Why didn't he restrain his hands from wandering over her ample breasts? And wasn't that a plastic smile on her face, or were his eyes too closed?

Suddenly as they were locked in their passionate embrace, they heard the lock in the front door turn. For a moment they stared at each other in a protracted, stiff silence, unable to move. Their magic moment shattered into a million pieces as Pauline's African boyfriend walked in.

"What the fff...?!" he began marching towards them.

"Let me explain..." Johnny began.

"Yeah, yeah, yeah," the African said, raising a bulky fist and sending it crashing into Johnny's left eye.

"Ouch!"

Being angry with Pauline for making things bad for him wouldn't help. It wasn't anger, anyway, or pride, or anything like that. Johnny was not proud. He was hurt though, his eye throbbed like crazy and it had begun to swell up. Sometimes the only way you can deal with hurt is through comfort. By the time Lesley got back with Winnie from visiting her mother in her new Volkswagen Golf, it was already midnight and Johnny was in need of some tender loving comfort. Christmas Day had been a painful one.

He told Lesley that he had walked into a parking meter on the street. He didn't know whether she believed him, all he wanted was for her to hug him. Too afraid to be rejected by her yet again, he hoped that she would realise it of her own accord.

Winnie was tired, but not too tired to go up to her room

and test out her new boom box, before going to bed. Jacob was asleep in his cot. Johnny and Lesley sat next to each other on the sofa, the closest they had been for months, watching TV. It was a live satellite link with Jamaica, where the station was allowing people to send their Christmas wishes to their friends and relatives back in the UK. The programme was sponsored by the Jamaican Tourist Board who were trying to attract more people to visit the island. A recent TV documentary portraying Jamaica in a negative light had resulted in a twenty-five percent fall in holiday bookings for the year and the entire island had united to rebuild the damage done by the film. As a result, holidays to Jamaica were currently very cheap.

The scenes from a hot Jamaica on Christmas, got Johnny dreaming. "Wouldn't it be great if we could take a luxury trip to the Caribbean or somewhere like that? And when we get older we can retire back home. We can get a little house up in the hills, with a cool stream running by and a few goats and rams in the yard. The quiet life, you know."

"I'm tired of helping you dream your dreams, Johnny. Stop dreaming and just sort your life out."

Lesley may have been delighted with her Christmas present, but she wasn't that grateful.

"...And anyway," she continued, "when I think of the future, I don't always see you there. I don't know if we will grow old together. Sometimes I think I want to be in love with someone else."

"Wh...what? When did you decide that?"

"Oh the decision was made for me the moment I learned that I could never trust you."

"There you go again," Johnny protested, "you keep downing me and expecting me to do wrong."

"That's because I know you Johnny. I keep saying that and you don't realise just how much I know you. I know what you're thinking even before you've thought it. I've caught you so many times looking at other women's chests on the street. Or you think I don't notice? Don't worry, I know it's not your fault, everybody notices another human being. I notice handsome men as well, but I just know that you'll never change. I know you expect people to pick up your mess after you Johnny, but you have to take care of that and to ask yourself some serious questions. You need to look in the mirror and take a good look at yourself."

Having the baby had changed Lesley's life. Johnny hadn't realised just how much. Like most men he assumed, during pregnancy that his woman's thoughts were consumed by the first swelling, what colour the nursery should be or what brand of nappies she should use and because she had been in labour before and knew all the signs, he figured he didn't have to be around twenty-four seven as he had been when she was carrying Winnie. Once she had given birth, Johnny assumed she was content with washing nappies and breastfeeding.

It had been ten years since her last child however and Lesley had totally forgotten how painful breastfeeding could be. But she was still doing it after nearly a year nevertheless. Jacob was always keen to get at his mother's breast and more often than not, rejected the bottle in preference to Lesley's natural milk. Eventually she had to bandage her breasts, so that he couldn't smell them but he would still tear at her clothes to get at them. All in all though, she was enjoying motherhood much more this second time around. She was more motivated than she had been when Winnie was a baby. Maybe it was because she was older, or that she was just a naturally pushy mother. She hadn't been able to cope with the hectic lifestyle of a mother the first time around, because she was too insecure. Now all that was gone. Even though there were still times when she wondered whether motherhood was all it was cracked up to be or whether the sacrifices were too great, Jacob was a special child and his birth made her a new woman. A Superwoman.

By the time she wanted to go back to her job as a proof reader for a local newspaper, her job no longer existed. The paper had been taken over and they said they were deploying her to a new office and that the entire company was being reorganised and computerised. Though she had been very respected in her old job, her new boss, a woman, didn't believe she could handle the responsibilities any more. That first day back, she took Jacob to the child minder on her way to work, and broke down in tears. She couldn't believe it herself. She had grown so attached to him and felt dreadful leaving him. That and the fact that Lesley didn't fancy travelling to Surrey every morning for a job she no longer enjoyed, made her mind up for her. Besides, she was having to pay so much money for a nanny to look after Jacob when she was at work, that she was hardly making any money at the end of the month. She was working to stand still and not even enjoying it.

She still wanted to work with something however and she now knew exactly what that something was. She had spent so many hours at home with Jacob that she had watched her fill of Breakfast TV. In the afternoons, she usually listened to an afternoon play on the radio. They always thrilled her and one day she decided, "I can do that."

When Lesley put her mind to something, she usually followed it through. After a few cursory enquiries with friends of hers at the BBC, she discovered that you didn't need any special qualification to write these radio plays. In short, anyone could do it, and they were always looking for new talent. So she set about, putting her ambitions into practice. She started off by getting out some books on radio scriptwriting from the local library. To her surprise, there were several. And they were most informative. There was really nothing more to it, but to sit down and see it through. So she drew up a timetable, which she would stick to as much as Jacob would allow. Whatever else she decided, Jacob always came first and his desire to be fed or to have his nappy changed took precedence over everything else. She didn't like the term 'quality time', because whenever her son needed her, she had to be there for him. She just had to be totally flexible in the way she planned to lead her life, that was all.

She usually woke up at about 7 am just as Johnny was waking up downstairs. While he fed the kids, she would don her tracksuit and run for about four or five miles. Whenever her mother was around, she would take the opportunity to nip down to the local gym for a workout followed by a sauna and steam bath. She discovered that the jogging not only kept her fit, but it even cleared her mind and allowed her to think. She had even come up with the plot for her play in the steam room. And when her mother occasionally took Jacob overnight to give Lesley a break, she got even more work done.

By the time Johnny was off to work and Winnie had departed for school, she was at her word processor, with Jacob in her arms being breastfed as she typed out her story. In the afternoon, while Jacob took a nap, Lesley liked to concentrate on her writing projects. She would sometimes space out in the middle of the living room floor, reading through the work she had already typed out. When all was said and done, she concluded, working from home was the best option for a mother, but it wasn't the easy option financially. So it was a good job that Johnny was making a financial contribution to the household.

On the televison, Christmas in Jamaica was over for another year and was followed by Casablanca with Bogart and Bacall. Johnny's left eye had swelled so much, he could hardly see out of it now. If Lesley wasn't going to be nice to him after all he had been through tonight, she never would. What about the Volkswagen Golf, hadn't that softened her enough to make her nice to him? What about the fact that it was Christmas, the season of goodwill... What about that?

Once again he protested:

"What do I have to do to make you believe that I've changed. I'm not interested in other women. I want to make something of our relationship Lesley, I really do. I really want to make up for all the things I've done wrong. But when you keep downing me like this... It's frustrating, you know."

Lesley heard the quiver in his voice as he pleaded and decided that whether Johnny believed in the season of goodwill or not, she ought to at least try and be charitable. She took his hand in hers and spoke softly:

"There's no need to say all those things Johnny, because talk is cheap, don't you see? I know things aren't going to change between us. Oh, it would be great for a few weeks or a month or two, maybe even a year, but eventually things would be right back to the same square deal. They always are. That's the way it is with relationships. I've been doing a lot of research recently..."

Johnny could see she was convinced by her research and nothing he could say would change her opinion. She was an angry black woman who wouldn't let her man get away with anything. She had suffered too much to be other than but suspicious and take the whole thing with a pinch of salt. Okay, she didn't have any faith in him, okay, but she ought to know that it wasn't always going to be that way. That he was going to get his shit together. Meanwhile he just wished she would give him a little more air, a few more breaks and trust him a little bit more.

"I can't even trust you with money!" she exclaimed. "If you live in this house, you've got to pay your way. That's what we agreed when I took you back. So why am I having to make up for your shortcomings nearly every week? You've got no excuse, you're earning enough from the shop aren't you?"

"I manage to keep my head above water," he said defensively.

"That's because wood floats," she replied quickly.

"Are you trying to make a fool out of me?"

"Why should I take the credit?"

How could he tell her? How could he tell her that most of his money was going to maintain his baby mother's extravagant lifestyle? He couldn't tell her, so he had to accept that he was terrible with money and agree that if it wasn't for her they would be broke, they would lose their home and all their possessions. He even had to admit that it didn't seem to make sense when he added up all his income and his outgoings, it just didn't seem to make sense where all the money went. He made a mental note that in the New Year he would pay his friend Mr Bookies a lot more visits.

"Whatever else you want to say about me, you have to admit that I was always good in bed wasn't I?"

She admitted that he was good in bed but so what? "Life ain't just about satisfying your woman in bed... And by the way, your shit ain't that hot..."

Johnny was truly shocked to hear that. "What...?!" His shit wasn't that hot! What did she mean by that? He had to laugh, he was so embarrassed. It was the first time he had ever heard a criticism of his performance in bed. Lesley said that she hadn't wanted to say anything before because she didn't want to upset him too much – she knew that it would be hard for his ego to take.

"I'm two thousand times better than you, Johnny. In everything. You think you're so great in bed, and you probably are for a man. But you see, I can turn you on a lot easier than you can turn me on? Does that sound like you're better at sex than me? If you are so good at sex, how come you can you never last the full course? Why did you always leave me so unsatisfied?"

Johnny almost choked. Lesley was going too far now. He didn't mind her being two thousand times better than he was, that was fine, because he could always use that in his defence whenever he made a mistake in anything, but, "Bwoy!", he wasn't expecting her to go this far. He told her that she was saying all this from a long-faded memory anyway. How long ago was it since they last made love? How could she remember what he was like?

Lesley smiled at him mysteriously, looking deep in his eyes. At the same time the phone rang. He jumped up to reach it, but Lesley beat him to it. Johnny sat back down on the sofa deflated. Only one person could be ringing this late on Christmas Day. He waited nervously for Lesley to explode with anger.

But it didn't happen. It was Lesley's friend Alison, who just had to ring in the middle of the night, because she was feeling lonely having to spend the whole of Christmas night on her own, when everybody else was with their loved ones. Alison was a nurse at one of the big London hospitals and had worked a shift which lasted all of Christmas Day. Lesley tried to cheer her up. They were cracking jokes and exchanging stories. Lesley informed her friend that she was now an official car driver, while she sympathised with Alison that her boyfriend was far away in Gambia.

"Don't worry Alison," Lesley said, loudly enough for Johnny to hear, "A good man in Gambia is worth two wot'less men in Brixton... What? You have to go to bed with a teddy bear? I have to take a game with me. I've been taking the crossword to bed with me since my baby was born..."

"Ouch!" That one hurt Johnny almost as much as the swelling of his eye. There was no need for Lesley to tell everybody that nothing was happening sexwise. Johnny drowned his shame in a glass of Dragon Stout, but he really needed some chronic to help banish all the negative vibes from his mind.

Lesley spoke to her friend for another few minutes. Then a strange thing happened when she came off the phone. She simply turned to Johnny with a smile and without saying a word, took him by the hand and led him slowly up the stairs to her bedroom. Once inside, she proceeded to strip him naked. She unzipped his jeans and lifted his arms out of his shirt. His manhood stood to attention, almost bursting out of his briefs like the cannon on an armoured tank. Though he knew what was happening, Johnny was too afraid to ask why, in case he shattered the magic of the moment. But he couldn't hold off for much longer. It had been so long since he last slept with a woman, if he didn't enter her soon he was going to explode!

Before long, they were under the duvet together, she on

top of him.

"I'm a single woman and I can do as I please, when I please. Aren't you lucky that tonight I'm feeling pleased," Lesley smiled.

Johnny smiled too. He could hardly restrain himself, he had waited so long for this. But he had to restrain himself, he had to perform his best. Everything depended on it. As he entered his woman for the first time in nearly a year, he heard her earlier words ringing in his ear: "Your shit ain't that hot... YOUR SHIT AIN'T THAT HOT...'"

As they made sweet love together, the memory of all the doubts she had had to go through with Johnny came flashing back to Lesley. She remembered that first worrying suspicion that he was sleeping around. He thought she hadn't noticed when he came home time and time again, the smell of cheap perfume oozing from his neck and a hint of dark crimson lipstick on his upper lip. But she hadn't said anything. She had waited for him to explain it, but he hadn't said anything either. She wanted to confront him, but she knew that he would deny it and it would end up, as it often did, in an argument with Johnny protesting his innocence and claiming that she was paranoid or something. So she didn't mention her suspicions, but gave him the benefit of the doubt by saying nothing. She didn't want to row. She had just got confirmation from the clinic that she was pregnant and she wanted it to be a joyous occasion.

That was her first mistake. Her suspicions pursued her. All the more so because Johnny was regularly spending evenings away from home. Even while he kept assuring her that he was ecstatic over her pregnancy, he seemed not to understand that she wanted him there at home, with her every step of the way. It was too late for that now. The strain of trying for so long to make him want her had left her feeling lukewarm towards him. He would probably never really know how much she had loved him. As he fondled her breasts delicately, memories of love and passion flooding through his mind, she remembered how much he loved her breasts.

"I know I messed up, but I didn't plan it," Johnny whispered blissfully as he rocked her gently, determined to wipe the bad memories out of her heart for good.

Lesley put a finger up to his lips, "Shhhh, don't talk..."

She was so beautiful. He wanted to feel every part of her inside him. "Baby, baby, baby!" he moaned over and over. They were finally reunited. His eyes were moist with tears of joy. It felt so good.

In the background, soft music floated in from Winnie's room across the landing.

Before long, Johnny was moaning in hushed tones as he came to a wonderful orgasm.

"Oh, it was so beautiful... so beautiful," he whispered, kissing her all over, "you're the best... It was the most... It was..."

"It wasn't love, Johnny," Lesley interrupted. "It was sex."

NEW YEAR'S EVE

The fuller the moon, the brighter it shines and tonight, the full moon would shine bright over Brixton.

It was early evening and yet the High Street was bumper-to-bumper with traffic and everybody was sounding their horns. It was New Year's Eve and the whole of Brixton was weighing up the options for the evening. There were so many things to do.

After eating a hearty breakfast of porridge and fried dumpling and callaloo at the rastaman's shop in the market, Johnny had spent the day scouring the FM dial and taking notes of the raves advertised on the radio stations, legal and not so legal, listening out for the functions which sounded like they'd be pumping heavy around the midnight hour. He had just been down to Red Records to browse through all the flyers in the shop. There were 'nuff choices. Too plenty to mention. Johnny narrowed the options down to a handful. Night clubbing was an option, but Johnny would prefer to not go up town as he didn't like the fact that the reggae at those clubs got diluted the nearer to the West End you got. And because money was not in abundance, a party might be a better idea. On New Year's Eve, gate fees doubled.

Though he ignored the significance of the day, and if anything, he celebrated the Ethiopian New Year on January 7, Johnny couldn't ignore New Year's Eve night, because that was the day he and his friends met up, as was tradition. Nothing was allowed to stand in the way of their annual night on the town, neither history nor *her*story, nor a swollen eye.

When he had narrowed things down to one or two places, Johnny looked around for a phone box to call Beres as arranged, to show him what he was dealing with.

Johnny entered the call box and dialled the number. Beres came on the line sounding sleepy.

"Yes, me lion!" Johnny greeted him. "Wake up man, it's New Year's Eve. Wha' you ah deal wid?"

"Wha...? Oh sorry," Beres said with a yawn. "I've been so tired, I must have fallen asleep for a minute..."

"What! Are you not getting enough sleep?" Johnny joked. "Don't tell me Caroline has got you sleeping on the sofa!"

Realising that Beres had uttered no reply, Johnny thought it best to cut short his chuckle. He changed tack to the matter at hand: "I bet you haven't even bothered about checking out any parties tonight."

Beres admitted that he hadn't. He had altogether forgotten that they were going out raving.

"Aawww man!" Johnny cried. "What's wrong with everybody today? I called Gussie up and it was the same there. Said he'd been checking some woman last night, and she sweeted him up so, he was still recovering. Why do I always have to take care of the man dem?"

"So what are you planning for tonight?" Beres asked."Any ideas?"

"Yeah man. How you mean? Me have nuff ideas... Figured we should reach a hot club for the night..."

"Where? Up West?"

"Nah man, you know how dem places up there stay; they play too much pop and soda pop music."

Beres agreed. They needed something stronger for the New Year.

"So what about Linvall?" Beres asked.

"Yeah man, that's another thing... You waan see, I spoke to him earlier. And guess what? He says why don't we spend the night in for a change, and go around to his house for a chill evening. Because he can't make it out. Can you believe that? After all our arrangements. Says he's under manners, he's got to babysit."

"Well you can't blame him, that's not his fault."

"But his yout's a big boy now. Eleven-years-old, you know. He can look after himself. Linvall's getting distress from his woman if you ask me. That's what this is all about."

What incensed Johnny the most was that Linvall knew how important their annual raving on a New Year's Eve was.

After five years, it had become a tradition and as far as he was concerned, New Year's Eve wouldn't be New Year's Eve if he wasn't out painting the town red with his three spars. Beres was not as attached to tradition. He repeated that Linvall's predicament was understandable:

"At the end of the day, there's nothing wrong with us spending a quiet New Year's Eve together."

"Aaaahh, you're saarf!" Johnny interjected.

"It's got nothing to do with being 'soft', I'm just trying to be reasonable. Surely, the tradition is more about the fact that we four friends always try to see the New Year in together, rather than having to actually go out raving? And anyway, Gussie didn't show up last year either. It's no big thing, as long as the majority of us are there. If someone can't make it one year, that's alright."

Johnny wouldn't be put off that easily. He reckoned that they could still drag Linvall out. If they swung by his yard on the way out and reasoned with him, he'd see sense.

So it was, and round about eight in the evening Beres and Gussie, all spruced up in the former's car, arrived at Johnny's place. It would take them another hour to reach Linvall's, because after all Johnny wasn't quite ready. He still needed to "hol' a fresh" and didn't come out of the shower until he looked good and smelled good.

"Bwoy, what happened to your eye!" Gussie laughed when Johnny eventually emerged, sporting his shiner.

"I walked into a parking meter," Johnny replied sheepishly.

"Nah, that don't look like a parking meter to me," Gussie continued, laughing. "That looks like somebody t'umped you in the eye!"

Johnny warned Gussie to behave himself before climbing into the car. Then they sped off towards Linvall's.

Not being able to make it for the weekly football game was one thing, but not taking time out to see your spars was a separate matter altogether. Gussie had said as much to Linvall on the phone only a few days earlier, when his friend hinted that he might not be able to make the annual New Year's Eve night out with the lads.

"Yeah, I know you're under manners, man. I can understand. You're not able to get out and make moves as much as you used to. But come on Lin, this is us I'm talking about. The 'lads'. We go way back, man. Most definitely. And it's been weeks since anyone saw you. Don't tell me that doesn't bother you."

Linvall had to admit that it did. "But you can't understand what being 'under manners' means where Marcia's concerned, man. He who feels it knows it. This isn't just your normal stress factor. Marcia is much more subtle than that... Even when I come out of the bathroom, it's like she's got a stop watch on her and she can tell me exactly how long I've been in there..." he tried to explain.

"So what? Don't tell me you can't deal with that," Gussie teased down the phone line. "Believe me, when it comes to women, nobody knows the stress I've been through. Nobody knows but Jesus..."

There was a momentary pause on the line. Linvall understood that Gussie was referring to his record-breaking short marriage. All Linvall knew was that Gussie had married Chantelle in that memorable triple wedding with himself and Beres and that the marriage failed early on their honeymoon night. Gussie wouldn't say any more than that and although the rumours had been widespread, Gussie had made it clear on more than one occasion that he didn't want to talk about it. Linvall was too much of a friend to remind Gussie of his marriage.

"So what are you saying," Gussie asked eventually, "you gonna make an effort to make it on New Year's Eve?"

"Yeah, I'm gonna try," Linvall confirmed. "I'm gonna try, but it depends on how much room I get to manoeuvre in."

"Jeez!" came the frustrated exclamation down the line.

"Look, I said I'm gonna try, okay. Don't worry, I'll have everything under control."

"Well, the ball's in your court hombre."

"Don't worry," Linvall said again, "you'll hear from me, okay. Peace out."

Linvall replaced the receiver and sat down for a moment with his hand holding the sides of his temple in deep thought. He felt guilty, he really felt guilty. But at the same time the fellahs had to understand that his family was more important than his friends. Things had changed in his life. He still wanted to be the free spirit, raving and going out and everything else, but losing his family was too high a price to pay for doing those things. He didn't want to lose his friends either, so he tried to work out a compromise.

To Johnny, it still sounded like a cop out. Wasn't it Linvall who had been the most dismissive of Gussie when he didn't make it for their New Year's Eve ravings the previous year?

"What is the point of committing ourselves to seeing in the New Year as a foursome – forever – when someone always fails to show up? There have been times when I've found it difficult to make it too, but I've always come through nevertheless because I enjoy the opportunity to have a good time with my friends, dance to some music and admire the talent on display at the New Year's Eve raves. Sitting down at home having a drink together isn't the same thing."

Linvall opened the front door.

"Surprise!" Gussie cried raising the magnum bottle of champagne he had brought with him, and easing his way into the house past Linvall.

The friends made themselves comfortable in the living room. Linvall had been sitting by himself watching the TV. Lacquan was up in his room reading a book before bedtime.

"So how come you're babysitting? Wha' happen to Marce? And what happened to your old man? I thought he was staying over to babysit?" Johnny asked.

Linvall explained that his wife had insisted that she was going out this New Year's Eve, because for the past ten years she had sat at home babysitting Lacquan. This was her turn to go out and enjoy a New Year's Eve with her friends for a change. As for his father, the old man had said that he wasn't going out for the evening and would be able to stay at home with his grandson, but had changed his mind earlier that morning.

"Said an old friend of his had called to invite him over for a few drinks. But that's way up in the Harlesden side of things. Basically, I got stuffed."

"Dat couldn't happen inna fe me yard!" Johnny sang. "That's why I'm always showing unuh that you've got to manners your woman dem. Ah you run t'ings inna fe yuh yard. Every man is a king in his home. You see my woman, she couldn't tell me that I cyaan go out with my bredrin. No sah!"

Gussie had to agree and added that if that was what married life was all about, he wasn't in a hurry to try it out again. Then he went into the kitchen where he found a few glasses and helped himself to four cans of cold beer in the fridge. He returned to his friends in the living room and they each cracked open a can.

"My advice," Johnny continued, "is that we wait until Lacquan falls asleep and then we chip. There's a party I know about down in Camberwell. It's bound to still be running hot."

Linvall wasn't convinced with the suggestion. He had worked hard over the last few months to show Marcia that he was prepared to do his bit as a father for Lacquan. That kind of thing would just confirm her suspicions. It wasn't worth the distress.

"So wha', she pussy whip you?"

Linvall took umbrage with this. There were no weals on his back, he insisted. And from the state of Johnny's eye, it looked like he was the one who had taken a whipping. His impatience with Johnny was further increased when the latter pulled out a ready-rolled spliff from his jacket pocket and proceeded to light it. Why couldn't Johnny go out into the garden if he wanted to roll a spliff.

"Because you share a back yard with the police station,"

Johnny answered naturally. Then added, "You are pussy whipped and you know it. Bwoy, what some men are prepared to do for women!"

Linvall said he was more concerned that his father would come home and smell ganja in the place. And he didn't want Lacquan smelling it either. Not when they were trying to keep him on the straight and narrow.

"Wha' you ah deal wid?" Johnny asked. "Just remind your old man that the sacred herb was from creation and that if Peter Tosh can go an' light up his chalice inna Buckingham Palace, me don't see nut'n wrong with burnin' my fire, iya. As for 'Quan, man, dat yout' is safe. I don't know why you're worried about him so much. My smoking herbs ain't gonna do him no harm, neither is him staying at home by himself. He's eleven-years-old for crying out loud, if you're not careful he's going to grow up into a *maama* man."

Linvall insisted about the smoking. And with pressure from Beres and Gussie, who were telling him not to disrespect the man's house, Johnny reluctantly stubbed out the best part of a particularly wicked spliff. Still he was pretty charged already and made a mental note to commend his weed vendor for the quality of the product. He was even inspired to hum a verse or two of a popular ode to the sensi:

> *Drink up the Guinness, smoke up the chronic*
> *Gal start to bawl when you give her the tonic..."*

Johnny was in playful mood.

"Yaow, check this out," Gussie said, picking up the boxed game on the coffee table. He read the label: " 'Frustration'... So all the distress in your domestic life isn't enough, Linvall? You have to go out and buy a game called 'Frustration' to put you in the mood?"

"Naah, that's Lacquan's Christmas present," Linvall explained. "Wicked game though. You can laugh at it, but if you play it, I'm telling you, you won't stop playing until... until..."

"You're frustrated?" Beres offered.

"Exactly!"

Johnny took that as a challenge. There wasn't a board game invented which he couldn't win. Gussie took Johnny's challenge as an even more audacious challenge. He reminded his friend that that was what he had claimed before Gussie soundly thrashed him at chess, even though Johnny introduced some impromptu house rules such as 'black always moves first'.

The others laughed. They were all well aware of Johnny's Afrocentric view of the world.

"And it ain't no joke neither," Johnny said sombrely.

"No but it's funny," Gussie teased, with a wink of the eye.

Johnny didn't think it was funny either, but sipped at his beer thoughtfully, unsmilingly.

"In my yard, black always moves first and that's the way it's going to stay."

The atmosphere had suddenly sunk. It was only a game; why did Johnny have to get so serious, and on New Year's Eve and all? To lighten things up, Linvall took up the earlier challenges and threw in one of his own. None of them could touch him when it came to 'Frustration', he said. The others laughed. That was a challenge none of them could refuse.

The game was basically Ludo, except that you couldn't block the game up by putting two men on the same square. Gussie, Beres, Linvall and Johnny took positions on each corner of the board, with four counters each which they had to take around the board before returning 'home'. Each move was decided by a throw of the die. Each counter needed a 'six' to start. If you got two 'sixes' in succession however, you could only move one man at a time,

The first problem they encountered was getting that first elusive 'six'. Beres was the first to score. To Johnny's frustration, he was the last. His frustration was made worse by the fact that the others predicted his throw with shouts of "One!" "Four", "Two", as Johnny tried to 'will' a 'six'.

The others meanwhile, were steaming around the board.

Linvall showed his expertise with a few skillful moves, but Beres seemed to be flying homewards. Gussie was doing alright, but seemed to be spending more time reminding Johnny of his inability to get off the starting point.

"Forty-seven goes and nut'n nah gwan!" he said in an exaggerated patois. And then when it next came to Johnny's turn, "Forty-eight goes and nut'n nah gwan!" and so on.

In between teasing Johnny, they found time to chat and have arguments,

It kicked off with Linvall explaining that his son had to go to bed early because he was under a curfew for misbehaving in school. Then each of the men got to thinking about their schoolday memories.

"Things have changed though," said Linvall regretfully, "because in our days the teachers were allowed to give you licks and kicks and boxes too and it wasn't no soft licks either, but good old-time father licks... I remember one teacher we had – maths teacher, Mr Lloyd – he would put me and a next man in detention every dinner time and to go with it, he always used to give you a neckback, one that you could fry an egg on – guaranteed. And him no partial; girls got it as well. He loved to lean back and give it to you with all his strength, feel no way. He used to say, Henry, bwoy, I t'ink ah gwan arrange a caning fe yuh bwoy...Stop combing your head, bwoy, it's empty as it is!! If you said, Sir, I've got a toothache, he'd say: 'Good, I hope you die'! As a child hearing that from a teacher it was kinda heavy, you know..."

The other three nodded with recognition. They all remembered teachers like that back in the day. Even Beres who went to a public school remembered singularly sadistic members of staff. Johnny pointed out cheerfully that the few black teachers in those days always seemed to be the most wicked. Black teachers would think nothing of giving you a karate kick or a kung fu chop for the slightest misdemeanour.

"I remember this one Jamaican teacher, Mr Banton. We called him Judge Dread. 'Cause all he ever used to say was,

'Hush up, hush up! Order in my class!!' More time he didn't even bother with the words and just went straight in with the corporal punishment. All you had to do was cough in his class and that was a detention. And if he heard one word of protest it was a twist of the ear and so on. He had a list of punishments for every crime you could possibly imagine a pupil committing. Everything from a shove in the back for walking too slowly out of his class. So, of course, he wasn't that popular amongst the pupils and we were always planning to do him something bad. His favourite phrase to the pupils was 'I gwan to fix you, yuh know'. He was always saying it, so behind his back we would whisper 'We gwine fix you'. Our chance came the day he forgot his detention book in the classroom. Somebody grabbed it and everybody just went crazy. We scribbled all over it, every page. And in the euphoria one particularly mischievous boy even wrote inside it, 'Mr Banton, you is a eedyat, you is a fool, foo-foo eeedyat...And your face like a dog backside. I, Patrick Augustus, seh so. And don't try neck-back me again, 'cause a guy dead fe less than that...Seen?!' That was Augustus' big mistake, because he didn't know what we were going to do with the book. We didn't know either, until we walked pass this little MG convertible with a plastic rear windscreen that Mr Banton used to drive. Somebody got the idea first and in the next moment we had pushed the detention book through the plastic. The next day at school Augustus says to my crew, 'I'm not sitting next to you lot in Mr Banton's class today because you're always getting detentions and I want to go to lunch early'. He didn't have to worry about where he was going to sit however, because when it came to Mr Banton's class, he only managed to get one foot through the classroom door before the teacher had him by the scruff of the neck and was dragging him to his desk with one hand and reading from the detention book in his other: 'Mr Banton, you is a eedyat... Mr Banton, you is a fool... Mr Banton you is a foo-foo eeedyat... Mr Banton, your face like a dog backside...' And during each pause, Banton delivered a double whack with the book on each side of the boy's head and told him, 'I gwan to arrange a caning for you bwoy'. Augustus didn't know what was going on, but he got a good idea when he turned his head and he saw me and the others in my crew laughing our heads off. But I tell you, that boy had the last laugh. Because he knew he was going to get caned anyway, he turns around and tells Mr Banton that he wasn't the only one who scribbled in the book. And he started naming names. By the time he was finished, half of the class were lined up waiting to be caned. And you might think that Mr Banton's arm got tired as he went along, but it was just the opposite. I was one of the last ones to get caned, and he gave me the living stripes across my backside, I'm telling you."

Beres who had been to a minor public school hadn't had the benefit of a black teacher. What he remembered from those days, was the constant battle of wits between the teachers and the pupils. The teachers took every opportunity to write on the blackboard hoping that while their backs were turned, somebody would misbehave, allowing them to spin round and send a heavy blackboard rubber sailing through the air in the direction of the pupil's forehead. But Beres had one thing in his favour, he was the only black pupil and when it came to sports the entire school depended on him. And although he was an exemplary student, he was called to the headmaster's office a couple of times to receive corporal punishment, at which time he pulled out his trump card: "Sir, if I get the cane I won't be able to run for the school anymore."

Once they all got to recollecting their schooldays there was no stopping them. But Johnny had still not managed to cast a 'six'. With mock-sympathy, Linvall offered that all his 'frustration' would stand him in good stead any time his woman put him on a sex-rationing 'recession'. Johnny was quick to point out that he and Lesley were very active sexually ("thank you very much") and that they were making beautiful love together. "We've got a special kind of love."

Thereby began a discussion about women. Gussie said that as a born-again bachelor his sex life was of course very active. For the record, Beres noted that although Caroline was away in Belgium during the week, by the time she came home at weekends they were both steaming for each other and generally spent the next two days in a passionate embrace. Only Linvall would admit that things were not as they should be and that he was itching all over for his old days of a different woman every month.

Get four black men together in a room and they'll soon start to chat about women and 'fitness'. But feel no way, the women are the same. Get four black women in a room and they won't stop chat about men. But that's alright. It's healthy. That's the way nature planned it. If women lived up in the sky, men would learn to fly. And they'd learn to fly quicker if those women happened to be wearing a sexy outfit. That was a fact that neither Gussie nor Beres, Johnny or Linvall were prepared to admit to their women

"You know what marriage is," Linvall said, "it's an organisation that is run by women and financed by men. One way or another women always get paid. And when you're married you pay the most. I don't know what I was doing in that church saying 'I do' and 'goodbye' to all my freedom. I've been married four months and I'm bored already. I used to go out to parties every weekend and meet exciting women and take them to romantic hotels where we'd make love all night long..."

"Why don't you just find a woman to have on the side?" Gussie suggested. "A woman who doesn't want more from you than that. Like the women I meet, I tell them straight away, 'Here's the deal, I'm only out for a good time'. They either say 'yes' or they say 'no', The main thing is that they're not going to try and get inside your head and mess up your mind like your wife. And I know about wives, most definitely. I made a mistake once, remember? Just find yourself another woman."

Linvall said he had considered it, but it wasn't that easy.

"Sometimes I feel guilty just thinking about it."

"Understand your woman, Linvall, that's the secret." Beres was worried that his friend had become too cynical about love since his marriage. You couldn't talk about love in terms of percentages, he reasoned. Nor could Linvall compare marriage to single life by walking around with a score card to jot down the pros and cons.

"The way you're going about it is totally wrong," he said. "You can't evaluate marriage on a scale of one to ten."

Johnny felt that Linvall was thinking too hard about the wrong things. "How do you know your woman's not cheating on you right now? How do you know she isn't kissing some man under the mistletoe while you're sitting at home on New Year's Eve? That's what you should be concerned about."

Linvall was surprised that Johnny could even think of it. "I've got no worries in that department, I know my woman well enough."

Johnny doubted this. He wondered whether any of them in that room could honestly say that they knew their woman wasn't being unfaithful at that very moment. "Women cheat too," he declared, "it's just that they do it better than men and they don't get caught."

Linvall frowned. Again he stated that he knew his woman and Johnny didn't.

The game had consumed their interest such that they had all forgotten that it was now technically a New Year. They only realised after Johnny in a quick succession of lucky throws, managed not only to get his four counters off the start line, but to send the others back to the start line and to win the game. That was what the game was about – 'frustration'. As a victorious Johnny reminded his friends gleefully, "No game is over until the mampie lady sings."

After recriminations were hurled from one man to the next, about how the game was won and lost, Johnny suggested that if they started making tracks soon, they'd still be able to reach to the party in Camberwell. It was only three a.m and he had heard that there was going to be " 'nuff dutty rub-up inna the area." He added, "Me trash an' me ready an me still alive, so what happen?"

Linvall finally relented, but only after going up to his son's room to make sure Lacquan was asleep. He figured it couldn't do any harm. But he wouldn't be staying too long at the party, he insisted. That was okay with everybody. Within minutes, they had grabbed their coats and were out on the street.

As they had all had too much to drink, Beres left his car parked up. It wasn't far to Camberwell and the walk would do them good and help to clear their heads.

The party was jumping when they arrived. It was being held in a large four-storey house in a quiet road just off the Green. The rumble of the bass from the stereo could be heard all the way down the street, but it was cool, this was New Year's Eve and nobody complained.

The house was packed to the seams. Entrance cost no more than an invite. It was essentially a revival party, with a touch of soul, hip hop, ragga and jungle; a joint birthday party between Patsy, Pepsi, Pinky Jennifer and Michelle and security was by the notorious Rottweiller Security of Brixton.

Nevertheless, Johnny managed to get them in past the two big belly men on the door through knowing somebody who knew somebody. Downstairs, a local sound system was holding court in the pitch darkness of the double-size living room, where the ravers had gathered in increasingly greater numbers. It was hot, the thick crowd of ravers seemed to be enjoying themselves, but could hardly move and couldn't make room for four more people, even if they wanted to. Within minutes sweat was running down Beres' back. He peered in the living room, but he couldn't see much, he could only hear the incessant drum beat crashing through the speakers. Everybody wanted to be 'in da house!' Unfortunately the living room was not designed to hold a thousand people, so others were upstairs, drinking the bars dry (the fad of the evening was to purchase a bottle of the best champagne and guzzle it down in less swallows than the next person). So it was from out in the hallway that Johnny, Linvall, Beres and Gussie took in the music and even there, things were tight with people passing by in search of the kitchen for refreshments or the lavatory for their convenience.

From the moment they got inside Linvall and his spars knew that this was the place to be. It seemed like there was nothing but pure woman in the place. The men didn't seem to matter to Johnny who was allowing the brew to rule his brain. All he could see was a house full of man-hungry women. He thanked the Lord as he eased his way through the crowded hallway. Soon he would be stumbling and trampling on people's feet, but for the moment he was simply merry. *I shouldn't have had that second drink*, he told himself, *I shoulda known better, I always handle alcohol bad*. Through the haze in his head, he sighted a few of his bredrin and hailed them. "Yush! Benji, Rupie, Junjo, Rizla... wha' ah gwan?" Then he saw a slightly-unsober but irie-looking sister in a black PVC wet-look raincoat, giggling to herself at the end of a spliff and he told himself, *Me ah go check dis daughter later*. She called out "Happy New Year!!" to nobody in particular. Johnny assumed that she was calling to him and returned an equally inviting smile, casually unbuttoning the top two buttons of his silk shirt, to reveal his hairy chest. "You see, me getting hot dis year," he winked at the others, "what dem ah go do fe cold me?" Those few words cost him dearly for at that moment, an even smoother guy with a pinstripe moustache and slick-backed processed hair had scooped up the woman and was gently but firmly escorting her out for a night of passion.

The selector behind the wheels of steel had 'nuff requests for the night, but he couldn't resist teasing the crowd with how many versions of a particular tune he had. It was the legendary *Full Up* rhythm, originally built at Studio One on Brentford Road. In the thirty years since it originally surfaced, there must have been one thousand versions under different titles by various artists. So far, the deejay had played a dozen versions and the room was steaming. Then suddenly, the entire ground floor of the house shook as the speakers exploded with the sound of the legendary rhythm in an even newer style for the nineties. Johnny and Gussie exchanged knowing glances, their eyes wide with expectation as the bassie rode the riddim tight through the opening bars. By the time the drums finally dropped in and the vocalist began voicing his lyrics, all four friends were slapping each other's palms and touching each other's fists in excited acknowledgement that this was definitely a 'boom track':

> *I didn't know what I was doing when I made this one*
> *I didn't know one rhythm would last so long*
> *Mighty Diamonds call it 'Kuchie'*
> *And now every singer want to touch it*
> *I am the original bassie*
> *No sound can string up and nuh play me*
> *I nevah mek much money from dis one yah, but I still feel good.*
> *'Cause everytime a sound box string up, Leroy Sibbles in your neighbourhood*
> *I am the original 'Full Up', 'Full Up', 'Full up'*
> *Haul and pull up, pull up, pull up.*

The tune by a veteran of the reggae industry, literally tore up the place. It was amazing that this riddim which used to 'buss-up' dance back in the day when it was first released, was even now, more than a quarter of a century later, kicking up a rumpus in a dance when you dropped it at the right time. It was especially appreciated by those who understood the sentiments of the lyrics and the fact that the singer was a 'don dadda' in the reggae music business. An original. For even though artists in America and all over try to pirate their sounds, everybody knows that reggae originated from Jamaican musicians.

The deejay took the needle off the record mid-track, to

make a public announcement:

"Calling D.J. Pickney... Yuh wanted, at the I-trol tower... D.J. Pickney... whe' yuh deh? Yuh wanted, IMMEDIATELY!"

Despite being interrupted in mid-dance, there was an excited buzz amongst the gathered ravers and even more people came down from the other rooms in the house, to catch a glimpse of the up-and-coming MC who everyone in London was talking about.

After thirty or so seconds, an adolescent voice burst through the loudspeakers in breathless rapid-fire:

"Yeah, greetings in the name of the Most High - Jah! Rastafari... Ever faithful ever sure, y'know. Look to the East for the coming of a black king...'Cause right now nice and decent people, you're tuned into the number one juggling sound of Goldfinger International with Musclehead and full crew. 'Nuff respect to my selector, otherwise known as Mr. Groovy. Anytime Mr Groovy play, everything's okay and that's the order of the day, from your boss deejay... And big up yourself Doreen, the promoter and all man like Asha, Bunny and Linton the Lone Ranger, best behaviour is essential... Seen?!"

By now the ravers were almost incensed with anticipation. Few of them could see the diminutive figure of the D.J. in the darkness of the room, but from the way he sounded on the microphone, he was a professional at his game despite his youth, and he knew how to whip up a crowd. D.J. Pickney continued with his introductions a moment longer, before the selector dropped the tune. A cut of the Capleton hit *On Tour*. Showing that he was a match for the Jamaican MC who originated the pattern, D.J. Pickney dropped the same lick with a different lyric:

Selassie I liveth every time... King Solomon, liveth every time...
Seven hundred wife, three hundred concubine, I sing...
If yuh waan me fe marry dem, just say de word
Dem ah the sheep, me ah the shepherd
As long as dem 'member it's my show

And if dem nuh like it, dem bettah go
...Well I was born to be free
To have a whole heap ah queen around me
Whole heap ah queen, whole heap ah queen around me...
And who have eyes dem will see.

One t'ing I get to overstand
Most the man dem inna de place have over seven 'ooman
Inna the north, south, east, west ah London
Manchester, Leeds and Birmingham
Well it coming like the woman dem cyaan tek it no more
Instead of keeping one man, dem ah keep four
If slackness ah the illness, the bible ah the cure
...Cause I was born to be free
And have a whole heap ah queen around me...
Who have eyes dem will see.

The young MC couldn't get through any more verses because by now the crowd were in uproar, shouting their approval and firing their imaginary shots in homage to the youngster

"Gwan my yout' fe real..." someone called out.

Again there was a musical pause as D.J. Pickney's pint-size voice came through the loudspeaker with his 'special requests':

"Yuh see me, me is a deejay who don't fool around music. Me is professional, seen? Cause the youth of today is the man and woman of tomorrow. Special request to the man like Nardo, a.k.a. the Upsetter, big up yourself every time... Happy new 'ear to all the African daughters in da house, love how unuh flex...every time...All the dancehall massive... All Jamaicans, big it up. All English, all Yankee, all Egyptians, all Africans in the house... big it up. From Goldfinger inna the place, big t'ings everytime... Upfront music, you could never refuse it...niceness guaranteed. An' we don't shoot an' miss, 'cause we finger 'pon the trigger we have to lick the target. So come down my selector with da riddim, an' like I told you, never walk without a version two..."

Without further ado, a cut to Tiger's *Seen, Come Again*, filled the loudspeakers. Again the youthful MC displayed that he could drop a lick in the same style to the original but with a new lyric:

> *Hey bad bwoy and your idren dem*
> *Coke an' crack ah yuh best friend*
> *Then when yuh done you sell it to the children*
> *Before twenty-one dem life ah go end...*
> *Seen? Come again...*
> *Bad bwoy stop influence the youths dem*
> *Dem ah carry gun instead of a pen*
> *Nuff cyaan count from one to ten*
> *Renk and feisty to the teacher dem...*
> *Seen? Come again...*

Some people called it ragga, but to Johnny it wasn't no ragga, it was strickly dancehall. He and Gussie had been to enough dancehall sessions in their time to know that the up-and-coming D.J. Pickney was going to make it all the way to the top.

"I like the way he rides the riddim, his tone of voice and I like the cultural injection in the lyrics. Although it's past his bedtime."

Linvall had managed to push his way through the darkness of the living room to the front by the turntables. D.J. Pickney sounded too close for comfort. He knew his own son's voice when he heard it Sure enough, in front of the turntables surrounded by a cheering crowd of partygoers was Lacquan.

WHERE HAVE ALL THE GOOD MEN GONE?

Gussie couldn't remember much about the last three days. He had hit the bottle in a serious way. He had been vomiting all morning and felt nauseous. He didn't have much time to dote on his hangover however, before the phone rang. It was Brenda.

"Gussie, I think you need to come down here now."

Gussie groaned and said it was impossible.

"No, I mean it," Brenda repeated, this time more urgently.

"What's so important that it can't wait until tomorrow?"

"Your business? There are two bailiffs here who have come to seize everything. Apparently you haven't payed your VAT."

Gussie sobered up quick. The VAT! He had forgotten about it!

"Tell them to hold it, I'll be there in fifteen minutes... Just make sure they don't take anything."

Gussie jumped off the bed into his jeans. Within seconds he was out of the door with a crash helmet.

When you've got to get somewhere in a hurry on a motorcycle, you don't notice the traffic. Gussie was at his shop if not within the fifteen minutes he promised, then only a few minutes later. The two burly guys were waiting impatiently. Not even Brenda's abundance of cultivated charms could bring a smile to their faces. Somehow, Gussie managed to bluff his way. Said he had been away from work. He forgot the deadline for the payments. He would pay the money straight away. Even without thinking about it, Gussie wrote out a cheque for £10,000. The men phoned through to their boss who said they could accept it on this occasion. Then the men left.

It was only later that Gussie started thinking he had better check out his account. He phoned through to the bank to get a balance over the phone. The clerk at the other end of the line informed him that, "Actually Mr Pottinger, the bank manager would like to see you as a matter of urgency..."

Patrick Augustus

Could one man really have so much bad luck in the same day? Gussie found himself having to sit in his bank manager's office explaining why his overdraft had gone several thousand pounds beyond the agreed limit. Gussie explained that business had been a bit up and down lately. The manager accepted this and would allow the overdraft to remain at the present level for the time being, just as long as it didn't increase. Gussie had no choice but to agree to this, even as he considered how he was going to find £10,000 to cover the VAT man's cheque which was due to clear in just a few days time. Why oh why had he allowed Courtney to talk him into throwing away good money on a boxer!

He kissed goodbye to the Harley and placed an ad in Loot. But only diehard enthusiasts would ride in the middle of winter. He got a straight five Gs for it, instead of the nine or ten it was worth. After that, he spent several hours in a mad panic trying to raise the rest of the money. He called his sister Evelyn first. There was only the answering machine at her house informing him that they were still on holiday in the Canary Islands. Then he called out to his closest friends, Johnny, Linvall and Beres. It was the same story each time. The Christmas and New Year's festivities had cleaned them all out and they were as broke as Gussie was. The more he rang around and heard that story, the more Gussie realised that he was running out of options. He finally decided to swallow his pride and call Angela.

Yasmine answered the phone.

"Oh hi Gussie, how are you? Fine. Fine. Yes, I enjoyed that night too. You want to speak to Angela? Yes, she's been expecting you..."

Gussie's first words to Angela were hesitant. He asked her how she was and made some irrelevant comment about the weather.

"So have you been thinking?" she asked.

"Yes... yes..." he muttered. "Yes I've been thinking and you know... to help a friend out and everything."

"Good," she said. "And relax, don't worry about a thing.

I'll have the agreement drawn up by my solicitor."

She was about to put down the phone...

"Er, there's just one more thing. That money...?"

"Oh you want the money now? I thought you were a rich diamond merchant? Okay, what figure did you have in mind?"

"Well, what figure did you have in mind?"

"A grand."

"A grand! Is that how little you value my seed?"

"Okay, two grand. But don't push it, Gus."

Gussie said he was thinking more like four. She said two and a half and they met at three.

"But you're only going to get half up front. You'll get the second half when a pregnancy test proves that you're not firing blanks!"

In this take it or leave it situation, Gussie had no choice but to take it. The whole thing was very businesslike and formal but that's the way she wanted it. It was the same when he went there later on that evening for the first sex session. It wasn't lovemaking so much as babymaking. There was no need to perform, she told him, she wanted the sperm of a man not a monster. Straight sex would do. Nevertheless, Angela nearly tore off his hide by clawing at his back as she came in orgasmic ecstacy. The whole thing had a coldness about it which made Gussie feel like a machine.

"We'd better arrange for a second session. Just in case today was a dry run..." Angela said afterwards. She picked up her filofax and flicked through the pages. "Next Tuesday is good for me. Why don't you drop by around eight in the evening. Please, try to be on time, I don't want my black man letting me down on only the second date."

In the back of the cab home, Gussie pulled out a cigarette and smoked. He had recently developed the habit and he needed it's calming, soothing effect to forget his troubles if only for a moment. He didn't consider the health risks. As the driver steered his vehicle southward, Gussie peered out of the window with a blank stare, his mind wondering off into the future. That night he was unable to sleep well and tossed and turned for most of the time.

The next morning, he woke up and switched on breakfast TV. Winsome was there as usual, giving the weather, after which the newsreader turned to her for their customary chit-chat.

"It says in all the morning papers that you are to get married, Winsome. Well on behalf of us all here on the morning news programme, we wish you all the best... So what's he like, your husband to be?"

A coy Winsome was being evasive. But the newsreader pursued the point and eventually Winsome admitted that she was to marry Augustus Pottinger, a diamond merchant of Hatton Garden.

Gussie was stunned. For a moment, he thought he was dreaming, that he was still asleep. But when he pinched himself, he realised he was wide awake.

He immediately tried to call Winsome at the studio. But they wouldn't put him through. She was on air. Gussie spent the next two hours trying to reach Winsome on her mobile. He finally got through.

"What's all this about?"

"All what about Gussie?"

"The papers... the TV all the publicity about us getting married?"

"Didn't you want the publicity, dear, I'm sorry about that. There was nothing I could do. A journalist spotted me in the wedding gown shop, getting measured out and from there the news leaked out."

"What?! Wedding gown! Please explain, have I missed something. When did you decide that we were getting married?"

"Me?" came Winsome's horrified answer. "You asked me to marry you, remember."

Gussie remembered, even if it was in a moment of passion. He had to talk to her seriously, urgent. They arranged to meet up.

So many things were going through his mind when he jumped into the cab and headed for the TV studios in West London. He sat bolt upright in the taxi sweating, as the realisation dawned on him. He was being steam-rolled into marriage. True, he liked Winsome enough to marry her, but he wanted to take it slowly.

At the studio, Winsome's producer, a particularly abrupt woman by the name of Lucy Fry, was waiting for him at the reception.

"So you're Augustus Pottinger," she said. She congratulated him and said that she used to go out with a black guy once, until she came to realise that all black men were bastards. Apparently, her ex had promised her the world and lied. "A lying bastard in other words," she said.

Gussie ignored her. Her problem wasn't his. Still jabbering away, she led him to the lift.

"Why is it that all you black guys think about is sex?" she asked him. "This guy I used to go out with, that's all he was interested in, sex, sex SEX! He was also trying to use me to get a job in television, but I saw through that. What's wrong with you black guys? Can't you make it on your own, without exploiting your women?"

Gussie couldn't believe what he was hearing. He wanted to kiss his teeth, but decided to be on his best behaviour, and was relieved when the lift doors finally opened. Winsome was standing waiting on the other side. As soon as she saw him, she threw her arms around his neck and hugged and kissed him.

"Alright, alright," said Lucy Fry. "Don't get carried away. Remember you're on air after the one o'clock news." Then she hurried away down the long corridor.

"Bitch!" Gussie mumbled. Then remembering himself, he turned to Winsome. "Not you. I meant her..." he pointed to Lucy Fry who was just disappearing into an office halfway down the corridor. "What's her problem?"

"Oh, you've obviously heard her views on black men. That was a bit quick. Usually it takes her about fifteen minutes to get onto the subject. Apparently she used to go out with this black guy that did the dirty on her and she's been that way ever since."

"Poor guy," Gussie sympathised.

"Yes, what was his name again...? Linton? Linvall? Yes, that's it Linvall...?"

Suddenly a thought struck Gussie. "Not Linvall Henry?"

"Yes, that's right. Why, do you know him?"

Gussie spluttered a moment then finally mumbled something about having seen a newspaper story about the woman and her ex-boyfriend. It didn't seem like the right time to boast about his friendship with the culprit.

"So," Winsome said, "you needed to see me. I hope you're not having second thoughts about marrying me. Or is a gentleman's word no longer his bond? Anyway, I've already booked the chapel and the hotel for the wedding reception. The invitations are being printed as we speak. I've already told my parents and my dad has promised that he'll make it a wedding to remember."

Gussie mopped the sweat off his brow with his handkerchief. To say he was stunned was an understatement. He couldn't believe it. He raised a reproachful eyebrow. "Don't you think you've gone a bit too far?"

No, Winsome didn't think so. How could she go too far when Gussie had asked her to marry him and she had said, 'yes'.

"Okay, but I mean, let's take it one day at a time."

"And give you the chance to change your mind? You've got to realise Gussie, I'm a good catch, as good as you're going to get. I'm not a fool to go waiting on any man."

Gussie spluttered some more. He said something about how difficult it was nowadays with all the pressures of marriage in society. Perhaps they should be engaged for a while and go courting in the old fashion sense.

"Yes, maybe it's a good idea to go steady for a while before getting married."

"If I'm good enough to get engaged to, I'm good enough to marry. Why should we wait? It feels right as it is now."

There weren't any customers at the book shop on the weekday morning when Johnny got the call.

"Hello, is that The Book Shack?" asked a youngish-sounding man with a heavy Sottish accent. The man introduced himself as a researcher on *The Janet Sinclair Show*, the most popular of Channel 5's chat shows. He said he had got Johnny's name through a friend of a friend who had suggested that he might be a good guest to have on the show for the following week. The topic for the show was 'Male Bonding' and the researcher had heard that Johnny was one of the Brixton Massive FC football team and he wanted to invite him along as well as a couple more people from the team.

There was a pause for a moment as Johnny took it all in. TV? Channel 5? *The Janet Sinclair Show*? Of course he had heard about it like every other member of the black community. He had even seen a couple of shows and knew that Janet Sinclair, or the 'weave queen' as she was known by those with less charity, was the hottest chat show host on the airwaves. A spot on such a popular live TV show could be the break he needed. He agreed to do it and at the same time decided to get a T-Shirt made with The Book Shack logo on it to wear.

"But let me make one thing quite clear," Johnny was at pains to stress to the researcher, "I don't know nothing about the 'bonding' bit. I want to make it quite clear that I'm only close and tight with my spars in a manner of speaking. I'm not literally tight with them yuh understan'? So let's just make that straight first."

The researcher said that it was fine and assured Johnny that he wouldn't have to do any kind of 'bonding' in front of the cameras.

For the next couple of days, Johnny's head swelled-up big time. He could hardly wait to get into the studio and become a TV star. At the back of his mind, he was convinced that some TV producer watching would sign him up for one of those big film contracts when they saw him on *The Janet Sinclair Show.* "Bwoy, me can act you know star," he said aloud as he admired himself in the mirror the next evening as he waited for the cab to pick him up from home to drive him to the studio for the taping of the show. He was dressed in his most expensive two-piece, a dark green silk number with a glittering motif on the trousers and jacket. He looked stunning, even though the jacket buttons were undone so that you could read the words *Book Shack, Peckham,* on the T-shirt underneath..

Lesley was busy for the evening and couldn't make it, but she promised that she would record Johnny's TV debut instead.

It was the first time Johnny had been inside a television studio. He was met at the studio gate by one of the researchers, a charming and attractive sister called Natalie, who treated Johnny as if he was already a film star. 'Yeah, maybe sump'n can gwan here,' Johnny thought to himself and made a note to check her later after the show.

The Janet Sinclair Show was taped live every week in front of a live audience which though mixed, was about half black. The guests were always seated on a raised platform, with the audience seated around them on three sides. Not as intimidating as the rival *Marcus Ho Show*, the set of *The Janet Sinclair Show* was styled more like an intimate forum than like 'the devil's anus'. Natalie led Johnny through the rows where an eager and hushed audience waited for the show to begin, up to the guests' seats on the platform. To his surprise, Johnny saw his friends Gussie, Linvall and Beres all sitting there waiting.

"Wha'?" he said, addressing them, "how comes you guys are here?"

"We could ask you the same question," Gussie replied.

"I got a call from the TV company yesterday. Said they wanted me to come and talk about 'male bonding'."

"Me too," Beres confirmed. "But they didn't tell me you guys were going to be on."

"Me neither!" Johnny exclaimed.

They didn't have time to chat any more however, because just then the stage manager called out: "Quiet on the set!! Five, four, three, two, one...Cue music!"

At the sound of the familiar theme tune to the show, the primed audience began their applause. A moment later, Janet Sinclair walked in boldly and confidently to the number one camera with a microphone in her hand and dressed in a glittering black outfit. Her trademark weave sat on her head in a new style. She stood amongst the audience, waiting for the rapturous applause to die down, and smiling into the camera, introduced the show:

"Good evening and welcome once again to The Janet Sinclair Show. This evening, my guests think they have been invited here to talk about 'male bonding'. Well we've got a surprise for them. The real subject of this show is 'Where have all the good men gone?' Go to any cafe or bar in London, go to any party or rave go to any college, any workplace and you'll see the same thing – single women who would rather stay single than settle for second best. And I'm not talking about men who can't satisfy you sexually... Ladies, you know what I mean by 'second best', he's the type of man you cook and clean for and do everything for, and then when you need a shoulder to cry on, the man's sneaked out and left you for some bimbo!"

The majority female audience exploded with clapping. On the platform, Johnny and his spars began to feel a bit uneasy.

"So, this evening ladies and gentlemen, I will be pointing fingers. Let's meet our first guest. His name is John Lindo."

"Hey Janet," Johnny interrupted, "just call me Johnny Dollar, seen?"

Taken aback, Janet turned to Johnny and smiled. An uncomfortable ripple ran through the audience.

"Alright Johnny Dollar, tell me, you currently have three

children by two different women – at the last count, and you believe men have a right to 'go forth and multiply' with as many women as they want but you disapprove of female infidelity. What is so unique about men that makes it alright for them to, in your words, 'spread their seed'?"

Johnny was taken aback by the amount of facts Janet had about him at her disposal. If he had known the secrets of TV, he would have known that one of the show's researchers had done a little checking up on him and was now priming Janet with questions through the earpiece in her left ear.

"Oh you're lost for words?" Janet asked. "That's unusual."

"You've got your facts there," Johnny replied, "but that's how I used to be. I've changed my views now. Because me and my woman are trying to work things out."

"But tell us about how you used to be then. For the sake of my viewers, how did you justify your own polygamy?"

Johnny thought about the question for a moment longer, a nervous smile on his face.

"Well," he began, "a man can have as much women as he wants and if any of them become pregnant, as long as they are faithful to him, they know who the father is. No dispute. But in reverse, if a woman sleeps with Tom at nine o'clock, Harry at ten o'clock and at midday she has Dick, and they each have the same blood group and they also look alike, it is very difficult for you to know who the father is."

There was a disapproving murmur in the audience. One middle-aged Pentecostal woman in the front row muttered: "He must don't hear about AIDS. Is man like him catch AIDS!"

"Don't you think you're being derogatory about women, Johnny?" Janet asked.

"Not at all, it is women who initiated polygamy in the first place because there was a social imbalance where they determined that every woman deserves the right to have a family. Also polygamy is the only way forward to safe sex."

Some of the women in the audience got hot when they

heard that. So far, most of the men in the audience were silent.

Janet Sinclair offered the Pentecostal woman the microphone to ask Johnny a question:

"Young man, you're too girlie-girlie. Don't you know that the Lord disapproves of you galavanting around the place having affairs? You must only have one woman!"

'First let me stress, that this is how I used to think... I'm not speaking for myself now, but how I used to think was that affairs are quite nice. After all everybody I've spoken to who has affairs seems to enjoy it It is nice and healthy, I think everybody should have them. And you read your Bible carefully and you see how many women some of those guys had. At the end of the day women are just like men and like to have affairs too. At the end of the day, ask anyone here, whether if someone came along who was better in their view than their partner, they'd probably have an affair. Anyone who doesn't agree with that is a liar. Remember, it takes two to tango."

The Pentecostal woman had a look of disbelief on her face.

"My next guest," Janet continued, is someone who knows Johnny intimately. Sharon has been having an affair with him."

The audience gasped and Johnny almost fell off his seat as Sharon, his regular customer at The Book Shack walked confidently on the stage and took a seat opposite Johnny.

Johnny was shaking his head. He knew this meant trouble.

"I know it's hard for you Sharon, to talk like this on live TV, but tell us something of your relationship with Johnny."

Dressed in a pastel coloured trouser suit, Sharon looked more like a film star than a secretary. She started talking slowly.

"I met Johnny when I bought books from his shop. We became friends over a period and started seeing each other every day. He told me everything about himself, but he didn't tell me that he already had two baby mothers when we started making love."

At this point, Sharon pulled out a handkerchief and dabbed her watery eyes. "You see, I'm a good woman and I truly believed that Johnny was a good man. I thought he was serious. But now, I know the real truth." She stifled a sob.

"And you've got something else to tell him, haven't you?" Janet Sinclair prompted.

"Yes," Sharon turned to Johnny. "I'm two months pregnant!"

The revelation was a shock. Johnny threw back his arms in mock horror and tilted his seat too far back. It fell with a crash backwards. The audience burst out with laughter. A few of the women could be heard saying, "Serve him right for being a dog!"

"So Johnny," Janet demanded, "you may soon have four children by three different women? How are you going to pay for them?"

Johnny got up quickly and sat back down on his righted chair. He held his head in his hands and let out a long sigh. But he couldn't answer. He didn't know how he had allowed himself to be duped like this.

Okay, it was true, he had made love to her twice. He was desperate. He had been without sex for so long. Sharon had become a friend when he was at his lowest ebb and they simply got a little bit too close, when she showed up at The Book Shack one evening after work, just as Johnny was about to shut up shop. They had made love in the back room. For Johnny, it was sexual healing, but for Sharon it was more than that. It wasn't that he didn't fancy her, because he did, it was just that he didn't want more than the occasional grind. Anything more was too much to ask. When he realised that she wanted more, Johnny wanted to cut things off. Sharon didn't know what was up with him and he didn't come right out and say it either, but she sensed that something was up. When she finally managed to drag it out of him he admitted that he wanted to end the relationship.

She was stunned and for a moment just stared at him wide eyed, a tear ready to fall down her face but unable to. The stare bothered him, he couldn't avoid it. He saw deep in her eyes her anguish as she realised that their night of passion together had been just that. But she did come by once more after that, just before closing time and before he realised what was happening, they were enjoying a repeat performance.

Janet Sinclair turned to the camera with a smile.

"My next guest, Marcia Henry..."

Linvall jumped up from his seat and looked about him terrified. Janet continued:

"...She says there's no such thing as a good man and that all men are dogs and once a dog always a dog!"

The women in the audience cheered rapturously as Marcia stepped up on stage in a long evening dress. She acknowledged the cheers of her sisters in spirit. She sat down next to Linvall.

"Now Marcia, you're sitting next to your husband and yet you say all men are dogs. Don't you know that men get vexed when women say things like that?"

"Good!" Marcia replied to thunderous applause. "I don't care if men don't like it. It's true. The best way to make sure that your man doesn't do the doggystyle, is to never give him the opportunity. Because men can't control themselves. You have to stop thinking of your man as 'my man' and start thinking about him as a man, because that's how he's going to behave, not as your man. So even though Linvall's my husband and the father of my son, I watch him every minute of the day. And it works. He hasn't been unfaithful to me since we married."

The audience applauded. Some of the men could be heard making comments such as "outta order" and "woman nuh run t'ings!", but Linvall said nothing. He just stared ahead in a trance.

Again Janet Sinclair smiled directly into the camera.

"My next guest is coming to us on a live satellite link

from the European Courts of Justice in Strasbourg, where she's fighting a very important case..."

At this, Beres shifted uneasily in his seat. The audience turned to the video screens above their heads. Caroline's image came up. Next to her was a handsome athletic looking black man with a pinstripe moustache and dressed very elegantly in a dark suit.

"Caroline, can you hear us?"

"Yes, I can hear you very clearly," was Caroline's reply.

"I believe you have a message to give to your husband Beres, who is sitting here in the studio."

"Yes," Caroline stated, sounding official. "Thank you for giving me the opportunity to introduce my soon to be ex-husband to my fiance, Jean-Pierre, sitting next to me here. Your previous guest was right; all men are dogs. Because I'm a lawyer and I'm not easily duped. I thought Beres was a 'good man' – the best. But now I know he's nothing but a dog."

Beres was speechless.

Seeing what had happened to his friends had made Gussie extremely nervous. But it wasn't his turn, not yet."

Black woman MP Anna Stuman was the next guest. She had been abandoned by her husband who later went and did a "kiss and tell" to the tabloid papers for a lot of money. Stuman sat on the panel chair beside Johnny, her face almost livid with rage as she stared into the camera. Her face told the story of a woman who had been wronged and was going to make someone pay. Black men, all of them were going to pay the price. Johnny didn't see the look on her face, because he was looking into the camera.

"Welcome, MP, Anna Stuman," Janet said. "Now, you're one of Britain's top women MPs, representing a large Afro-Caribbean community in South London. You have seen the damage done to your constituency by men going off and sleeping around the place and you also have a personal experience in the matter."

"Well, I don't need to tell you all my story," Stuman said

bitterly. "I'm sure you've all read my husband's side of things in the gutter press..."

The audience responded with a nervous giggle.

"But what we're really talking about here, is men who behave like animals. I mean, you don't expect a dog or a rabbit to control their libido, but you do expect a fellow human being to be able to control it. After all, that's what separates us from the lower animals. Some people say intelligence separates us, but as you can see from this example of hu*man* sitting next to me, I have a pussy which has more intelligence than this man's infantile brain."

The audience gasped with relish. This sounded good and entertaining. A resounding applause rang out for the MP.

"Just hold on.... just hold on," Johnny struggled to make himself heard over the cheers from the women in attendance. "Why are you starting on me, what have I done to you? I'm not the one who left you with a pickney you know!"

The audience 'oohed' and 'aahed'.

"And another thing," Linvall interjected, "when you say 'pussy', do you mean a cat?"

There were a few sniggers from the handful of men in the audience. Stuman ignored Linvall's question and Johnny's reference to her much publicised personal life and continued...

"What *you* and men like you have done, is destroy the black family. Time and time again, you show that you have little understanding of what is really going on out there for black families. When was the last time you took a walk around some of our neighbourhoods?"

"What are you talking about," Johnny said, raising his voice, "I live in Brixton don't I? And my feet is my only carriage, seen? So I'm walking about all the time."

"Yeah," Stuman retorted quickly, raising her voice, "but you obviously don't have your eyes open!"

"Ah wha' de bumboclaat...!" Johnny cried out from his seat. He couldn't take it any longer. He had heard enough and wasn't able to contain his emotions. He felt like a 'claat' just sitting there listening to all this foolishness from the MP. "Me personally tek responsibility fe *my* family, yuh understand? So don't come yah with no bumboclaat 'bout how *me* destroy any family!"

Janet Sinclair had learned her art well and knew how to stir up her guests so much that it became 'interesting television' and more importantly, she knew when to intervene in what looked like it could develop into a slanging match.

"Alright, alright!" she commanded. "This is my show, and the rules are, no personal attacks...unless you can't help it..."

The audience shouted their roar of approval.

"Tell us anyway Anna," Sinclair said with an air of familiarity and a tone of sympathy in her voice, "how did you feel when your husband abandoned you with your new-born baby and went off with a younger woman?"

"I felt like cutting his balls off!"

The audience exploded in applause and cheers and whistles. Johnny winced with pain. Gussie crossed his legs anxiously and Linvall looked on in frozen horror at Stuman.

"But you know what...?" the MP continued, raising her hand for quiet, "what really hurt me wasn't the fact that he left me after I had cooked for him and cleaned for him and given birth to his child at the same time as bringing home the larger part of the family income and working bloody hard in parliament, but the fact that he left a pair of his dirty underpants behind..."

Everyone, including Janet Sinclair laughed.

Then Stuman added seriously, "I had hoped that time would wound all heels, but it looks like he's going to get away with being a dog."

Janet smiled to the camera. My next guest, is our celebrity guest. She says that men are now redundant and that with the advancement of science, women no longer need men for anything. Please welcome TV personality Angela Braithwaite.

Gussie held his head in his hands. This was it. This was definitely it! It was his turn to get dissed.

"Angela, why have you decided that men are redundant?"

"Well because they are just a burden to women most times. The only reason we ever really needed them as women, was when we wanted children. Now, with scientific advancement we don't even need them for that. All we need is the sperm."

"And you say that you have recently had some sperm donated so that you could get pregnant," Janet said.

"That's right. And I just heard the good news yesterday from my doctor. I am pregnant with twins."

Despite himself, Gussie fell over backwards on his chair.

"Well, I was going to present Augustus Pottinger as my next guest, but he seems to have passed out. I hope he's alright, because he's marrying weather girl, Winsome Scott. While our staff are reviving him, lets talk to someone in the audience. Are there any men here who think they understand women?"

The diminutive figure of Free-I, the rastaman rose up from his seat in the audience, his huge tam on his head. Seeing that this was likely to be 'good TV', Janet gave him the microphone. The rastaman spoke in gentle compromising tones:

"Bwoy t'ings ah definitely go on a way now you see sah and it coming like a pure box-box, everybody get box up. Like Beres, him get kick out. Him have a nice pretty gal like Caroline, who is an upstanding lawyer an' member of the community and he disrespeck her still. Look 'pon it, bwoy I tell you, some man deal wid madness nowadays, you see sah. Imagine, him t'row away a woman who most man would die for. He must be mad! And Johnny now, it look like him tell the 'ooman dat him don't want to be with her no more, but the 'ooman possessive and it coming like a fatal attraction, you see sah. The woman just tek set 'pon Johnny a way and it coming like Johnny ah the honey an' she ah the bee. An' yuh know how bee love honey. Me sorry fe him. Bwoy. But Marcia, I tell you the truth now, me kinda deh 'pon your side, but you have to treat Linvall a bit better than dat... An' to dat 'ooman who says she don' need a man, all she needs is him seed, ah wha' you a deal wid? Me know seh ah you produce the yout', but if you use smaddy seed fe get pregnant, the yout' still have a father! You know what I mean? Yeah man. Certain woman deh 'pon the street ah gwan 'bout dem no have no baby father... Dat a joke man, because certain ladies don't mek the baby father see them babies. Yuh understand dat part deh, Janet?"

Janet Sinclair nodded, but didn't have time to respond. A voice in her ear told her that there was just time to thank her guests and the audience and to tell the viewers that she was back same time, same place next week.

BESTSELLING FICTION

I wish to order the following X Press title(s)

❑ Single Black Female	Yvette Richards	£5.99
❑ When A Man Loves A Woman	Patrick Augustus	£5.99
❑ Wicked In Bed	Sheri Campbell	£5.99
❑ Rude Gal	Sheri Campbell	£5.99
❑ Yardie	Victor Headley	£4.99
❑ Excess	Victor Headley	£4.99
❑ Yush!	Victor Headley	£5.99
❑ Fetish	Victor Headley	£5.99
❑ Here Comes the Bride	Victor Headley	£5.99
❑ In Search of Satisfaction	J. California Cooper	£7.99
❑ Sistas On a Vibe	Ijeoma Inyama	£6.99
❑ Flex	Marcia Williams	£6.99
❑ Baby Mother	Andrea Taylor	£6.99
❑ Uptown Heads	R.K. Byers	£5.99
❑ Jamaica Inc.	Tony Sewell	£5.99
❑ Lick Shot	Peter Kalu	£5.99
❑ Professor X	Peter Kalu	£5.99
❑ Obeah	Colin Moone	£5.99
❑ Cop Killer	Donald Gorgon	£4.99
❑ The Harder They Come	Michael Thelwell	£7.99
❑ Baby Father	Patrick Augustus	£6.99
❑ Baby Father 2	Patrick Augustus	£6.99
❑ OPP	Naomi King	£6.99

I enclose a cheque/postal order (Made payable to 'The X Press') for

£ _____

(add 50p P&P per book for orders under £10. All other orders P&P free.)

NAME _____

ADDRESS _____

_____

Cut out or photocopy and send to:
X PRESS, 6 Hoxton Square, London N1 6NU
Alternatively, call the X PRESS hotline: 0171 729 1199 and place your order.

X Press Black Classics

The masterpieces of black fiction writing await your discovery

❏ The Blacker the Berry   Wallace Thurman   £6.99
  'Born too black, Emma Lou suffers her own community's intra-racial venom.'

❏ The Autobiography of an Ex-Colored Man   James Weldon Johnson   £5.99
  'One of the most thought-provoking novels ever published.'

❏ The Conjure Man Dies   Rudolph Fisher   £5.99
  'The world's FIRST black detective thriller!'

❏ The Walls of Jericho   Rudolph Fisher   £5.99
  'When a buppie moves into a white neighbourhood, all hell breaks loose. Hilarious!'

❏ Joy and Pain   Rudolph Fisher   £6.99
  'Jazz age Harlem stories by a master of black humour writing.'

❏ Iola   Frances E.W. Harper   £6.99
  'A woman's long search for her mother from whom she was separated on the slave block.'

❏ The House Behind the Cedars   Charles W. Chesnutt   £5.99
  'Can true love transcend racial barriers?'

❏ A Love Supreme   Pauline E. Hopkins   £5.99
  'One of the greatest love stories ever told.'

❏ One Blood   Pauline E. Hopkins   £6.99
  'Raiders of lost African treasures discover their roots and culture.'

❏ The President's Daughter   William Wells Brown   £5.99
  'The true story of the daughter of the United States president, sold into slavery.'

❏ The Soul of a Woman   Zora Neale Hurston, etc   £6.99
  'Stories by the great black women writers'

I enclose a cheque/postal order (Made payable to 'The X Press') for

£ _____

(add 50p P&P per book for orders under £10. All other orders P&P free.)

NAME _____

ADDRESS _____

✂ **Cut out or photocopy and send to: X PRESS, 6 Hoxton Square, London N1 6NU**
  Alternatively, call the X PRESS hotline: 0171 729 1199 and place your order.